1 HABIT™ FOR A THRIVING HOME OFFICE

KILLER HABITS OF THE HAPPIEST ACHIEVING HOME-BASED BUSINESS PEOPLE ON THE PLANET

STEVEN SAMBLIS

DEBBIE ROSEMONT

HABIT PRESS
EST 2019
A VOICE FOR BRILLIANT MINDS

1 Habit™ For A Thriving Home Office

By Steven Samblis, Debbie Rosemont and many Happy Achievers.

Published by 1 Habit Press, Inc.

Copyright © 2020 by 1 Habit Press, Inc. All rights reserved.

No part of this book may be reproduced in any form or by any electronic or mechanical means, including information storage and retrieval systems, without written permission from the Author.

The publishers gratefully acknowledge the individuals that contributed to this book.

1 Habit™ and its Logo and Marks are trademarks of 1 Habit Press, Inc.

1 Habit Press, Inc.®

(310) 595-1260

30 North Gould Street

Suite 7616

Sheridan, WY 82801

www.1Habit.com

Copy Editor & Design: Steven Samblis

To my Daughters Lindsay and Kaitlyn

- Steven Samblis

To my husband, Rob, and children, Sarah and Eddie - you inspire me daily

- Debbie Rosemont

FORWARD

Welcome to 1 Habit for a Thriving Home Office!

As a Certified Professional Organizer and Productivity Consultant who has happily worked from home since 1999, I was thrilled to have been asked to Co-Author this book. I am passionate about helping people experience joyful productivity, the idea that Habits are life and business changing AND about the benefits of working from home. Being able to Co-Author this collaborative project that I knew would be a valuable resource to so many was a no-brainer for me.

Working from home can save time, money, energy, stress, the environment, and much more. Having worked from home for over 20 years at the time of publication, I know I have experienced a reduction in stress (no traffic in my commute downstairs), more time (saving a couple hours a day with no commute), money (gas, parking, purchasing coffee and lunches out, wear and tear on my car, dry cleaning), and an increase in focus, energy and attention.

Anyone can work from home, but this book is full of ideas to help you do so successfully and productively. The chapters in this book offer the best Habits of a wide variety of happy achievers that, when implemented, can help you have a thriving home office.

Habits are things you do innately; that you do not have to think about doing. They are established in your routines, and engrained in the way you go about your work and your day. Habits can help or hinder. It is my hope that you find in this book a selection of Habits to consider implementing that will help you achieve your goals, work more productively, and thrive in your home office.

You will also read about "un-Habits" -- these are Habits that the contributing authors suggest you stop doing or break in order to succeed and thrive while working from home. Considering, identifying, and discontinuing Habits that do not serve us well can free up brain space, energy and resources to intentionally adopt Habits that contribute to your success instead.

Here's to your productivity in a thriving home office!

Warmly,

Debbie Rosemont

CPO® & Productivity Consultant

Simply Placed

THE CREATION OF THE 1 HABIT™ MOVEMENT

My name is Steven Samblis, and it is my honor to present to you "1 Habit for a Thriving Home Office". I hope this book will have a profound effect on your life.

To help you to get the most out of this book, I feel it is essential that I share with you how the 1 Habit™ Movement was created, and more importantly, why it was created.

I say the following with absolute certainty. Taking ownership of just one of the Habits in this book will have a profound effect on your life. I know this because when I learned about the power of Habits and instilled the first one into who I was, my life changed forever. I know the same can happen to you, and here is where it gets exciting. Add on another Habit and another after that, and you will find your life taking off on automatic pilot to the greatness that you were born to achieve.

The Beginning

From the time I was a young man, brand new to the business, I knew the way to be successful in my chosen field was to find successful people that came before me and do the things that they did. I was a stockbroker at the time. I would find the most successful stockbrokers in the business, study what they did, and do the same thing. I then began to do the same things they did. I would start my day at the same time. I went to lunch at the same time. I ate dinner at the same time. I went home at the same time. I made calls when they where making calls and studied the market when they did. After the end of doing this for six months, I was mentally and physically fried. Something was missing.

One of my heroes at this point in my life was a stockbroker named Al Glover. Al worked with me at a Dean Witter in Cocoa Beach, Florida. It was the early 80's. Cocoa Beach was a sleepy town where you could buy a charming home for under $50,000.00. Al was making a few million a year in commissions.

Al's office was right across from mine, so I every once in a while I would pop in his doorway and ask him how he became so successful, hoping to find the key. On one particular day, Al told me to sit down, watch, and listen. As he stood behind his desk, he picked up the phone and called a client, whom he later told me was a huge client but somewhat challenging to deal with. She always over-analyzed his recommendations, and by the time she was ready to pull the trigger, it was usually too late. "Mrs. Rooney, we have a terrific tax free bond yielding 8%, and I thought you would be interested." Al delivered the words, sat down, and shut up. It felt like an eternity went by as he sat silently on the phone, waiting for her response. "I have worked with you for many years, and during that time, you have missed out on incredible opportunities, which would have made you a great deal of money. This will be one of those. You have the money sitting in your Money Market, making a few points taxable. If you do not take this position, I am not doing my job and will no longer be able to be your Financial Advisor. I will pass your account on to somebody else." Al then stopped talking and waited. Another eternity went by until Al said. "Great, we will buy $200,000.00. I will place the order for you in the morning. Great decision. Talk to you soon."

I looked at Al stunned. "You were willing to throw away one of your biggest clients if she had said no?" Al went on to tell me that he had created a nightly Habit. Every evening at 6 pm, he looked at his book of 2000 clients and picked the five most difficult ones. He then called each one and gave them one shot to turn the relationship around, or he would dump them. He told me that this 1 Habit gave him a tremendous sense of peace. As it turned out, most clients just needed a little nudge to understand what a good position they were in having him manage their money. From that day forward, their attitudes and how they worked with him was dramatically improved.

As I left Al's office, I was inspired. I was motivated and worked hard, but motivation is just the thing that gets you started. It is Habits like Al's 6 pm calls that keep you going and drive you down the pathway to success.

Habits, once a part of you, are automatic. They don't drain your energy. They guide you along the right path to the life you want to live.

I went to my office, sat on my chair, and bounced up and went right back to Al's office. "Al, this is an amazing Habit, the 6 pm calls. However, I don't have 2000 clients. What one Habit could I make part of me that would get me to that 2000 client number?" Al took a moment and told me in a very matter of fact way. "Every night before you go home, map out your next day. If you have clients or prospects you will want to call tomorrow, make a list before you go home. If you have a trade ticket that you need to place in the morning, write it out before. Set yourself up for success every day by preparing the night before."

Wow. He was so right! I started with that 1 Habit, and it was a game-changer. I eventually instilled other Habits. This, in turn, led me to my goal. Within five years, I was managing over 2000 clients.

Fast forward to 2 years ago. I was filming interviews at Greg Reid's Secret Knock. This incredible gathering was attended by some of the highest achievers on the planet. As we prepared to roll the interviews, a thought of my friend Al came to me. "Habits." I was about to talk to very high achievers, let's roll the dice and see if these incredibly successful people had unique Habits that guided them to success. I decided to ask each person the same question. One question and one question only. "If you could instantly instill in a child, one Habit, what would it be and why?" The first answer was perfect. The second one was great. As I listened to each answer, I thought to myself, "What would my life be like if these Habits were a part of who I am?" I also notice that many of these successful people from many different walks of life had the same Habits.

Although I realized my videos were good, I knew there was something more. As a book, the reader could skim through it and land on a Habit and say, "That is a Habit I want to make a part of me." They could instill the Habit, and once it is part of them, they can flip through the pages and find the next one.

With the idea in hand, I set out to find 100 extremely high achievers from many walks of life to contribute to our first book. I was amazed by the extraordinary people that were willing to work with me and offer their Habits. I still have such gratitude for them, believing in me enough help me make this dream a reality.

The 1 Habit Movement

After we published the first book, I watched as the incredible contributors to the book began telling stories about how they became a part of the book. They talked about how excited they were about its extraordinary potential. One contributor emailed me and said, "Steve, what you have created is more than a book. It has become a movement."

The Power of Collaboration

One of the most exciting parts of creating the first 1 Habit book was spending each day talking with some of the most inspiring people on the planet. Even more exciting, we were receiving more Habits, then we could fit into one book.

I began to see groupings of Habits that fit for particular demographics. It was at that time that I decided 1 Habit would become a book series. I would take the processes I used to create the first book and replicate it for each book going forward.

If I were to create a book series, the bottleneck would be finding people for each book. I found the solution. I would team up with a co-author for each new book in the series. It would be their responsibility to bring in contributors to the book they where working on.

Each co-author is an expert in a particular field. Co-authors find the Contributors and then organize their submissions.

As of this writing, we have twenty new 1 Habit books in process with twenty incredible co-authors. My goal is to publish once a month, each for particular groups of people.

Steven Samblis – Co-Author and Creator of the 1 Habit™ Book Series.

HOW TO MAKE A HABIT YOUR OWN

The Cycle of a Habit
All Habits follow a specific path

By Steven Bamblis Creator of 1 Habit

The Habit

The trigger that ignites the Habit

The reward - All Habits have rewards attached

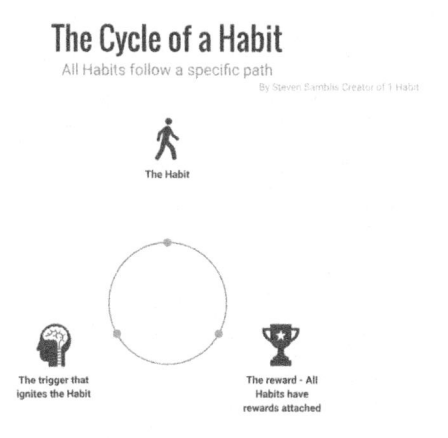

1 Habit - Envision Media Partners

Before we get into how to make a Habit your own, it is important to understand the cycle of a Habit. With this simple understanding, you will find it easier to make a Habit your own.

There is a cycle to all Habits. The cycle has three steps.

1st step: The Habit. It is the behavior you want to change, add, or remove.

2nd Step: The Reward. It is the payoff you get from the Habit.

3rd Step: The Trigger. It is the thing that makes you perform the Habit.

Keep this simple cycle in mind as you begin laying out your road map to making a Habit your own.

If you've ever tried to create a new Habit and have felt overwhelmed in the process of making even the slightest change, know that you're not alone. It's normal for emotions to come up when you're doing something new. It's also normal to want to QUIT and go back to your comfort zone, despite knowing those old Habits don't support your highest vision. As humans, we crave certainty. It makes us feel safe.

But safety doesn't always lead to success, and sometimes, risk is the best thing we can do to reap the rewards of leaning in and doing something different.

Realize that your *hands in the air* mentality when it comes to change won't serve you. Despite what you might think based on your old patterns or society's conditioning, you are capable of achieving anything you desire, and it starts with ***choosing yourself first*** and creating NEW Habits to fuel you forward, no matter what.

The Habits in all of our 1 Habit™ books have been carefully sourced by some of the most successful people to help you upgrade all areas of your life. The steps outlined below, as well as the inspiration laid out for you throughout these pages, *work if you work them*. So before you toss this book aside and let it collect dust, understand that this is not your typical "ra-ra" book. This is a book to challenge your beliefs, show you that what you want is on the other side of your fear (inaction) and that anything's possible when you commit to the process of change/upleveling.

If you think about your day to day routine, it's made up of Habits, right? And yes, some are better than others. That's okay! Change is possible, and you are more than capable. All of your current Habits, including the way you think, were created based on consistency - by YOU! So if you're feeling frustrated and wishing you could just (insert desire here), I am here to tell you that you absolutely can, and this book will help you get there... *faster*.

At this point, you might be evaluating what your current Habits are, and if you're not, I'm certain you will be by the end of this book. An important characteristic of a Habit is that it's automatic - you don't even think about it - so changing them takes conscious effort. Having awareness around how you spend your time and energy can be humbling, but it's necessary if you want to step into something greater. The truth is, we waste so much of our precious resources on things that don't move the needle forward because we've gotten so used to doing things a certain way.

The good news is, you have the power to change that at any time!

So how do you create new Habits that *stick?* Well, I've compiled a list of 30 steps that are not only proven to help you get started but also beneficial in supporting your long-term success. Before you read on, though, please understand that I am not asking you to do all of these things at once. I'm not crazy (and neither are you!). What I am inviting you to consider is that the way you're doing things right now isn't working (or you wouldn't be reading this book!). And more importantly, you can make positive changes in a short amount of time, starting small and gradually upgrading your daily Habits as they become a natural part of your routine.

After all, your morning coffee... your bath before bed... your need to answer every email as soon as it hits your inbox... the lack of time set aside for your workouts... even the route you take to and from work... all of these *Habits* were created *by you*, which means that only YOU have the power to change them.

Are you ready? Good! Let's get started.

1. Set yourself up to win. How many times have you told yourself you'd "start tomorrow" only to have tomorrow never come? I get it! Instead, focus on creating time and space and understand what needs to be present for you to achieve the goal you've set for yourself.

2. Practice compassion. You are not perfect, and you never will be. That's a beautiful thing! So if things don't go exactly the way you envision, understand that there's a lesson there and honor where you're at, while acknowledging where you still have room to grow.

3. Be clear on your WHY. One of the biggest mistakes and reasons for failure is a lack of clarity around *why* you want to make the change in the first place. When your *why* is big enough, nothing can stop you - not even YOU!

4. Choose curiosity over judgment. Ugh, the infamous "judgment". Let's be honest; how well does that work for you?

Instead, when you mess up (because you're human!), get curious. How could you have done it differently? How could you have shown up better? Who could you have asked for help? What needs to change to have a more positive result next time? Then rework your plan to support this new information.

5. Choose gratitude. *Gratitude turns what we have into enough.* Ever heard that saying? It's true! With everything and everyone that comes into your experience, give thanks for the opportunity to learn, grow, expand yourself. Remember to say THANK YOU for it all, and that includes having gratitude for yourself.

6. Stay consistent. The statement, *never skip a Monday,* could not be truer! When creating new Habits, it's important to keep your eye on the prize. If you want to get back to a regular workout routine, commit to moving your body *every single day* for 30 days. Skipping days while trying to create a new Habit will only make it harder to stick to. You'll notice that once you've completed those 30 days, your mind will be wired for movement (or whatever Habit you're implementing), and just like that, it's now part of your routine.

7. Find an accountability buddy. Everything is better with friends, right? Habits are no different, especially if it's a Habit that you want to create, but that feels reaaallllly hard to make happen. Grab your bestie and set up a check-in schedule, and make it fun!

8. Use visualization. Did you know there are now brain studies that show the power of our thoughts? In fact, it's been shown that our minds are capable of producing the same mental instructions as our actions.[1] Yea, how's that for some serious motivation! What we think, we become so think good thoughts and visualize them in the present moment as if they've already come to fruition. Add to that: *action,* and you'll be unstoppable.

9. Have a mantra. No, these aren't just for yogis. Think back to the *"Why"* you decided on (the reason you want to make this new Habit a reality). Create a statement or come up with a word that embodies the result you're working towards, or the way you want to feel in the process of instilling this new Habit. This can be an I AM statement (I AM capable... worthy... unstoppable...) or like I said, a single word like, HEALTHY. Whatever resonates for you, choose that. There is no right or wrong here.

10. Notice your self-talk. Every time a thought comes into your head that doesn't feel extra supportive, ask yourself: would I say this to my spouse... my child... my parents... my friends? If the answer is no, it's time to flip the script and create a more loving internal dialogue.

11. Ask for support. Yes, this might feel vulnerable. But just remember that people intrinsically want to help, so by asking for support, you are allowing others to give and getting in the practice of receiving. If this is uncomfortable for you, even better. Creating new Habits isn't meant to be easy; it's meant to challenge you and show you what you're made of, which is far more than you may realize.

12. Identify your triggers. Oh yes, the things that set us off and have us grabbing for the ice cream, or blowing our budget on a new pair of shoes! What (or who) are they? Write these down.

13. Come up with positive responses to your triggers. Now that you know what (or who) they are, how can you set yourself up to win if (when) they show up?

14. Start small. Small changes over time can make a massive impact. If you haven't worked out in years, saying you're going to run a marathon in a month probably isn't a great idea. Instead, can you commit to walking for at least 20 minutes each day and gradually increasing your time and intensity until you get where you want to go, physically? Decide what that looks like. Write it down.

15. Choose ONE Habit to implement at a time. I have a feeling you're ambitious, and you probably have a laundry list of things you want to achieve. Good for you! But instead of trying to do all the things immediately, choose ONE thing. Getting a win under your belt releases dopamine in the brain (that feel-good chemical) and will inspire you to keep going!

16. Celebrate your wins. So now that you've got that dopamine swirling around CELEBRATE!! You did it, and that is amazing... YOU are amazing!

17. Keep a journal. It's okay if you're not a writer, the point of keeping track is to look back and see how far you've come. Writing down the emotions throughout the process can be an interesting gauge, and can provide a really beautiful space for growth and healing.

18. Be specific. Do you want to lose weight, or do you want to lose 10 pounds? The more specific you can get, the easier it will be to create a plan to set yourself up to win - and be able to recognize when success happens.

19. Create a plan. How are you going to achieve this? Who can help keep you on track? What needs to change so you can replace an old Habit with this new, more supportive one? Write it down.

20. Have a reward in mind for when you succeed! Have you been putting something on hold just waiting "until"? Now is the perfect time to allow yourself permission to indulge in the reward you've been pawning over. *"After I workout for 30 days in a row, I'm going to get myself those new shoes I've been eyeing to celebrate!"* Or maybe it's a trip you've wanted to take, or whatever it may be... let this be your permission slip to reward yourself for your hard work and celebrate the new Habit you just implemented into your life.

21. Believe that it's possible. Because it is! And you are far more capable than you may realize. *Whether you think you can or you think you can't, you're right. - Henry Ford*

22. Be so committed that nothing can stop you. Eye. On. The. Prize. That new Habit is not going to happen on its own! How bad do you want it? I hope you said something like, *more than anything*. What is not doing this costing you, your family, your life?

23. Record your affirmations (and use them!). Use the voice memo on your phone to record your mantra, an I AM statement, your "Why," something that PUMPS YOU UP and encourages you to stay the course. Listen as often as you need to in order to keep pushing, even when the going gets tough.

24. Share with a loved one. This is different than having someone do the work with you to reach your goal (that new Habit!). Simply stating your intention and plan to make it happen and asking others to support you in your efforts keeps the fire burning a little hotter. As humans, we want to know that people care and that they're proud of us. Letting your spouse or kids know that you're going to be making some changes can inspire the entire family to get on board. Pay it forward!

25. Get plenty of rest. We all know that feeling tired doesn't exactly lend well to motivation. Commit to getting uninterrupted sleep each night.

26. Drink a ton of water. Maybe don't drink a gallon of water before bed, but nourishing your cells with proper hydration not only helps you sleep better, it helps you stay energized and fueled during your day while helping to transport nutrients to your cells and wherever else they're needed. Water is the ultimate brainpower! And healthy brains make better decisions.

27. Nourish your mind, body, and soul. Surround yourself with people that will encourage and uplift you. These are the real angels on earth. We become the five people we spend the most time with, so make sure your circle supports the Habits you're looking to cultivate.

28. Avoid situations that would tempt you to "cheat" on yourself. If you know that joining everyone for a Happy Hour on Friday is going to cause you to indulge when you're committed to "clean eating without alcohol," do yourself a favor and skip it! There will be plenty more opportunities to partake in these things once you've gotten your Habits in check.

29. If you mess up, find the lesson, and keep moving forward. You are human, and you will mess up. Totally okay! Beating yourself up, harsh self criticism, and unwarranted negative self-judgment are not supportive, and just don't feel good. Let it go! And commit to doing better next time. Now, if you find that you use this mentality as an excuse to keep repeating mistakes, that's a different story. This is meant to forward you, not sabotage your progress.

30. Don't start without a plan. If you were driving cross-country, you'd probably pull out a map, right? The same goes for creating Habits. If you want to get from point A to point B with ease, see step 1 and set yourself up for success! Fail to plan, plan to fail. It's that simple.

So there you have it! Thirty steps to help you not only upgrade your Habits *but make them stick!* If you are serious about living your best life, your Habits are imperative to your success. Our intention for the 1 Habit™ series is to make this as easy as possible for you in the way of motivation, empowerment, and support.

You're an intelligent person, so I am confident you are fully aware that, as much as we'd love to make these changes for you, it's not possible. But our hope is that by laying out the foundation for you, you will not only begin to see how simple it can be - but also be inspired to get to work!

On behalf of myself and all of our contributors, WE BELIEVE IN YOU! Now get out there, create some new Habits, and achieve your dreams.

Resources:

https://www.psychologytoday.com/us/blog/flourish/200912/seeing-is-believing-the-power-visualization[1]

ARE YOU A HAPPY ACHIEVER?

For years, my life was focused on being a high achiever. Success was all I could think about. And success meant one thing and one thing only, how much money I made.

Throughout my journey, I would go out of my way to meet respected leaders in business, culture, and social change to learn their secrets and apply them to my success.

But, as I set out to create 1 Habit, I learned something even more amazing. It turns out, my desire to achieve was on target, but I measured it all wrong—in dollars and cents.

I realized, no matter how much money I made, I wasn't as happy as I thought I'd be; there was always going to be someone making more.

One day it dawned on me, I needed to redefine what success meant to me. Money was not the right measurement of success. Money may be how others measure my success. Why should I give them this power?

I soon realized that happiness is how I wanted to measure my success. My happiness is something I am in control of. The way to reach happiness is to perform at your highest level in all plains of existence. The people that came together as contributors for 1 Habit all did this. These amazing people were all operating at the highest levels, Emotionally, Spiritual, their physical character, the way they live, and of course, financially. Happiness through the balance of performing and living at your peak in all those areas of their lives.

From that day forward, I would keep score based on the time I spent with my family, my friends, my hobbies, exploring the world, and realizing my passions and dreams.

I knew what I wanted to do now but did not know what to call this new category of a person that achieved highly at all levels and, as a result, were some of the happiest people on the planet.

Ask, and you shall receive

Whenever I have a question or a problem, I put it out there, and the universe always seems to give me the answers when I need them.

I was sitting with a friend who started out creating marketing campaigns for companies like ATT. He moved from there to head up a company that produces the marketing campaign for all the major Hollywood studios. If you saw a movie in the last 20 years, there is a high likelihood that Mike Tankel was part of the reason you walked into that theater.

I told Mike about my new way of keeping score in life with happiness, not money. I no longer wanted to be a singular high achiever. I was something more. This thing was "the" more.

With little effort, it rolled off Mike's tongue. "You don't want to be a High Achiever. You want to be a Happy Achiever". And there we have it. A "Happy Achiever."

So now I ask you, my dear reader. How do you keep score in life? More importantly, how do you *want* to keep score in life?

I hope you will join us and live your life to the fullest on all planes of existence. I hope you, too, will become a Happy Achiever!

Steven Samblis

Creator of 1 Habit™

DEFINITION OF HABIT

Habit: A behavior pattern acquired by frequent repetition or physiologic exposure that shows itself in regularity or increased facility of performance.

- Merriam-Webster Dictionary

IMPORTANT NOTE - HOW TO USE THIS BOOK

1 Habit books are created to help you to find and instill new Habits that will change your life forever. These books are different from other "Self Help" books in the way they should be used.

Do not pick it up and read it from cover to cover.

The best way to use this book is as follows...

1. After you have read "How to Make a Habit Your Own", flip through the pages and let a Habit find you.
2. Decide if the Habit will enhance your life. If the answer is "Yes," go to step 3. (If not go back to step 1)
3. Follow the steps in the chapter "How to Make a Habit Your Own."
4. Once you have done so, and the Habit is a part of who you are, go back to step 1 and repeat.

Continue these steps, 1 Habit at a time, and you may change your life forever!

CONTENTS

Forward   5
The Creation of the 1 Habit™ Movement   7
How to Make a Habit Your Own   13
Are you a Happy Achiever?   23

Definition of Habit   27
Important Note - How to Use this Book   29
1. Compartmentalize Your Day; Separate Work Time From Personal Time - Debbie Rosemont   35
2. Prepare For Tomorrow's Success Tonight - Steven Samblis   41
3. Do Things That are Difficult - Alan Berg   45
4. Set up a Second Monitor in Your Home Office (and use it!) - Randy Dean   49
5. Stay Focused on Balance, Marketing, and Goals - Michael A. Gregory   55
6. Respect the Space - Darlene Law   61
7. A Ball & a Wall - Christopher Jossart   67
8. A 30-Minute Healthy Lunch Break - Louise Tyrrell   73
9. Create Space That's Your Own - Kathy Gruver   79
10. Be Your Dream Boss - Mary Nestor   83
11. Generate Creative Inspiration - Katie Goodman   89
12. Forget About The Idea of Work / Life Balance; Create Work Integration - Reade Milner   95
13. Pray and Affirm Daily - Kamia Kindle   99
14. Inspire! - Irene Zamaro   103
15. Find Fun and Joy in Each Day - Kirsten Jarvi   107
16. Cultivate The Capacity To Be Alone - Gaurav Bhalla   113
17. Create an Invigorating and Separate Workspace - Cynthia A. Peel   119
18. Be Consistent - Jennifer Mastor   125
19. Minutes Of Movement - Heather Denniston   131

20. Cultivate Curiosity - Tabitha Colie	137
21. Continue your Education - Regina F. Lark, Ph.D.	143
22. Use Your Phone to Help Build a Routine - Scott Schweiger	149
23. Make Your Space Beautiful and Inspiring - Melinda Slater	155
24. Take Your Eyes Off the Clock - Jim Hessler	161
25. Create a Curated Written to-do List for the Next Day - Liz Jenkins	167
26. Create A Trigger For Your Work Day - Kelly Smith	173
27. Stick to a Workday Schedule - Lauren Burgon	179
28. The Right Daily Task List - Silvia Peterson	183
29. Finish Your Key Priorities by Noon, Every Day - Dan Faulkner	187
30. Promote Your Higher Self to CEO - Jessica Riverson	191
31. Make a Daily "Results" List - Aubrey Armes	197
32. Get Your Daily "Dose of Happy" - Laurie Nichols	203
33. 60 Second Morning Mirror - Erik "Mr. Awesome" Swanson	209
34. Create Your Work From Home Routine - Brooks Duncan	213
35. Find What Works For YOU - Kirsten Sandoval	219
36. Set Expectations With Family About Your Home Office - Jen Taylor	225
37. Choose the Right Tools - Lori Vande Krol	231
38. Treat Your Home Office as a Sacred Space - Jill Nichols-Hicks	237
39. Create Structure and Space to Support Working From Home - Yvonne D. Hall	243
40. Be Intentional When Setting up a Home Workspace - Gazala Uradnik	249
41. Be Like Phineas: Speak Your Plan Aloud! - Ron Rael	255
42. Stop Worrying and Make a Decision! - Kristin Bertilson	261
43. Start Your Day Strong With Movement - Stacey Sorgen	265

44. 5-10 Minute Morning Meditation to Start the Day and Get Centered - Jackie Ramirez	271
45. Be Clear on How You Spend Your Time - Nicole Mangina	277
46. Uproot your Boot(y) - Reisha Holton	283
47. Be Profound - Daphne Michaels	289
48. Diversify Your End Market and/or Your Customer Base - Ashok S. Ramji	295
49. Start Working Iteratively - Andrew Hinkelman	301
50. Creating Space Anywhere To Think And Let Go! - Leona Thomas	307
51. Set & Honor Time Boundaries - Sarah Frink	313
52. Get Up, Dress Up, Show Up - Lisa Fischer	319
53. Make Daily Nature Breaks Part of Your Schedule - Rose Harrow	325
54. Play the Right Music - Jeff VandenHoek	331
55. Move Your Body Daily - Mindy Garrett	337
56. Dress For the Office Every Day! - Cynthia Lindsey	343
57. Keep My Eye On My Why - Betsy Matias	349
58. Mindfully Disconnect, Every Day - Neelu Gibson	355
59. Be More Productive by Integrating Personal Tasks in Your Workday - Andrea Duffield	361
60. De-clutter Your Physical and Virtual Desktops - Janine Sarna-Jones	367
61. Leverage Your Peak Productivity - Shannon McGinnis	371
62. Make Time for Connection - Denise Lloyd	377
63. Plan For the Right Balance of Individual Work Time Versus Virtual Meetings - Jennifer McKibbin Harris	383
64. Take Your Dogs to the Park, Every Day - David Schwartz	389
65. Start Each and Every Day with Gratitude - Mike Nakamura	395
66. Arrive Like a Boss - Whitnie Wiley	401
67. Practice 10-10-10 - Andrea Heuston	407
68. Use A "Maybe List" to Keep You Focused - Denise B. Lee	413
69. Be Super Organized for Super Success - Brandon B. Kelly	419

70. Move Your Paper! - Sharon Davis	423
71. Create a Space That Speaks to the WHOLE Person - Mind & Body - Paul Andrés Trudel-Payne	429
72. Time Batching - Kamelia Britton	435
73. Focus on the Value and Not the Money and the Money Will Come - Robert J Moore	439
Acknowledgments	443
About the Creator of the 1 Habit™ Movement	449
About Co-Author - Debbie Rosemont, CPO	451
Available From 1 Habit Press	453

1

COMPARTMENTALIZE YOUR DAY; SEPARATE WORK TIME FROM PERSONAL TIME - DEBBIE ROSEMONT

Why: It is tempting and easy when you work from home for work to bleed into your personal life and vice versa. While nice to have the flexibility to start a load of laundry in the middle of a workday (a luxury you don't have when working in a traditional office), it is also easy to get distracted by personal tasks and not accomplish priority work during the workday.

Conversely, since the "office" is just down the hall from the bedroom or kitchen, it can be easy and sometimes tempting to work around the clock. After all, the work (and office) is "always there." Primarily compartmentalizing work into the workday and personal tasks into off-work hours helps create more focus and better results in both areas of your life.

To compartmentalize, establish a daily plan and adhere to it with as much consistency as possible. Have a start and end time to your workday. Work in the same place in your home each day; ideally, a dedicated home office, but that's not always possible. As long as it is a place that you can work consistently, clear of clutter and distraction, the space can signal your mind that it's time to focus on work (i.e., when I sit in this chair, I work). You can even signal the transition to work by getting dressed for work or with an accessory or particular clothing item, donning a "work hat" or "work scarf" for the workday.

Block time on your calendar for the different types of work you perform, meetings and appointments, and priority work. Do the same for your personal commitments. Honor those times and stick to your schedule as much as possible. Planning and prioritizing your next day as you wrap up the current one means when you enter the office the next morning, you're ready to hit the ground running and can focus on your most important work.

Build a transition into your daily structure. Just as you would during a commute to or from work, have some "transition time" to ease into your workday or back into your home life. For example, five or ten minutes of transition time at the end of your workday can help with compartmentalization. Activities, like listening to a particular song, checking personal email or social media for fun, or checking in with your family, can help with the transition from work to personal time.

Compartmentalization can help you to thrive as you work from your home office and live your best life.

The Un-Habit: Stop Procrastinating

Why: We procrastinate for any number of reasons and in a variety of ways. In fact, I teach a workshop titled "What Are You Waiting For?" that details ten top reasons people procrastinate (and what to do about it).

Compartmentalize Your Day; Separate Work Time From Person... | 37

Some of us are expert procrastinators. We get very creative and get lots of "busy (but not productive) work" done to avoid priority work.

When you work from a home office, it can be tempting to make many trips to the kitchen to get another snack, to the laundry room to fold a load, to the mailbox to check the mail, to the cupboard to organize your linens, or to our email inbox (though we were just there a minute ago) to see if any new email has come in, all to avoid priority work.

While it is nice that we CAN do personal tasks in the middle of the workday, compartmentalization leads to greater productivity. We need to be thoughtful not to use personal tasks or low priority work as distractions or excuses to procrastinate.

Fight procrastination by identifying your highest priority or the number one task that when accomplished, would make the biggest impact on your work, your clients, or your goals. Do that work first thing in your workday.

Author and Speaker Brian Tracy calls this concept "Eat a Frog for Breakfast." His idea is that if someone held a frog in front of you (representing the highest priority, and possibly the toughest thing you'll need to do all day), and told you that you had to eat it at some point that day, wouldn't you rather get it down for breakfast than have to stare at it all day, with dread and anticipation, eventually having to eat it anyway?

Doing the hardest task or most significant work first thing in the day builds momentum and means that you are less likely to get lost or distracted by other things. It ensures you work proactively instead of just re-actively (i.e., by starting your work in your email inbox and then looking up at the clock at 5:00

realizing you didn't get to anything but responding to email done from your list).

Stop procrastinating by identifying your highest priority every day and then completing it before anything else (distraction, avoidance tasks, or reactivity) gets in your way. Refill your coffee cup or check email AFTER you accomplish your highest priority, as a break before engaging in your next best work.

Fight procrastination to increase your productivity and thrive in your home office!

About Debbie: Debbie Rosemont, Certified Professional Organizer and Productivity Consultant, has run her company, Simply Placed, from her thriving home office since 2003. Simply Placed helps clients increase productivity, maximize efficiency, and bring balance and control into their work and lives. Simply Placed associates work with individuals and businesses to create effective organizational systems, clear clutter, successfully manage time, focus on priorities, and achieve goals. They help people work smarter, not harder, to increase their bottom line and peace of mind through consulting, organizing sessions, group training, and It's About Time, a virtual productivity membership program.

Debbie teaches individuals and groups productive Habits and organized systems that allow them to maximize their email, time, tasks, teams, and work-space, resulting in improved client service, employee retention, revenue, and reduced stress. Simply

Compartmentalize Your Day; Separate Work Time From Perso... | 39

Placed can help you and your business focus on what's important, ultimately helping you achieve a level of efficiency that allows you to get not just more, but more of what you want, out of business and life.

Rosemont is an engaging speaker, an effective consultant, and trainer, and has been interviewed numerous times for TV, print, radio and online media. She is also the author of the book Six-Word Lessons to Be More Productive (available on Amazon) and the creator of several information products (available at www.itssimplyplaced.com/shop).

Rosemont is one of a small number of Certified Professional Organizers in Washington and was a founding member of the Seattle chapter of NAPO. She is an active member of NAPO (National Association of Productivity and Organizing Professionals) and Women Business Owners (WBO). She was a proud finalist for the 2015 WBO Nellie Cashman Business Owner of the Year award.

Rosemont, who wears many hats in her own life as a wife, mother, volunteer, and business owner, understands that "life happens" and that it can be a challenge to get and stay organized. However, she's seen the benefits of an organized life and wants that for her clients. Her goal is to save her clients time, money, and stress ultimately, and allow them to focus on the things that matter most.

Simply Placed, and Debbie Rosemont can be reached by phone at 206-579-5743 or by email at debbie@itssimplyplaced.com. More information about the company, services, and products and programs can be found at www.itssimplyplaced.com.

You can also grab her free "Rock Your Work From Home Guide" at www.itssimplyplaced.com/wfhguide

2

PREPARE FOR TOMORROW'S SUCCESS TONIGHT - STEVEN SAMBLIS

Why: When working from home, you need to be organized, or else you will lose the divide between home and work life. This Habit will help you to organize and give you peace of mind at night to enjoy your home life.

This Habit is also very fast to instill but will result in a substantial positive impact on your life.

I learned this Habit when I was a brand new stockbroker.

Here is how it works...

Every night before you go home, map out your next day. If you have clients or prospects you will want to call tomorrow, make a list with their names and numbers. If you have a trade ticket that you need to place in the morning, write it out the night before. No matter what it is you are doing tomorrow, there is an opportunity to prepare the night before. It is even a great idea to set out clothes for the next day.

Make this the evening Habit that you do in a couple of parts. When you finish your workday, take a moment to plan tomorrow's workday. This lets you close out each workday with a calm, organized spirit.

When you are ready to retire for the evening, take a moment and plan out your wardrobe for the morning.

Doing these things puts you at peace and lets you even get a better night's sleep. This simple 1 Habit can be a massive game-changer in your life.

The Un-Habit: Stop Listening to Your Well-Meaning Friends

Why: When you work from home, you will probably interact more with family and friends than business associates. This can be good and bad, depending on who those people are.

This is a Habit that was given to me by Queen Latifa, while I was interviewing her and Dolly Parton together for a movie called Joyful Noise.

I have interviewed over 1000 of the top actors in the world on camera for a show called Cinema Buzz. One day I realized that I was sitting across from the most successful people on the planet, why not tap into that and learn more from them than just who they played in their movies.

As I sat across from Queen and Dolly, I asked them... " You are two of the most successful women in not just Hollywood, but in business in general. I have two daughters. What would you tell them is the key to your success?"

What Queen Latifa said to me stuck with me maybe more than anyone else I spoke to. She told me that when she was growing up and told her well-meaning friends that she wanted to be a singer, a rapper, an actor, they told her, "Don't be silly. You will never do that. Stick to what you know."

She realized that those well-meaning friends and family members could very well be the biggest obstacles to her getting out of her situation and becoming what she dreamed of.

Sometimes we surround ourselves with people that will enable laziness. That will allow you not to try. To give up. To not dream. A lot of times, those people are family and friends that we grew up with.

I know this is a difficult one, but this is a Habit that you need to change, and it could be a pretty painful move.

These family and friends that will give you the comfort to be Ok in your mediocrity do so from a loving place but also a place of fear.

There is a story about Crab fishermen. As they bring up the cages, they throw the crabs into a bucket with no lid. The reason they can do this is that if one of the crabs tries to get out, the others will grab him and pull him back in.

Sit back and look at the people you surround yourself with. Are they pulling you back in, or are they lifting you up? As painful as it may be, once you have the answer, you must either help them to change, or you need to make a change.

About Steven: Steven Samblis is the creator of the 1 Habit book series.

He is the founder of 1 Habit Press. Before creating Samblis Press, Steven had a meteoric career in business that saw him go from being ranked among the top 50 rookie stockbrokers at Dean Witter, to speaking before 250,000 people for The Investors Institute. He has spoken before congress on shareholder's rights representing T Boone Pickens' "United Shares Holders Association."

In 1989 he founded "The Reason For My Success." which grew into one of the largest sellers of self-improvement programs in North America. The Company expanded into production where Steve collaborated with Chicken Soup for the Soul co-creator Mark Victor Hansen on the audio program. The program was called "The World's Greatest Marketing Tools."

As a consultant, Steve created a new name brand for a struggling gym in Dover New Hampshire called Coastal Fitness. He then created a $9.95 a month business model, which helped to turn the single gym into one of the most successful fitness franchises in North America, Planet Fitness. In November of 2015, Planet Fitness went public with a 1.6 billion dollar market valuation.

For six years, before launching Envision TV, Steve hosted Cinema Buzz, a television show syndicated in North America and the UK. On the show, Steve has interviewed over 1000 of the biggest actors and directors in entertainment one on one on camera.

Resources: www.1Habit.com/StevenSamblis

3

DO THINGS THAT ARE DIFFICULT - ALAN BERG

Why: Are you the best you can ever be? I don't think so. It's easy to put off things that seem difficult, things that stress us out, and things that scare us. But once you do them, your perspective changes, and the other stuff looks easy. So, do the difficult things first, while you have the most energy, don't wait until you're tired from the day to day grind. None of us knows what we're capable of, that is until we try. Then, once we do something we've never done, we forever move the bar higher, and higher.

I started Tae Kwon Do when I was 39, just to get into shape. After achieving my 1st degree Black Belt at 42, I went on to get a 2nd degree Black Belt at 44. At 24, I never would have imagined that I'd ever have a 1st degree, no less a 2nd degree. There were many times where I was pushed way beyond what I perceived was possible (like breaking 30 boards in 36 seconds), and pushing those boundaries is what kept me going.

I decided to become conversational in Spanish when I was in my early 50's, just to be respectful of the people whose countries I would visit. The more I learned, and the more I practiced, the more I wanted to keep going. There were many times I wanted to quit... because it was hard. What kept me going was the fact that is WAS hard. When people in other countries would ask me why I decided to learn Spanish, I tell that "Porque es difícil" - because it is hard! I've now presented on stage in 5 countries in Spanish.

You are capable of so much more; all you have to do is try. As the T-shirt that I got after going skydiving (at age 50) says: "What's the worst that can happen?"

The Un-Habit: Stop Saying "I Can't do That" if You've Never Tried

Why: Each of us is capable of so much more than we give ourselves credit for. You can be a better father, mother, husband, wife, partner, boss, employee, friend, son, daughter... if you try. Each little triumph can propel you forward. Conversely, each time you say, "I can't do that," you're defeated. And, if you try, and don't succeed, try again, and again, and again. The most valuable things in life deserve more attention and shouldn't be easy. Relationships are hard but don't give up so easily.

When I did Tae Kwon Do, our Master would hold up a board a way we've never seen, and ask us who can break it in a way we'd never seen. Half of the class would say: "I'll try," and half would say: "I can't do that." The Master would ask: "But you've never tried, why do you say you can't do it?" And they would say that they can't. Then he would add: "I would never ask you to try something if I think you'll get hurt. Now, who will try? And the same half would say they will try, and the same group would say they couldn't do it. They may have been physically strong, but they were mentally weak.

Can you remember a time in your life where you tried something you'd never done before, and you succeeded, and how good that felt? Maybe you mustered the courage to approach that cute guy or girl and didn't get rejected. Perhaps you achieved a new milestone in a sport or personal best score on a game. You didn't get there by giving up. You didn't get there by saying: "I can't do that." You got there by doing what was hard, knowing it was hard and pushing through. Don't try to be the best you can ever be. Just be the best you've ever been, every time.

About Alan: Alan Berg has been called "The Leading International Speaker and Expert on the Business of Weddings & Events." He's a Certified Speaking Professional, the highest earned designation through the National Speakers Association, and one of only 36 Global Speaking Fellows in the world!

After publishing two wedding magazines, Alan was the Vice President of Sales for The Knot, the largest wedding website in the world. He now serves as an independent education expert for WeddingPro, the education arm of The Knot Worldwide, which has websites in 15 countries and publishes 17 regional and one national magazine. Alan also consults for major wedding websites in Ireland, the UK, India, Dubai, and Australia.

In addition to his contribution to 1 Habit, Alan is the author of 5 books: "If Your Website Was An Employee, Would You Fire It?", "Your Attitude for Success," "Shut Up and Sell More Weddings &

Events," "Why Don't They Call Me?" and his newest book "Wit, Wisdom and the Business of Weddings." All are available in English and Spanish, Kindle and on Audible (and yes, Alan did the narration).

He's presented and done sales training in 14 countries, on five continents – 5 of them in Spanish. In addition to speaking, Alan does sales training for companies in the wedding and event industry, privately and in small one-day Mastermind groups. Through his consulting and website reviews, Alan helps clients, large and small, around the world, improve their conversion through his division: "Your Personal Sales Trainer." The best athletes in the world have coaches and trainers because they want to always be on top of their game. Alan helps companies and their sales teams, large and small, sell more through the Sales Circuit: 1) Get their attention 2) Get the inquiry 3) Have a conversation 4) Make the sale.

4

SET UP A SECOND MONITOR IN YOUR HOME OFFICE (AND USE IT!) - RANDY DEAN

Why: I have been teaching time and productivity management, using technology for nearly 30 years. One of the best productivity tips/Habits I can share with a home-based business owner is to invest in a second monitor for their primary workstation in their home office.

I not only have a home office, but I also travel extensively. Therefore, I have a hybrid laptop that can be "flipped" into tablet mode – very helpful in situations where a full laptop is a bit clunky. But when I get back to my home office, I usually plug in my second monitor via USB to my laptop, and tile to a second screen.

Why? Well, do you do any cross-referencing while working on your computer? Are you trying to check your calendar and e-mail at the same time? Or your calendar and task list? Are you pulling info from one document or spreadsheet to another? Are you comparing information or prices from more than one web site? Do you regularly do any of these activities? The estimates vary, but a popular productivity study found that moving from one monitor to two can increase productivity by 9 – 50% per employee!

When you consider that second monitors, depending on size, run from $100 - $200, that means the typical business owner, at a reasonable hourly rate for their time, can pay for that second monitor in JUST A FEW HOURS or less!

I understand that, especially at start-up, home-based business owners are often "cash-starved" and want to avoid all potentially unnecessary expenses. However, I would argue that to be a successful entrepreneur, you need to quickly realize that your most valuable asset is your TIME, not your money, and any investment that you make that will allow you to see a 20-30% return on your time/effort is one of the very best productivity investments you can make.

In my Outlook and Gmail programs, I even recommend that working professionals have their regular primary set up of their dual monitors with their calendar app on one screen, and their task list app on the other. That way, by default, that person sees their time (calendar) and daily tasks first and most, so they can keep their focus on their most important projects, tasks, clients, activities, and actions.

I DON'T recommend you keep your e-mail open except for when you are actively checking it – otherwise, that second screen might turn into a regular and never-ending distraction – SQUIRREL!

The Un-Habit: Don't let the second monitor become a distraction!

Why: This leads into a couple of important potential "un-Habits"

– first if you are like me, I sometimes like to change my physical location working from home. By design, I have my home office in a somewhat secluded area, so when I'm trying to get some work done when both teenagers are home and if my wife has visitors, I can go into my "dungeon" and keep my focus. However, when the kids are at school, and my wife is at work, I like to "come up for air" and work in our well-lit kitchen or an upstairs bedroom with nice windows, and see a bit of the sun!

I have to keep a close watch on myself when I decide to work in one of these different places in my home because if I am going to be doing something on that laptop that requires cross-referencing, I should either move back down into my home office for that action or if I think I'll be doing it for a few hours. I want a nice window view; I should grab that second monitor and move it up to that kitchen island for maximum productivity.

The time to move the monitor from my office (and back when I'm done) is usually paid for in a matter of a few minutes when compared to the time saved when doing those cross-referencing activities. In short, make your "place" – wherever that is -- as productive as possible, and be willing to quickly move or change that "place" to enhance your productivity.

The second "un-Habit" I recommend is to carefully watch what is truly going on with that second monitor and to make sure it doesn't become yet another distraction. I mentioned above that I don't recommend keeping your e-mail open as that will likely become a productivity distraction rather than a productivity booster. Well, you could have your favorite social media open, or your favorite news feed or streaming service, or your favorite video game, or your real-time stock ticker, and your productivity might plummet!

That second screen could EASILY become a squirrel! Never forget that if you are not actively multi-tasking/cross-referencing, and that if you'd instead entirely focus on one thing (project, client, activity, event, action, task), you can unplug that second monitor and make this crazy productivity-enhancing Habit called SINGLE TASKING. (I know – crazy concept, eh?)

About Randy: Randy Dean, The E-mail Sanity Expert®, is a professional speaker and expert on time & e-mail management, effective organization, and related technology use. For more than 25 years, Randy has been leading training and speaking programs for major corporations, universities, associations, and government audiences. Obsessed with time management and personal productivity, he left a successful career as a graduate program admissions director, professional marketer, and manager to become a leading speaker and trainer. The author of the recent Amazon bestseller, Taming the E-mail Beast, and producer and creator of 6 time and productivity management-related video self-study courses, he has led programs for thousands of satisfied and inspired students, managers, and professionals on being more productive with their time and life. His highly informative and entertaining speaking and training programs leave audience members with immediately usable tools, strategies, and skills to better manage their time, technology, and information overload following their program experience.

Randy is best known for his programs on time, project, people, distraction, office clutter, and especially e-mail management using popular tools like Microsoft Outlook, Gmail/Google Apps, and smartphones & tablets. His speaking and training programs are consistently some of the highest-rated programs for the many clients he speaks for, including major conferences/conventions, Fortune 500 organizations, top universities, governmental agencies, and leading nonprofits -- basically, anyone struggling to manage better their time, e-mail, smartphone/tablet devices, Google productivity apps, and Microsoft Outlook. (And he makes these topics fun and engaging too!) He shares strategies and techniques in popular software tools and devices that working professionals use every day, allowing them to find extra time and productivity every day.

He has previously been interviewed by the Washington Times, Detroit News, The Globe and Mail, Business Week Online, and numerous other media outlets, including radio, television, newspaper, and blog sites. He is a member of the National Speakers Association (NSA) and Michigan Society of Association Executives.

5

STAY FOCUSED ON BALANCE, MARKETING, AND GOALS - MICHAEL A. GREGORY

Why: Focus is the key. Working from home is nice on several fronts, but when you have an office in the house, there can be distractions too. To have a thriving home office, three elements are presented for your consideration. These are balance, marketing, and the bottom line.

First, have a balance in your life. Your home office is for work. Keep it that way. Set up your schedule. Have a rhythm on how you start your day, go to work, and work in your home office. Structure is very important. Have a set closing time. That's when your day is done. Keep track of your time. Not just billing, but your actual work time. Determine how many hours in a day or week are right for you. Eat right. Get enough sleep. Exercise. Practice meditation, prayer, yoga, or reflection at least 10 minutes a day. Focusing on work in your office while addressing these four elements with your life outside of work will set you up for success.

Second, if you are setting up your home office to run your business, you need to reach out to three people every day for marketing purposes. It's that simple. If starting a new business, try and get in front of five people a week for coffee, tea, or lunch. This was the best marketing advice I ever received. Yes, I know it is hard. Be creative. Be prepared to reach out to others up to three times with an email, a call, and with a handwritten note if necessary, to have someone break out to meet with you in person. If they still won't accept that, realize it's not about me and move on. You have to get out of your home office regularly to meet, greet, and be with others to expand your network.

Third, set goals for yourself. Focus on your major goals, and don't sweat the small stuff. Determine your top priorities related to work and focus on them. You have to meet business metrics to keep the home office viable. Follow your business plan and pause quarterly to reflect on where you want to be two years from now changing course as appropriate. If you don't know what a business plan is, go on the internet, read about it, and develop one. Ensure you have goals for customer satisfaction (under promise and over deliver), your personal satisfaction, and business results. Finally, just do it. Learn what works and doesn't work. Adapt, be flexible, and continually improve.

THE UN-HABIT: LIMIT DISTRACTIONS AND WHAT YOU PERCEIVE AS NEEDS

Why: When you have a home office, you will be tempted with plenty of distractions, both personally and professionally. No one else is watching. Be careful here.

You had distractions at the office. Now you have some new ones at home. Consider your refrigerator down the hall; a TV in the other room; social media right in front of you; pets, kids, spouse, or a significant other that could pop in at any time; and other distractions. With your home office, you need a policy for yourself and others. For example, when the door is shut, that indicates that you are working. This tells others to limit interruptions. Even if you are by yourself, shutting your door can psychologically help you. If you don't take preventative actions, time will easily slip away, and at the end of the day, you will wonder what happened.

It is quite easy to get caught up with email and social media (Facebook, LinkedIn, Twitter, Instagram, etc.) that may even have professional applications. For example, you may want to focus on a specific amount of time each day (say one hour at the start of your day and then 30 minutes in the middle and near the end of your day) on social media. That way, you can really focus on your work and give yourself a break for these types of items as appropriate. If you don't, you may squirrel away hours with related items, that don't focus on the items above.

However, some interruptions are well received, but be aware of both your needs and the needs of others. For example, if you have a spouse or significant other that works outside the home, consider your and the other person's needs. After arriving home, give the other party time to settle in, unwind, and to stop by when the other person is ready. Remember to listen and to give the other party time to unwind. This is a great time for a nice hug and to check in with each other. If you have been in a home office all day, the first thing you might want to do is share your day and enter a conversation. Be respectful and wait for the other person to decompress. After all, they had to commute, and you did not. Avoid the distraction of speaking up right away. This can actually improve your personal relationships.

ABOUT MICHAEL: Michael Gregory leads two firms, The Collaboration Effect® and Michael Gregory Consulting, LLC.

The Collaboration Effect® is a professional speaking business.

Mike's keynote speech entitled, "It's Not About Me", is for organizations that are looking for an inspirational, dynamic and entertaining speaker.

As a result of Mike's presentations, clients often share that their people are more focused on the tasks at hand, have more control in navigating difficult decisions, and more peace in their professional and personal relationships.

After participating in presentations, participants leave with actionable items they can apply immediately on the job and in life.

Michael Gregory Consulting, LLC is a consulting firm dedicated to overcoming conflicts with the IRS and others, and provides focus by applying The Collaboration Effect® to increase revenues, reduce resources and strengthen relationships.

Much of Mike's work is designed on how to mediate, negotiate, and collaborate for improved performance. Mike has completed over 2,500 mediations, given over 400 presentations and written 11 books including his three signature books, Peaceful Resolutions, The Servant Manager and Business Valuations and the IRS.

With 28 years at the IRS at all levels and having headed up business valuation nationally for 11 years at the IRS, Mike has real insights into the IRS. Mike has leveraged that experience and partnered with neuroscientists over the last eight years to enable him to be an expert in conflict resolution. He works with small businesses to Fortune 100 companies helping others to resolve conflicts and to promote new levels of cooperation and achievement.

As a result of his collaborative approach clients have saved nearly one billion dollars.

Mike has a B.S. from Valparaiso University, a M.S. from the University of Wisconsin-Madison and an MBA from DePaul University. This formal education has been enhanced by his varied work experiences as well as more than a decade of active participation in professional and legal negotiations and with hundreds of hours of continual professional education.

Mike is a qualified mediator with the Minnesota Supreme Court. He serves on the Minnesota State Bar Association Alternative Dispute Resolution Section board and is on the Ethics and Oversight Board of the National Association of Certified Valuers and Analysts (NACVA). He is Certified Valuation Analyst (CVA) with NACVA. He is also an Accredited Senior Appraiser (ASA) in business valuation with the American Society of Appraisers having served on the national Business Valuation Committee. He also is a reviewer of the Estate and Trust Journal.

On a personal note as a proud Grandpa, he loves playing with two lovely grand daughters every week.

Mike may be reached at mg@mikegreg.com and 651-633-5311.

6

RESPECT THE SPACE - DARLENE LAW

Why: As a certified Feng Shui Consultant, along with my work for AJL Communications Ltd, I know that the energy of our space impacts how we work in that space. A cluttered space wastes time as you are always interrupting yourself by shuffling papers and books around to find what you want when you want it. Physical clutter distracts us from what is important and leads to mental clutter which can stop us from getting into the flow of concentrating on important tasks.

When working from home, it is especially important to have a dedicated workspace (there are tax implications in this as well), not unlike what you would have if you worked outside the home. The energy of this space should support you and reflect on what it is you do. Your dedicated office should be just that – dedicated to your work. It should contain a good solid desk, a comfortable, ergonomic chair, good light – preferably natural light as well, and hopefully, be set away from outside distractions such as television. You should have easy access to everything you need to do your job without running around the house looking for your tape, scissors, or even your phone. Your office should be a place that you are comfortable and enjoy being in – otherwise, what's the point?

I like that I have a door that can be closed for private conversation. The closed door tells others that I am not open to interruptions.

I had always had a home office, even when I had an outside job. Ever since I started working exclusively from home over 20 years ago, I decided to never have the television on while working. Alvin – The "Talent" with AJL Communications prefers to have the TV on. Luckily our offices are on separate floors in the home, and the TV in the family room located outside my office is never on except for during the lunch break.

Not only do we respect the space that we work in, as well we respect the other person's space and how they like to work — a win-win for both of us.

The Un-Habit: Clear The Clutter

Why: Clutter is anything that we do not love or use. Clutter is stagnant energy that affects your personal energy and stops the positive energy from flowing freely around you. It can impact your mood as well as your overall health, relationships, and even finances.

Dust, old papers and files, expired coupons, flyers, items that are broken, burnt out light bulbs, outdated or broken electronics, cords that you don't have a use for all constitute clutter. Clutter distracts us from what is important and takes up valuable space.

Clutter that covers our desks and shelves invites in more clutter and slows you down. Books that we have read but won't read again, books that we have never read (and probably won't), business cards collected but never filed or added to our contacts all constitute clutter. Files of completed projects take up the space that new and exciting projects could use. Old financial files, receipts, and tax records may need to be kept for tax purposes but have no place in your current life just to remind you of old finances and keep you focused on the past. The past is the past; you need to focus on the present to be able to go forward to the future.

Clutter isn't about self-control, being a bad or lazy person. It is a manifestation of our inner life. If the stuff in your life is a problem then the stuff in your head is the problem. When we can't let go of something for fear that we may "need it some day," this is a sign that we don't trust ourselves to provide for the future. There are as many reasons for clutter as there are people, and one person's comfort level may not be the same as the next person.

Both physical and mental clutter take up space that could be better utilized. When every space is covered or filled with clutter, there is no room for anything new to come into our lives. That includes opportunities, people, and even money. By clearing the clutter, you open up your space, your life, and your mind to new opportunities and possibilities.

About Darlene: Darlene Law is "The Brains" of AJL Communications and is married to Alvin Law, "The Talent," Motivational Speaker, Author, and Musician. Darlene joined AJL Communications in October 1991 after moving to Regina, Saskatchewan, from Calgary, Alberta. She brought her extensive knowledge in office management and human resources and applied them to Alvin's growing, international speaking business. Good thing too, and just in time!

When Darlene first moved to Saskatchewan, Alvin made a promise that one day they would return to Calgary. That day happened in July 2000. Since then, Darlene has managed the office full time, is a partner in the company, and is the first point of contact when looking to connect with Alvin. Alvin does the speaking, Darlene does everything else. Early in their relationship, they made a deal that Alvin will stay out of Darlene's office, and Darlene will stay off the stage. So far, that has worked well for them.

In addition to her work with AJL Communications, Darlene studies energy. In 2005 Darlene graduated from Mount Royal College Feng Shui Practitioner course. She continued and expanded her studies and knowledge and is now a Certified Feng Shui Master. As a Feng Shui Master, Darlene works with both personal and professional clients to help them balance their space to help balance and enhance their lives. This could include space clearing, decluttering, or evaluating the space to eliminate blockages. She also uses this extensive knowledge daily in the managing of AJL Communications as well as in their personal lives.

In addition to Feng Shui, Darlene studies healing energy modalities. Healing Touch, meditation, and NLP Tapping are tools that Darlene uses to keep their mental energy healthy. Lately, Darlene's interests have expanded into Healing Touch For Animals with an eye on providing animal foster care.

Alvin can travel independently in North America, and that leaves Darlene time to get involved as a volunteer in the community. She has belonged to different organizations such as Kinettes (it's a Canadian thing), Junior League, and currently, is on the Board of Directors for Variety Alberta, A Children's Charity. Darlene loves to travel and gets to tag along when Alvin works internationally. They have enjoyed visiting Australia, England, Bangkok, Romania, and various other locations both professionally and for personal enjoyment.

7

A BALL & A WALL - CHRISTOPHER JOSSART

Why: At-home offices are fuel stations of productivity.

"I think better with my bat. Where's my bat?" So maybe that quote from Tom Cruise in the 1992 blockbuster film "A Few Good Men" didn't leave quite the impression in the same movie that Jack Nicholson's shout from the courtroom did. Even today, "You can't handle the truth" grows in playful infamy among moviegoers.

Cruise's baseball bat, however, served as a 'must-have' while playing Lt. Daniel Kaffee, an attorney in the Armed Forces. Kaffee did his best work from the confines of his apartment, preparing to defend two U.S. Marines accused of murder. There, he paced the floor with the bat in hand during the building of a case with two other legal colleagues. Part of those long days working with his defense team included a plan to call the intimidating Col. Nathan Jessep, played by Nicholson, to the stand. The goal was to get the egotistical colonel enraged enough to admit conspiracy. It worked.

For most of us, our daily grind isn't as dire as was the lieutenant's. That said, maximizing your craft from home, not at the office, is a shared connection to that movie. Let's look at two winning outcomes for entrepreneurs in establishing a home office culture.

First, working from home furnishes key aides in removing barriers to productivity, like Kaffee's bat. When stuck on an idea or the next sentence in a proposal, grab a ball, and find a wall. Sometimes "doing nothing" produces the next "something" you need to push a project closer to the finish line.

I'll often toss a tennis ball against a brick part of my house or sit and lob one softly at the fireplace for ten minutes or so. It's tremendous therapy—getaway, get renewed. For others, maybe a walk around the yard during a time in which you'd normally be at work will reset the mind. The next time you meet with clients, you'll feel energized, not emotionally drained, from having to "be on" all the time in an office setting.

Second, we feel most peaceful at home. Peace lessens stress, which in turn amplifies productivity. Find your peace point. Maybe it's a set of headphones compared to water-cooler chatter or noisy potato chip bags in an office. Entrepreneurs know what needs to get done; they should begin their start-up venture by finding where to do the work best.

The Un-Habit: Falling Into Unproductive

Why: Working from home builds new skill sets.

The refrigerator calls. You trip over the laundry. The golf bag is smiling at 80-degrees and a sunny sky.

In all likelihood, any one of these three persuasions would win against a pile of papers waiting for your attention as an at-home entrepreneur. In reality, hitting the fridge, doing laundry, and teeing it up will always be tempting forces when operating a business from your house. Ironically, if approached strategically, small business proprietors can enjoy all of these immersions and more.

Loose talk about the downfalls of working from home typically ranges from the call of domestic duties to gorgeous weather and a home to-do list (usually reserved for weekends). Successful at-home entrepreneurs follow their own weekend parameters.

That's the point. You call the shots under the premise that accountability rests on your shoulders. Accountability today is a lost skill because of social media and related technologies consuming our time. It also segues into skill-building in time management. If one day you want to hit the golf course, then learn how to manage what's teed up on your desk for the rest of the week. Then a rainy Saturday is treated as a Monday and is a chance to go to town in the home office.

At-home business owners excel in communication skills as well. They become sharper, more concise communicators resulting from less small talk that is always prevalent inside corporate walls. It's a learned balance of just enough at-home emails and phone calls with needed coffee clutches in face-to-face meetings that keeps business going in the right direction.

By working whenever and wherever we want at home as a way to integrate our passion with a profession, the possibilities are endless in terms of production.

What could you do with better skills in accountability, time management, and communication?

About Christopher: Christopher Jossart delivers game- changing messages on both paper and from the podium, and he's been doing so for 27 years.

In 2019, he was named Communicator of the Year on behalf of the National Council for Marketing & Public Relations (NCMPR). A 16-time award-winning writer and editor recognized nationally by NCMPR and the non-profit sector, Chris' work has appeared in international publications while overseeing thousands of news releases to publication.

Chris has earned distinguished status as a top 10 national nonfiction author, and his books have been used by a top U.S. law enforcement training program and have drawn media attention around the globe. His current read, Railroaded: Framed for Murder, Fighting for Justice, is being sold in markets worldwide and has become an audiobook based on its success.

On the speaking and training fronts, Chris has uplifted packed audiences with customized keynote addresses for many sectors, while training thousands of high school learners, college students, and business professionals on personal and professional branding. He taught communications courses for two decades at an accredited college and is a public relations management professional with more than a quarter-century of experience in developing speaking scripts and articles for corporate executives and faculty members with doctorate degrees. He has appeared regularly on national radio talk shows.

Chris' leadership helped an accredited college pass a $66.5 million public referendum by a two-to-one margin. He holds a

Master's degree in Managerial Communications, is an Honorary Member of the Phi Theta Kappa Honor Society Hall of Fame, a Professional Member of the National Speakers Association in addition to The Authors Guild, and is a certified Strategic Communication Management Professional on behalf of the International Association of Business Communicators and Global Communication Certification Council.

Learn more about Chris' critical thinking writing topics and bold employee development training programs by visiting www.christopherjossart.com.

8

A 30-MINUTE HEALTHY LUNCH BREAK - LOUISE TYRRELL

Why: Collapsing into bed that night, I wondered what was wrong? It was no busier than usual, and I hadn't driven that day – one of the joys of a home office! Initially, I thought that coaching online wouldn't be as helpful for clients as in person, but plenty of positive feedback and transformations reassured me their well-being benefited greatly. One call rolled into another, with the final one lasting longer than expected as Ann and I happily chatted about how her mood, energy, and focus improved since starting the Life Success Program.

Morning rolled into the afternoon, and at 6 pm, I realized I had forgotten all about lunch. Ignoring the signs and waning energy mid-afternoon, I was now feeling famished. I prepared a delicious dinner, and even though it filled me, my body was exhausted!

To avoid exhaustion, I recommend stopping for a 30-minute healthy lunch break. Common sense, right? At home, though, it's tempting to keep working without breaks. I believe this can catch up on us and lead to adverse health conditions.

There's no denying our bodies and brains need a break to rest and recharge. One hour would be wonderful, but beginning the Habit with 30 minutes for lunch, preferably at the same time every day will leave you feeling relaxed, revitalized, and rejuvenated.

Because our bodies and brains need fuel to function to their optimum potential, it's best to choose healthy, wholesome foods that will provide the required essential goodness. A protein-packed lunch will boost energy and vitality and help prevent the afternoon slump, sometimes felt when we choose carbohydrate packed lunches or sugary snacks. One nutritious, delicious, easy to prepare lunch is a Quinoa Salad. Gluten-free quinoa contains all nine essential amino acids and is high in many vitamins and minerals. On its own, it's a bit bland, but adding beetroot, broccoli, salad leaves, celery, cucumber, feta cheese, and olives offers you a very wholesome, healthy lunch, which will satisfy your appetite and boost energy.

It's also good to sit away from your workspace and switch off everything so that you can enjoy your lunch in peace and allow it to digest.

The Un-Habit: Working in your pajamas

WHY: I ran up Una's driveway dodging the drops of rain. It sure is great to work from home on days like this I thought, remembering how happy Una was to set up her home office a few months before. I rang the doorbell and she appeared in the doorway ... in her pajamas. 'Oh, are you ill?' I asked, 'You should have said, I can come back when you're well again.' 'I'm not ill,' she said 'I'm fine, what makes you think I'm ill?' 'Pajamas at 2 pm', I answered, 'I thought you'd be busy working.' 'I sure am busy and regularly work in my pajamas, sure nobody sees me,' she answered.

We walked into the living room and sat down. Having not seen each other for a few weeks, it was great to grab an hour to catch up. As she filled our cups with hot coffee, she asked me why I made a face when she said that she regularly works in her pajamas. My mind mulled it over as I didn't consider it wrong, and I didn't want to offend her. I replied, 'whatever you're comfortable in is grand, but I find that when I start my day with an invigorating shower and get dressed as if I was going out to work that my day is much more productive than if I stay in my pajamas. I usually reserve the pleasure of pajamas for Saturday or Sunday, so that I feel there's a distinction between working at home and relaxing at home'. 'Mmm....', she replied.

It was an unexpected but welcome invitation to Una's house for lunch again the following Friday. I prepared a delicious pot of homemade soup which I carefully carried up the driveway. I struggled to ring the doorbell with my elbow. Una opened the door and I nearly dropped the pot of soup with shock. She stood there in a beautiful blue dress with her hair tied back, smiling through delicate pink lipstick. 'Wow,' I exclaimed 'what a transformation.' 'Do you know,' she said, 'since last week I've gotten dressed up every day for work and I feel like a million dollars. I'm sitting more upright at my desk, speaking clearer, closing more sales, and generally getting on great, who would believe? What a difference a dress makes!'

About Louise: Louise Tyrrell works as a Transformational Health Coach, Stress Consultant, and Speaker, helping hard-working, ambitious executives and entrepreneurs who are busy and burdened by the stress and strain of modern living. Even though they're smart enough to know they need to slow down and take care of themselves, they just can't seem to find the time. Louise shares simple strategies and skills that you can sprinkle through your day, even if you are the busiest person on the planet! These tried and tested techniques will improve overall wellbeing so that you wake with energy and enthusiasm to enjoy every day, feeling calm, confident, and in control.

In her 20's, while recovering from a car accident, Louise became very interested in a holistic approach to health. "Even though I was feeling utterly self-conscious and completely out of condition, I pushed through the self-doubt and plucked up the courage to attend my very first Yoga class, and that was the day my life changed," she says. Fortunate to make a full recovery and no-longer needing the surgery that was planned, she began her studies in Yoga, Psychotherapy, Stress Management, Meditation, Mindfulness, and Holistic Healthy Eating. She traveled to the UK and USA to train with some of the world's greatest teachers; Tony Robbins, Dr. Deepak Chopra, Dr. Wayne Dyer, Bob Proctor, Eckhart Tolle, T Harv Eker, John Assaraf, Susan Jeffers, and Robert Holden and also learned a lot by tapping into her own strength and courage to overcome obstacles and adversities along her own journey.

Since setting up one of the first Holistic Therapy Centres in Ireland in 1999, she has helped hundreds of individuals, small businesses, large companies, and community groups to gain a competitive edge by managing stress and mastering health. She is the founder of ZenLife Mind-Body-Health and creator of WOW, Stress Mastery and FAB at 50 and beyond. Her work has been featured on RTE television, local radio, and in the Irish Times Health Supplement.

A 30-Minute Healthy Lunch Break - Louise Tyrrell

Louise recognizes how important self-knowledge and self-care are for vibrant health and wellbeing. With a wealth of personal and professional experience, a passion for helping others, and a calm, caring nature, she will help you to change the course of your health so that you can restore balance and harmony to live a full and happy life.

For your free gifts visit www.louisetyrrell.com/free-gifts

9

CREATE SPACE THAT'S YOUR OWN - KATHY GRUVER

Why: The advantage of having a home office as opposed to being in a building with other people is that you can create the environment to work. Even if you have a small amount of space, you can surround yourself with touchstones and reminders of what you want to achieve, who you want to be, and what your values are.

Get your systems in place first. Are you a piler or a filer? Figure out what is going to be most productive for you. Put the hot items closest to you; don't bury them in the drawer. Use labels, folders, trays, or colors to help keep yourself organized.

Have things close to you that you will need, whether it's Kleenex, nasal spray, lip stuff, or an inhaler. This will keep you from having to break your work cycle to dig through your house and find things. That is the best way to get distracted; you'll think, "I'll just go grab that one thing," and then two hours later, you're doing the dishes, watching TV, and playing with the cat. Stay at work during work hours. Then, have things in your environment to remind you who you are, and who you want to be. My desk is surrounded by things that remind me to be the most powerful, be the most productive, perhaps reminds me of supportive people or little gifts and tokens from people that remind me that I am loved.

You can create the perfect environment for you. Paint the walls, bring in a sound machine, or scented candles. Whatever is going to make this environment ideal for you.

I recommend affirmations, perhaps one a day, to inspire you and keep you on track for your goals. Make them short, positive and in the present moment as if you already have that thing or that quality.

Maybe you have your vision board on the wall or a photo of your dream vacation spot or car you want to buy. Our brain moves towards things that are familiar to us. Make your goals and dreams a 'known' and your brain will help you get there.

Create an environment that is ideal for you, that will up your productivity and skyrocket you to success.

The Un-Habit: Living in fear

WHY: Fear is simply False Evidence Appearing Real. Fear is about living in the future, projecting to a time that isn't even here yet. Let's face it; we can't change the future anyway. If something bad is going to happen, worrying, ruminating, and losing sleep isn't going to change it. Why suffer twice? Why ruin this present moment by being anywhere other than where we are right now. We are the only creature that does this. The only being that can drag around the past and project into a worrisome future.

We have the tools to do the best we can at this moment. And this moment is all we have. Our brains move towards that which we know, that which is familiar to us. So, if we are thinking about negative, scary things, that is what we are going to move towards. You know, those things we say we don't want.

What if we practice thinking only of those things we want, the things we truly desire? If we daydream and fantasize about those instead, then our brain will start lining things up to help us find those things.

I remember when I learned to ride a bike, my father told me to look in front of me. I was doing great until my mother called us from the porch. I looked to the right to see her, and sure enough, the bike veered, and I went careening towards her.

What we focus on is what we are going to move towards. So, what do you really want? And focus on that. Go for that. Stop dwelling and putting energy towards those things that you say you don't want in your life. Know what you, what you truly want, and think about that, move towards that. Let fear fade, stay present and rejoice for that which is right in front of us, in the here and now.

About Kathy: Kathy Gruver, Ph.D., is an international motivational speaker, two-time TEDx-er, an award-winning author, a podcast host, and hosted the national TV show based on her first book, The Alternative Medicine Cabinet. She has earned her Ph.D. in Natural Health. She has authored seven books including, Conquer your Stress at Work, Workplace Wellness, Body/Mind Therapies for the Bodyworker, Conquer Your Stress with Mind/Body Techniques, Journey of Healing, and she co-wrote Market my Practice.

She has studied mind/body medicine at the famed Benson-Henry Institute for Mind-Body Medicine at Harvard Medical School. She has been featured as an expert in numerous publications, including Glamour, Fitness, Time, More, Women, Wall Street Journal, CNN, WebMD, Prevention, Huffington Post, Yahoo, Marie Claire, Ladies Home Journal, Dr. Oz's The Good Life, First, and Women.

Dr. Gruver has appeared as a guest expert on over 250 radio and TV shows, including NPR, SkyNews London, Morning Blend in Las Vegas, CBS Radio, and Lifetime Television. Gruver has facilitated over 250 educational lectures around the world for everyone, from nurses in the Middle East to 911 dispatchers in New Orleans, corporations around the US, and teachers in her own backyard. Her typical topics are stress, mindfulness, communication, and ego state optimization.

She had the privilege of working on a project for the military to create and institute a stress reduction program and helped shut down underground sex massage parlors in her community.

She is the co-host of the hot new Fire and Earth Podcast and a past winner of NAWBO's Spirit of Entrepreneurship Awards. Kathy maintains a hypnotherapy and coaching practice in Santa Barbara, Calif. She has also produced an instructional massage DVD, Therapeutic Massage at Home; Learn to Rub People the RIGHT Way™ and is a practitioner with over 25 years of experience. For fun and stress relief Dr. Gruver does flying trapeze and hip hop dance.

More information can be found at www.KathyGruver.com

10

BE YOUR DREAM BOSS - MARY NESTOR

Why: A recent LinkedIn survey of 1 million employed US workers showed that 75% who left their job voluntarily made their exit because of a bad manager, not the job. You may have decided to go solo and strike out on your own for the same reason.

Home-based business owners can be tough bosses, too. So, now that you've set up your home office and you're the boss, you get to be the "dream boss" you always wanted. Here are some tips to form a Habit of being your own dream boss.

1. There is nothing more frustrating than a boss who doesn't know where they are going or how to get there. The dream boss has a clear vision, plan, and short-and long-term goals. Take some time each morning to think, plan, and set reasonable goals for the day. Then get moving.

2. Are you still getting up at 6 a.m., putting on your work "uniform" and logging in by 6:15? In your home office, you make your own schedule. You've always wanted a flexible schedule

with plenty of time for life. Finally, you've got the dream boss (YOU!) who agrees.

3. The boss and co-workers have been replaced by the partner, kids, and dog who compete for your time and attention. Now that you're the dream boss be decisive and assertive. Look for ways to use their talents to help keep your office running smoothly. Make your home office a harmonious, friendly haven where you are respected, confident, and are your own amazing leader.

4. Be kind to yourself. Home-based business owners can be their worst critics and hardest taskmasters. It takes time to get out of the mindset of going to an office or job controlled by someone else. You're the dream boss, remember? You can binge-watch Netflix one afternoon. You can read a story to your five-year-old or take the dog for a walk. Put some life in your work. Your dream boss wants you to be happy and successful.

The transition to a home-office based business takes time. I spent a lot of years in Corporate jobs with a lot of rules. I found that I was taking on the role of the toxic bosses I escaped. I had to learn to be comfortable with myself and my quirky, creative mind that got distracted by new ideas and opportunities. Be your own dream boss—the one that values your individuality, talent, and determination.

The Un-Habit: Limiting Your Home Office Space

Why: When I started my home-based consulting business, I spent some time and money, creating a home office with all the equipment and furniture that I thought was required. It was functional, comfortable, and convenient, with internet access, a desktop PC, and a combination fax/printer/copier/scanner. A bookcase and filing cabinet rounded out the functionality and ambiance I thought I needed to get down to business.

I got to work, and the space worked out well. But It didn't take long before I felt a little isolated in those four walls. I began moving to the dining room, using the large dining table to organize research for training programs, collate training manuals, and organize notes for speeches.

I had a cute, small breakfast room off the kitchen, with a high window that warmed up the space with the morning sunshine and seemed to light a fire under my creative mind. I would take a note pad and pen with a cup of tea to that room when I needed to generate ideas. The living room with its large picture window facing the busy street and a comfortable overstuffed sofa was the perfect place to sink down with my laptop and write. Ideas seemed to flow with the traffic and people passing by that window.

I have moved several times since then, and in each new location, I created what I called my home office. Each time, I found that I was creative and productive outside those four walls, too. In one recent move, I set up my "office" in the dining room, angling my desk so I could see the palm trees and lush foliage outside the windows in the front and the back of the house. There were no doors to close off the space, which flowed in all directions to the rest of the house.

Since I've gone solo in 1992, I've worked in lots of places in my home and neighborhoods. The buzz of a good coffee, people watching, and cool music at a coffee shop or bookstore can be a stimulating extension of your "home" office. You've been de-cubicled. Make it a Habit to find new and exciting ways to make your home an energizing space. Push the walls back to find new spaces that energize you, be creative, and make contacts. Make your home office anywhere you get down to business.

About Mary: Mary J. Nestor is an international speaker, author, seminar leader, and coach with a diverse background as a business owner, entrepreneur, freelance writer, author, and business executive. She is a certified speaker, coach, and trainer with the John Maxwell Group, holds the SHRM-SCP designation for human resources professionals, and a member of the National Speakers Association for over 25 years. She has worked with a variety of organizations, non-profits, and individuals over the years through MJN Consulting, an organizational change, leadership, and communications company she founded in 1992. Her company is a certified DBE in the State of Georgia.

Mary is an award-winning speaker, master evaluator, and executive coach. She has appeared on TV, radio and online as a motivational expert, career coach, and lifestyle contributor. She is past president of the Savannah Toastmasters Club #700. Mary is also a Dale Carnegie graduate and has worked with that organization to help others to achieve their goals.

Mary has over 25 years as a change agent, process improvement consultant, and technical writer. She was certified in Total Quality Management/Statistical Process Control by the British Standards Institute (BSI) and has led ISO 9000 certification projects for both Monsanto Company and Garrett Aviation (Augusta, GA). She conducted organization change projects for a variety of organizations, including August Technical College, Augusta, GA.

Mary is a freelance writer and author. In 2014, she published her first book, "Emily's Best Birthday Party Ever!." Her second book, "Say It Now! Say It Right! Tips To Handle The Tough (and Tender) Conversations in Any Business or Life Situation" (Motivational Press, 2016). She has written hundreds of feature stories, blogs and articles for The Savannah Morning News and various online business, career and personal development websites. She is a contributor to the Amazon.com best-selling book, "1 Habit for Women Action Takers," 1 Habit Press. She is currently working on a mystery/thriller novel.

Mary has designed and delivered hundreds of seminars on management/leadership, communications, customer service, and human resources management in the U.S. England, Scotland, Puerto Rico, and the U.S. Virgin Islands. She was a certified trainer for SkillPath Seminars and a career transition consultant. She has presented at SHRM National Conferences. Her topics include motivation, leadership, communications, customer service, personal and professional development.

After living on both U.S. coasts and a two-year stint in Saudi Arabia, Mary settled into a 1940's bungalow in Ardsley Park in Savannah, GA. She continues to write, speak, blog, coach, and consult with individuals and organizations on leadership, communications, and personal growth. Mary is a member of the CEAC Advisory Board for the Savannah/Chatham County Public School System and enjoys singing Alto II with the Savannah Symphony Orchestra and Chorus and the St. John the Baptist Cathedral Choir. She also loves spending time with her two grown children and five grandchildren.

You can learn more about Mary on her website: www.maryjnestor.com

Contact Mary at mary@maryjnestor.com Facebook: https://www.facebook.com/Nestormaryj Phone: 912-844-1794

Mary's books are available online at Amazon: https://amzn.to/2vPUpFZ

11

GENERATE CREATIVE INSPIRATION - KATIE GOODMAN

Why: When working alone as a solopreneur in a home office, the silence can be golden or it can be creatively deadly. How do you generate creative ideas when you're sitting alone without the hubbub of other energized humans?

As someone who teaches how to use *The 8 Tools of Improv Comedy* in every day life, I came up with these creative tricks because I was often in this situation myself.

Oh the terror of the blank page!

One of the first things to know is that no improv comedian loves it when someone says, "Okay, start a scene, no location, no premise, just pick anything! Go!" That absolutely doesn't inspire ideas. Having no parameters is a death sentence for creative idea generation.

<u>Constraint Breeds Creativity</u>: When we are stuck, what we need is *more* constraint, not less. For example, trying to come up with a blog for your business? Give yourself a constraint, such as: You must write about something that happened in the last 24 hours.

Or, you can only write about something that made you incredibly ticked off. Or, you can only write about something your parents taught you that you hated at the time but appreciate today. These constraints are much more likely to help you get inspired and come up with something good.

And then, allow yourself to be lost. You don't have to have the whole thing in your mind when you start. The same goes for a business plan, a marketing plan, an article, a novel, a song, a pitch: anything you are creating from scratch. Allow yourself to explore and play and generate creative ideas without knowing where it's going. This is a practice that improvisers must do every day to create their scenes. It's what business people do when they have a new idea no one's tried before. You can't possibly know exactly where things are headed. And if you get stuck with a preconceived notion of where it's going, it's very likely you'll persist down a useless path when you should be open and flexible and able to pivot when necessary.

The Un-Habit: Being Isolated

Why: As a solo-preneur, I work alone a LOT of the time. There are definitely days where it's like The Shining around here. I get a little cabin-fever-y and just simply lonely. I have worked in a home office for 30 years, but I'm also a highly social person. I'm a comedian, actor, writer: a *collaborator*. So in addition to working at home, I always made sure to have a co-working space or a fun little office situation with other creatives.

Many days were spent alone, and some were in rehearsal or writing with my husband... Yep you heard that right. Husband. He's my co-writer! "Yikes!" you might think. "How on earth do you work together??"

My great aunt was my mentor and worked with her husband for 40 years. She used to say, "I've never considered divorce. Homicide, yes, but not divorce." If you've worked with your spouse, you get this, *amirite*?

Well, Step 1: we definitely have different writing spaces. That is important. We come together, brain-storm and then get the hell out of each other's way. We also have a rule: No work talk in bed. Very smart rule.

Working together too much without any play or fun can end up wreaking havoc on a relationship. This can happen with any collaborative relationship, not just romantic partners, so you have to make sure you aren't actually *creating* isolation within the over-connectedness. It's complicated. You need to create some distance to actually have connection.

We all need connection. If we don't connect *enough* we get disconnected. If I don't go on tour often enough with my "Broad Comedy" show cast or head out and lead corporate improv workshops with engaged employees, then I get bored, uncreative, and lonely. So what's an entrepreneur to do?? I get out of the house A LOT. I meet friends for lunch more days of the week than not. I go to a gym with a fun group. I take walks with people and talk through ideas. I have two mastermind groups that meet monthly on Zoom calls. I GET OUT.

So have that home office. Make it gorgeous, playful, creative, cozy. But invite people over to it to work sometimes. Allow yourself to head to a coffee shop as soon as you starting thinking about writing "All work and no play..." all over your walls. Get an accountability group you can meet online. Connect with people in your field or phase of life and make sure to *stay* connected over time.

About Katie: Katie Goodman is an award-winning musical comedian, author, speaker, life-coach, and social activist.

She is a nationally touring keynote speaker on the topic of using the tools of improv comedy in everyday life.

Her musical comedy show, "Broad Comedy," runs Off-Broadway and tours across the country, where they have helped raise over 1.5 million dollars for Planned Parenthood by performing at their events and fundraisers.

She has been seen on Showtime's The Green Room With Paul Provenza, on Current TV as a pundit, and on TruTV. Her comedy videos, having amassed 3 million views, can be seen online. She received a Time Out New York Critic's Pick for Best Cabaret, and is signed with Comedy Dynamics, North America's largest independent record label. Her album "Halfway Closer To Dead" is available on iTunes.

Katie holds a philosophy degree form the University of Pennsylvania. As a keynote speaker, workshop leader, trainer, and life-coach, Katie has taught over 10,000 people the art of improvisational comedy. She certifies entrepreneurs in her 4-month program, "_The Creativity For Life Workshop Certification Program_," that teaches how to create a thriving, profitable and fulfilling business as a creative workshop leader.

She is a featured blogger for *The Huffington Post,* writes for *O, The Oprah Magazine,* and is the author of _Improvisation For The Spirit: Living A More Creative, Spontaneous and Courageous Life Using The Tools of Improv Comedy_, and the funny children's book, *The Night Our Parents Went Out.*

Katie was nominated for the MacArthur Foundation Genius Grant for her unique work in theatre.

Arianna Huffington says: "If Steve Martin and Julia Cameron had a baby and hired Samantha Bee to raise it, you might get someone as bright, funny insightful and inspiring as Katie Goodman."

You can read more about Katie as a speaker and workshop leader by visiting www.katiegoodmanspeaking.com.

12

FORGET ABOUT THE IDEA OF WORK / LIFE BALANCE; CREATE WORK INTEGRATION - READE MILNER

Why: As a husband and father, I am required to delicately balance my role as an entrepreneur who works from home with my responsibilities to my family. With two small children right down the hall from my office, this can sometimes be a challenge.

The life-changing moment for our family occurred when I stopped trying to create a "Great Wall of Work" around my office.

Not long ago, I started talking to my children about the work that Daddy does in his office. Though young, they are beginning to understand that it is a good thing to work hard because they can see me doing so every day.

My son often pretends he is "working, like Daddy" while playing on a computer (that he built using legos, of course).

Work isn't something that happens in some unknown place far away from them. It happens right there at home.

My wife and I have also managed to blur the lines between work and family effectively. She often helps me in my business by providing her time and skills that I don't possess.

This creates yet another shared experience between her and me and draws us even closer together.

On the other side of the coin is an imperative to decide on an end to the workday consciously. I'm not one who believes this has to be the same every day. Some days, I'll take advantage of my professional liberty and cut out early to pick up my kids from school.

Conversely, I may find myself working in the evening after the kids go to bed. I'm also not afraid to pull out the laptop while on vacation. It's the price we pay for freedom. I'm not draconian about my schedule. You can't be when your work and life are so intimately integrated.

The Un-Habit: Don't hide work from your family

Why: I understand why this Habit became commonplace during the latter half of the 20th century. For centuries, families were all involved in work together. This was by necessity. To survive in the early American agricultural economy, there was an advantage to having more hands to the plow. This often meant the children.

During the post-war 1950s, work took on a very different look. The father got up and commuted to an office or factory job, leaving mom and children home to attend public school. This disconnect created a separation between work and family that, I believe, harmed the family unit.

Forget About The Idea of Work / Life Balance; Create Work Inte... | 97

Fathers had difficulty relating to the rest of the family, and they, him. Fortunately, we are no longer required to create such a stark separation. We can include our families in the intimate details of our work and, in some cases, recruit their help.

I would argue this is not only good for family relationships but business as well. If you have more peace and personal satisfaction with your home life, you will perform better and more energetically professionally.

Research has even started to support this claim. Studies have been done to observe the effect of different factors on professional success. While factors like IQ and education seem to have little correlation, conscientiousness and life satisfaction are the most highly correlative factors that lead to professional and financial success.

What this means is that if you stop creating these unnecessary walls between your work life and your family life and, instead, integrate the two, you will end up with better performance and higher levels of satisfaction in both endeavors.

So, tear down those walls. Invite your children into the office. Get your spouse's input on your business. And finally, experience what it means to live a fully integrated life.

About Reade: Reade Milner is a husband, father, entrepreneur, and marketing consultant with over 10+ years in business. In that time, he has personally advised or driven results for over 250 businesses, ranging from startups to the Fortune 500. His insights into marketing and innovative business growth have enabled him to help his clients increase revenues by many millions of dollars.

Additionally, Reade serves on the Board of Directors for the Atlanta Chapter of the National Association of Insurance & Financial Advisors (NAIFA), where he leads marketing efforts and community involvement.

A lifelong Georgia resident, Reade graduated from Emory University in Atlanta, where he served as team captain of the basketball team. It was during that experience that he learned real personal accountability along with leadership skills that have and will help him in his current endeavors.

With a demonstrated heart of service and zeal for helping people, Reade is actively involved in his local community. He created a local storytelling platform called The Faces of Barrow County, where he and several other volunteers seek out and explore notable community members, helping to promote their stories via their social media channels and website.

Reade also serves faithfully in his local church, where he leads Sunday School and assists the pastor as a member of the Board of Trustees.

Personally, Reade takes great pride in his wonderful family, citing them as his greatest assets. He has often stated that leading his "Crazy Crew" is the privilege of a lifetime. Integrating his family and professional endeavors has meant an optimal quality of life that allows him to provide for the family he loves so dearly without having to spend so much time separated from them. His office is 15 steps away from the dining room table, meaning that no matter how hectic life becomes, he is rarely late for dinner.

13

PRAY AND AFFIRM DAILY - KAMIA KINDLE

Why: When building a thriving home office, your mindset is critical. For many of us, we start with a smaller business that will grow. In the beginning, when it is just you and that computer, you need to make sure you are mentally on the right path.

I was raised to always speak positively over my life; in fact, it's how I raise my two sons. Starting the day with prayer and affirmation sets the tone of the entire day. Prayer alone allows you to do the following: let go of yesterday and those things that cannot be changed; it will enable you to enter into a place of gratefulness and show appreciation for those things that matter in your life; it allows you to pray for peace and blessings towards everything and everyone attached to your life. Prayer brings a form of peace to your day that's irreplaceable.

Alongside prayer, making affirmations invokes self-encouragement. Affirmations speak alacrity, life, love, prosperity, and so much more into the very moment you begin to open your mouth! You feel and believe what you affirm as soon as you start to say it. When I make affirmations, they usually are the same things I have been saying for years: "I am healthy, wealthy, wise, and I have peace in my life. I am a great mother. I am a great steward of the precious things I have been given. I own and operate a fortune 500, multi-million dollar marketing agency. I am beautiful inside and out. There's nothing I can't do. I am unstoppable!" I repeat this to myself at least five times in the mornings before I begin my day. This is important because no one can pump you up better than yourself.

The truth is, my days are just not the same if I fail to start my day with prayer and affirmations. They are like medicine to my soul.

The Un-Habit: Dwelling on yesterday

Why: Yesterday has come and gone. A lot of times, we hang our heads on what happened, what could have happened, or why it happened. But if yesterday is gone, why do we find ourselves always thinking about it? We only have so many hours in our day. When we allow our current moments to harp on what's already gone, it is a waste of time.

Those close to me always hear me say, "Yesterday is over. There's nothing we can do to change it. Tomorrow isn't here yet, so don't worry about it. FOCUS on what's in front of you at this very moment and give your best for RIGHT NOW!" I say this because it's essential to put your best efforts towards what's here on this occasion.

I tend to compare the worries of yesterday to unnecessary baggage. I am not insinuating that we don't have anything good to take from yesterday, because we do. Our good memories/moments/times from yesterday, should be used as positive energy every now and then to help encourage us when needed. However, things of the past that cause us to lose focus are flat out useless. When we allow bad things from yesterday to take our energy, this is known as dwelling on the past.

It's important to get out of the Habit of dwelling on yesterday, and the simplest reasoning is because we cannot do anything about what happened in days gone. Use your energy and resources to make the most of the moment you're in RIGHT NOW! Are you in the grocery store shopping for your family? Well, take this moment to make it the best-dammed grocery shopping trip you've had in a long time. Breathe, relax, walk through the aisles thankful, purchase something new you haven't tried before. Grab a thoughtful gift for your kids or your spouse while you're there. Just enjoy the moment and be your best self.

Leave yesterday where it is. It's gone.

About Kamia: She is the founder and CEO of SPG, Web + Marketing LLC, in Kansas City, Missouri. Seventeen years ago, she had a vision for a marketing and design firm that not only produced cutting edge work but of an organization that reached out to the community far and near. Kamia knew that the ability to be artistic in such a niche market meant also being business savvy.

She is proud to have collaborated with such a wide base of local and national talent ranging from the home-grown resident Shawn Edwards (well-known movie critic and author) to other prestigious organizations such as CHEP and Pepsi Co. The accomplishment of designing well over 45,000 ads and email campaigns is one fact that she likes to remain extremely humble about.

Kamia received her undergraduate degree in Computer Information Systems in 2003. She possesses the confidence and ability to capture the intent of her client while maintaining her God-given, raw artistic talent. With over 20 years of experience in the graphic design and internet marketing solutions field, she is deemed as an expert. Kamia has been an entrepreneur since the young age of 16. Her company has received many awards, such as Supplier of the Year and Small Business of the Year, in Kansas City.

Project management, coupled with her ever-increasing industry knowledge in methodologies such as RICH-AC and Taguchi, make Kamia one of the industry's most progressive CEO's known today. Her education of advertisement psychology, attention to detail, and her diversity of clientele all lead to a firm that is infused with nothing short of success.

Granted, Kamia is a forever rising entrepreneur; she's also known for being an intentional and loving mother. She has two sons, Pierce and Jaycion, whom she adores more than anything. She firmly believes in family time and loving on her children daily. She's an active member of her local church, serving as a Sunday school teacher for two years now.

She's an entrepreneur at heart and is currently starting three additional companies. Kamia's hunger for building businesses from the ground up started at a very young age, and she doesn't plan on letting up any time soon.

14

INSPIRE! - IRENE ZAMARO

Why: I was always a nine to fiver. Wake up, battle traffic, and work to make someone else successful. We are all trained through life that this is what we are supposed to do each day. Eventually, I found I was never satisfied, my opinions and ideas were glossed over by managers, and I never felt like I was taken seriously. One day I became inspired, and I broke that chain by becoming self-employed.

I realized my passions and what gave me fulfillment. I broke free from the office chains and became an entrepreneur. Part of my inspiration was doing work that made me happy, to interact and meet exciting and driven people. However, my real motivation was being able to spend time with my children. Two of my children have a rare disease that deteriorates their eyesight. My oldest son is a military veteran who suffers from ailments that many soldiers like him have brought home. Being able to support their dreams and help them to be successful continuously inspires me to be better. If they don't accept excuses and find a way to live each day to its fullest, what reason do I have?

It's not easy, it takes much hard work, and we don't usually have a big office full of people to help and support us. However, the flexibility of being able to work from a home office, to help them during the day and finish work in the evenings brings a self-satisfaction you rarely see in the corporate world. Being able to work remotely or having the flexibility to shift my hours to allow quality time with loved ones instead of compiling vacation for one trip a year is priceless.

Some people believe this is taking a risk, and it can be scary and intimidating. I'm a single mom trying to care for my family and myself. There are struggles in anything you do, but when I see my children overcome their obstacles, it makes it all worth it—making it possible to have a flexible work-life balance.

The Un-Habit: Negativity

Why: If there is one thing, you must avoid its negativity. There can be no growth or creativity when negativity is there to bring everything down. I pride myself on my energy and optimism, but sometimes you find yourself in a rut. Take a step back when that action occurs and see what's changed to drain your energy, what has blocked your optimism, and clouded your mind from creativity.

No matter how you might want to celebrate positivity, there are always those specific people that cross your path and focus on the negative. They still have a counter of something terrible to your good…a rumor to plant doubt against people you enjoy… office gossip. This energy pulls away from your creativity, your energy… your smile!

Negativity can be the hardest when it comes from a great worker, a long-time friend, or someone you just ended up behind at the grocery store. This dark cloud, this pressure, creates a drain on you emotionally and pulls your energy and drive down before you realize it's happening. We allow that person, who might just be having a bad day or honks at us on the freeway to change our mood. We've allowed that person people in front of us in line who yells at the teller, to drag us down. Ultimately, it's our choice if we allow them to impact our lives and change our attitude.

Be aware of that negative cloud around us, take the high road, and don't become influenced by the negativity. Distance yourself from negative people, no matter how hard a worker or how long a "friend," that don't improve who you are. Find people and places that enhance your energy, and that will allow you to grow and prosper. You are the only one in control of how you feel and what you want to be... give yourself the opportunity to grow and be the best person you can be...do not allow the negativity of others to slow your creativity.

Be above it, and be fabulous!

About Irene: Irene Zamaro is a spark of light and a true professional driven by her passion for life and people. A native Californian, born and raised in Los Angeles, Irene, now continues her journey as a professional entrepreneur in Orange County, California.

First and foremost, Irene is a single mother of three beautiful children. She enjoys spending time whenever she can with her children and their families.

Engaging in their lives and interests provides endless pleasure, whether its braille with her daughter, scrapbooking, or racing cars with her grandson. Irene loves nature and the outdoors. Whenever there is free time for hiking or camping, she takes advantage of it. The peace and tranquility of the environment allow you to get to know yourself and keep your mind clear. Irene loves astronomy and enjoys using her telescope to wonder at the beauty and mystery of the moon.

Irene loves to help others and dedicates much of her time to charities and non-profit events. She organized and managed the Young Artist Academy Awards, coordinating entertainment, gift bags, and food service vendors for the next generation of actors. The reward is the joy of watching these children inspire others.

Irene enjoys traveling for events, and the opportunity to meet other like-minded and creative individuals never get old. It's energizing to hear the stories of others to learn of their struggles and the ultimate path to success. Utilizing her endless energy and spirit by supporting other individuals as they grow their brand provides real satisfaction. There is a world of unique and fascinating individuals, and Irene takes genuine pleasure in impacting the lives of others.

Irene believes that no matter what you do or where you go in life, bring your energy, and Don't Forget to Share Your Smile!

Inspirational Quote: California women are the engine driving the growth in California's economy; Women make the California economy unique and bright.

15

FIND FUN AND JOY IN EACH DAY - KIRSTEN JARVI

Why: I have experienced joy in leadership on multiple occasions in working from a home office. Creating happiness in a home office environment helps you align with the who rather than the how by creating innovative solutions and aligning with others who have massive transformative purposes.

The two hours in a car each day can also be harmful to our air quality, and it is a very much less productive use of time. Time is an incredible resource for being utilized in planning, creating content, and performance partnerships. Some of the most joyful, visionary, and innovative people I have met online, these people I would have never physically meet in an office environment.

Why? These people are in different time zones out about the nation, and some internationally. I have worked in both environments a home office and have traveled the country like a road warrior. I have experienced the joy of manifesting these new partnerships and relationships that happen early in the AM, many times with online meetings to collaborate and make critical decisions. Outside of the formal office environment. Not only is it good for the environment, but it also increases productivity and focused alignment, the key to creating clear intentions.

As a woman in science, with a growth mindset, when faced with a challenge, I say to myself, I am still learning, I may not do this entirely, but I am learning how to do it, a home office creates a great environment to do this in. Awakening joy to focused attention and intention. Following my heart's sincere desire to close down the noise amongst us. I have come back to the question: What do you hold as the purpose of your life? A home office is ideal to be genuinely present with the projects I have personally worked on with multiple teams, and our teams love this as well. Whatever motivates you to grow becomes the wind in the sails of the original invention or intention.

No one does it alone—the more inspiring our motivations, the more energy we can bring to fulfilling our intentions. If you want to appreciate or encourage others to value themselves, this is what you can do. Praise efforts, choices, and strategies, and do it with specifics. When you do this, you are telling your brain to do more of this. Giving precise details is essential; remember this in the future.

Developing appreciation, gratitude, and joy with this kind of unconventional Habit will provide you with the upper hand advantage. When failure comes, and it will, the ability to laugh at oneself is crucial to not taking ourselves too seriously and being out of touch with God-given being in joy. When we pause, reflect, and be grateful, we naturally return to who we are born to be—a brilliant, powerful human being.

Finally, some of the most prolific scientific inventors found their greatest inspirations from finding joy in failure. Until eventually, that spark of inspiration turns to discover incredible solutions! Your most significant barriers, or your circumstances, are simply an opportunity to look at solutions with an open mind and utilize resilience. There is a vitality a life force, energy, a quickening that translates through you into action, and because there is only one of you in all time, this expression is unique and original. And if you block it, it will never exist and could be lost. The world will not have it. It is not your business to determine how good it is or how valuable it is compared to other expressions. It is your business to keep it clear and directly to keep the channel open. The channel open to joy.

When we are living in our pure joy, we uplift ourselves at that given moment and move through life with ease. Being present, as well as thinking about the future, is how God wants us to be. Love another as we love ourselves.

Finding the joy and celebrating the fun- factor is a blessing we give to the world and, in return, creates leadership balance both in career, personal life, a home office is ideal for this.

The Un-Habit: Minimize complexity

Why: At one point in my life, I was continually thriving, moving, and wanting more with not ever genuinely being fulfilled. It was a Habit of complexity I created. I was not satisfied, even being super successful. I always thought there was more to life. Then a paradigm shift occurred more healthily. I slowed down and simplified to amplify. When moving too fast, I was distracted, not focused, in touch with my authentically. It was not until I slowed down in a home office environment and started practicing meditation; exercise life became simple.

As a healer, an optimist, and a visionary, being all of these things at once, yes, my brain sees patterns, before others do, this is a gift, but with too much complexity can be very self-debilitating.

I can create a positive flow in an instant in a home office. I accomplish skills and tasks much quicker in a quiet, focused environment. This consciousness helps to take something complex and turn it into something simple in a fun-loving way. The goal is to make an impact on people's lives. I love to learn when it is playful and fun. I find myself getting bored and distracted if something that is too complex and lacks clarity.

There is a genius in taking complex problems and making simple solutions.

As a visionary or overachiever creating time to Be---Then Do---Then Be in a home office is very easy to do. Listening and genuinely being authentic, I then come from a place of inner truth. And I write from this place too. In this fast-paced world, yes, technology is high-speed fast. There is a lot of data and information coming at us; how can we apply the knowledge is a pearl of more profound wisdom.

We must understand how the human brain works, moving fast; sometimes, it is hard for the human brain to slow down enough to know what matters truly. As a healer, it is so easy to get caught up in the every-day rush of business tasks, commitments, goals, and implementation, which can lead to burnout, if continually working.

It's appropriate to set boundaries. A home office makes it easier to do this and produce authentically.

Simplify to amplify. Breaking the Habit of complexity and aligning with other souls who commit to simplicity in implementing the new. You can tell the masters of this in design thinking.

About Kirsten: Kirsten Jarvi is an award-winning registered dental hygienist, author, founder, and owner of CERDH.com, she enjoys seeing others authentic leadership shine in action as well as finds joy in the calm of solitude.

Kirsten has inspired many healthcare professionals; she has worked with start-up companies and fortune 500 companies. She has built and implemented technology in business, education, and research environments. One of her favorite positions was building two Salesforce® platforms for innovative companies. To create tele-health collegiate teams to benefit dentistry and dental hygiene. Her values of high touch of social support with the high technology to access across the United States. Kirsten helped establish one of the first tele-health educational support teams for a Fortune 500 company. She recruited, hired, lead, and inspired women across the nation and supported small entrepreneurial, innovative dental offices implementing technologies into their offices.

Her intuitive nature helped her to inspire and recruit some of the best leaders in the nation to pursue advanced degrees in the dental hygiene profession. She inspired leadership at her almamater the University of California, San Francisco, to start the very first Masters of Science for registered dental hygienists in an inter-professional model. This innovation created a more interactive connection and respect for healthcare professionals.

She earned a degree from Sonoma State University in Biology. She continued her studies with a bachelor of science in dental hygiene, and a master of science at the University of California, San Francisco.

She has conducted interviews with Fox television, multiple independent dental hygiene companies, as a subject expert. She has written articles or been interviewed for dental hygiene industry magazines Dimensions, and RDH. She has sat on different key opinion leaders boards for multiple companies to implement innovative marketing strategies. "Kirsten finds joy in making an impact on humanity, she is good-natured, has strong leadership skills and would be an excellent asset to any company, I relied on Kirsten on some of my most difficult technical tasks." A leading researcher and world-renown NIH grant writer, Margaret M. Walsh, once wrote. Kirsten also believes in giving back to the next generation of healthcare professionals she has supported initiatives include funding of two scholarships, two for women who choose a healthcare career, and has coached young girls in soccer.

Being born on 11/11 Veterans day, she always remembers the responsibility of gratitude, honor, and service. She has a deep respect for our military leaders and veterans. Especially how they bring peace to the world and hope by teaching other countries the benefit of peaceful outcomes.

CULTIVATE THE CAPACITY TO BE ALONE - GAURAV BHALLA

Why: "Without cultivating the capacity to be alone, productivity and professional success is impossible."

It's rumored that a lady once asked the celebrated playwright, novelist, and short-story writer, Somerset Maugham if he wrote every day or only when inspiration showed up. Maugham replied, "Lady, I write only when inspiration arrives. Fortunately, she shows up promptly at 8 am every morning."

Maugham's witty retort unveils a powerful truth – steely discipline is non-negotiable for any meaningful achievement. This is especially critical for solitary undertakings. A writer must confront the blank page and write, inspiration or no inspiration. A musician must practice scales, for long hours, alone. A painter, a carpenter, a sculptor, a chef, a gardener, a golfer, all must show up and practice their craft for hours on end...alone...with no one willing them on, but their own desire and commitment. Without this discipline, all professionals mentioned above would fail to produce the quality and quantity of work vital for earning recognition and being considered successful.

Working from home is very similar to practicing a solitary art. Here's why. The discipline to show up, be at one's desk, and begin work at 8 am every day, day after day after day, is indispensable for anybody wishing to work from home. (The actual time a person starts working is irrelevant; what's at play here is pig-headed discipline and metronomic consistency). And to exhibit that discipline and live by it daily means a person must cultivate one indispensable positive Habit: Cultivate The Capacity To Be Alone.

Cultivating a capacity to be alone or getting warm and cozy with one's own company is mission-critical if a person wants to achieve success working from home. The issue is not introvert vs. extrovert, social vs. antisocial; the issue is very simply one of responding to the demands of our work in a manner expected of us, no matter how complex or how mundane the task.

Here is the bottom line: If we are to produce quality, error-free work – consistently – if we are to stand by our work, and feel fulfilled and satisfied with what we have produced, then we must pay attention to what we are working on, we must approach tasks and activities with focused concentration, and we must respond creatively because the world around is constantly evolving. All this requires shutting out people, which is what makes cultivating the "The Capacity To Be Alone" Habit crucial for any person wanting to thrive and succeed working from home.

The Un-Habit: Eliminate The Need For Constant Stroking

Why: "The need for constant stroking - recognition - diminishes creativity."

Creativity is a valued trait amongst a large number of professionals. Most people would be livid if denied a promotion because their boss thought they "lacked creativity." Yet, unknown to them, most people have no one to blame but themselves; they constantly erode their own creativity by incessantly chasing personal recognition.

This Habit can severely derail any effort to build a productive and thriving home office culture.

Alfred Adler, a contemporary of Sigmund Freud and Carl Jung, and founder of the school of Individual Psychology explained it in the following manner. According to him, all of life is comprised of two tents: The "Main Tent" and the "Side Show."

- The main tent is "What life is all about," work, earning a living, and earning recognition through one's own effort.
- The sideshow is running away, evading the demands of the main tent; it's all about wanting to be the favored child and craving for personal attention from other people.

The more time a person spends chasing sideshows, the less time they have for being truly creative and productive. No wonder they feel robbed. In reality, it's not another who has robbed them, denied them their dreams; they have robbed themselves. By craving personal recognition, by continually chasing the sideshow rewards of "wanting to feel good about me, wanting to feel loved, wanting to be accepted, wanting to be special for others," these people fall short of achieving their dreams.

Because they value "sideshow payments of recognition" more than what really matters in this world – "main tent achievements centered around work."

I've worked from home in some form or the other for over two decades. And during this time, the most common reaction I have encountered (still do) is, "Oh, I could never do that." When I probe and ask, "Why not?" I always get the same answer, "I need people around me."

No doubt, people and relationships are essential. But not if they cost us our dreams and achieving the demands made on us by the Main Tent. So, if you genuinely want a thriving and productive home-office, fire this baby-sitter, eliminate this 1 Un-Habit.

About Gaurav: Gaurav Bhalla, Ph.D. is a globally acclaimed 'thinker- doer' and trusted expert in Leadership, Strategy, Marketing, and Innovation. A provocative, charismatic, and entertaining speaker, trainer, and coach, he delivers insight-packed audience experiences that take organizations, teams, and individuals on transformational journeys of greater professional success and personal fulfillment.

In his 40+ years of global experience – 5 continents, 30+ countries – he has worked with a variety of clients, large and small, for-profit and not-for-profit companies in several sectors, such as Healthcare, Pharmaceuticals, Technology, and Financial Services.

A small sampling of his clients in these sectors includes Glaxo Smith Kline, Bristol-Myers Squibb, Blue Cross Blue Shield, Capital One, Axis Bank, Citi, MetLife, Bank of America, Legal & General, Caterpillar, Maersk, Audi, ESSAR, Deloitte, PwC, EY, JLL, T. Rowe Price, Randstad, Indian Railways, National Association of Broadcasters, Sprint, US Dept. of Agriculture, Hershey, Marriott, and Heinz.

Additionally, Gaurav has also designed and implemented executive education programs at leading Business Schools like Georgetown, Duke, Singapore Management University, University of Maryland, GIBS-South Africa, Indian School of Business, and at Corporate Universities of companies like Glaxo, Sprint, Kodak, Hallmark, Deloitte, IBM, Boeing, and Texas Instruments.

For a more comprehensive understanding of his professional and personal credentials, visit www.gauravbhalla.com

www.linkedin.com/in/gauravbhalla

In 2016, he won a global award, Executive Education Specialist of the Year, in recognition of his speaking and training services.

Published in both business and literature, his leading-edge thinking is reflected in his HBR article, "Rethinking Marketing," and his book, "Collaboration and Co-Creation: New Platforms for Marketing and Innovation." His latest book, "Awakening A Leader's Soul: Learnings Through Immortal Poems," presents a new human-centric narrative of leadership, "Soulful LeadershipTM, that reimagines leadership's purpose and reshapes its outcomes. It was launched globally in Sep. 2017. Additionally, he's also a novelist and poet. His novel, "The Curse and the Cup," was published at the end of 2014. He's also written and published two screenplays, several short stories, and numerous poems.

Currently, the CEO of Knowledge Kinetics, he has held senior management and C-level positions in Marketing, Strategy, and innovation at P&G (Richardson Vicks), Nestle, and TNS Worldwide.

What makes Gaurav unique are his growth mindset, his diversity of thinking and experience, his passion for action, and his WHY – his purpose – that values the humanity of people more than their executive brilliance.

17

CREATE AN INVIGORATING AND SEPARATE WORKSPACE - CYNTHIA A. PEEL

Why: Your home office needs to separate you from your other home life duties. When you work at home, the line is very thin and easy to blur, so you have to be diligent in making your separation, not only for tax purposes but for your sanity and productivity. If possible, make it a separate room, but if not, a small corner will do. I homeschooled four children, so I understand the challenge. But it can be done.

Your home office is a place that needs to inspire you to be your best self. I have my reasons 'why' I'm working posted on my office wall, a framed photo of my family. They smile at me and cheer me on as I work to help my clients reach their goals. My favorite color is on the walls, and I have special inspirational quotes and artwork posted to give me an occasional boost. Colors and pictures, sounds, and smells can all affect your mood and help you do your work. It might be surprising that something as simple as a well-placed plant can reduce your stress level. Create a space that energizes you.

If you are starting and don't know where to begin, ask yourself what is necessary? You should keep costs down, but keep your spirits high. YOU are your biggest asset. Start with the minimums and grow from there. Tactically, everyone needs to have their office system, furniture, and supplies that allow them to be organized and work in a way that makes sense and feels good to them.

For example, in my day to day in my business, I mainly interact with people on the phone or the internet. So I primarily need my computer and phone and some privacy to work. In my business, creativity and inspiration are important, so I have to keep moving to feel good. A great way to keep your mood and energy levels up is to stand at least every 45 minutes and move and do some deep breathing. It's been proven to help stimulate your mind and body. So I chose to have a counter height desk, where I can stand or sit in a bar stool chair. Fresh air and sunlight are also great mood boosters, they enhance serotonin, so I'm usually next to an open window.

You'll need to evaluate your specific needs and make this your special place to work. Keep it separate and design it to energize you. Choose wisely, and it will pay you dividends.

The Un-Habit: Letting piles of paper stack up!

Why: Paper is my nemesis, the kryptonite to my office superpowers. If I let my office get messy, I can feel it drain my mojo away. It makes me anxious, and I avoid my office because I know it's not going to be enjoyable working there. I'll find other things to do, like laundry, which won't pay the bills. However, I'm fortunate that my amazing husband, Derek, is a neat freak and such a great organizer. He comes in and saves me from time to time by helping me clean up and file papers when my office

Create an Invigorating and Separate Workspace - Cynthia A. ... | 121

gets too messy. If you tend to let paper get the best of you, you may need a 'Derek' in your life also. Find a person that keeps you in check or can clean it up for you. If not, make yourself accountable for cleaning up your own mess at least once a week. Put it on the calendar. It is a priority to keep your workplace happy and productive; somewhere you will want to be.

Better yet, something you can do to avoid the stack up altogether is to automate everything possible. There are so many wonderful free and low-cost programs that can help boost your productivity and help you remain calm and happier in your home office. Convert client files, get a customer relationship manager tool, and change invoicing and other routine tasks from paper to computer. There is a lot of storage available in your computer's hard drive and much more with various business programs on the internet cloud, like Google and Microsoft Suite. It is more secure than in an office cabinet drawer anyway. If you have an emergency, you can grab your computer and run, or know that your important files have already been securely backed up on the net.

If you still have to use paper, employ the old productivity rule to only 'touch it once.' Shuffling it around your office can be such a waste of time and drive you mad with the disorganized mess you make. Keep your home office space clean, organized, and as tech-savvy as you can muster, and you will be more joyfully balanced, and more empowered to add your unique gifts to the world. We are all anxiously waiting to see what you will bring to the party.

About Cynthia: Cynthia A. Peel, makes her home in Southern CA. She is the joyful owner of Peel's Maker Studio, and she is a Best Selling Author, Speaker, Knowledge Broker, and Small Business Coach.

Mrs. Peel graduated at the top of her classes with Bachelor's degrees in both Economics and Social and Behavioral Sciences. She earned multiple licenses in the financial services industry. She didn't stop there, always having a philosophy to never stop learning. Cynthia truly believes in self-education and is always happily taking notes in some new class. There isn't a subject that doesn't fascinate her. She gets excited when she discovers and then can share something beautiful and transformative. Tremendous fulfillment has come from her never-ending quest for personal development.

Mrs. Cynthia Peel's family is her greatest source of joy and inspiration. Cynthia and her husband, Derek, are the parents of four talented young men, aged from 12-19. When they first married in 1999, they had chosen for Cynthia to leave work and be a stay at home mom. She occasionally sold some products from home to make extra money, but just after the birth of their fourth baby, financial hardship caused a drastic reduction in their lifestyle. Cynthia started a new business helping protect families and businesses with legal and identity theft protection services and coaching others on how to start their home-based businesses. It helped restore their family to their previous lifestyle.

Peel's Maker studio was born in 2015 out of Cynthia's desire to create a business that matched her love for learning and her passion for teaching children. She had not only taught her own children, but had volunteered at the local schools and at her church for over 10 years. Peel's Maker Studio is a fun place for students to learn all things related to S.T.E.A.M. (Science, Technology, Engineering, Art, and Math) www.peelsmakerstudio.com Its mission is to inspire students to be excited learners and problem solvers.

Cynthia is especially driven to help other mothers, mompreneurs, earn an income so they can support their family's needs without missing important moments in their children's lives. She guides these moms to a more joyful, balanced business, and family life via online courses and mastermind groups. Over the years, she's been a real estate developer, a landlord, a financial advisor, a banker, an insurance agent, a teacher, and a salesperson. But her most important role has been a mother, and in her opinion, that's the role that any business should support. www.CynthiaPeel.com

www.facebook.com/groups/joyfulbalancedmompreneur

Cynthia Peel has served her community in countless hours of volunteer service for over 25 years and was honored by the city of Yucaipa for her efforts to coordinate the Make a Difference Day and Helping Hands days of Service. She has also been active in the local Faith in Action Committees to help solve the homeless issues. She truly believes that a group of committed and concerned citizens can make a difference and find solutions to any problem.

18

BE CONSISTENT - JENNIFER MASTOR

Why: Why is being consistent such an important Habit to have in your life? Why do you need to make sure you are consistent with how you work? Because when you have a home office and work for yourself, you don't have colleagues to help you remember. You don't have others that you can rely on to help you through a project. You have yourself. And you probably like it that way, or you wouldn't have gone into business for yourself. Think about it. If you ever worked for the public or private sector, you had others around you. You had someone else to rely on, to speak with, to share ideas with. And now, you have yourself. So, for you to be successful, the only person you can and have to count on is yourself.

So, let's look at how being consistent can improve your work Habits. Consistency is a patterned behavior. And we have all learned that to create a Habit, we must do it for 21 days, consistently.

So, for this example, I am using the adage, "Write it down," as being a consistent behavior for your company.

Can you imagine making sure you never forget what you are supposed to do! I was shown how to write down my agenda, my task, and needs every day at work on a calendar for 11 years at my first job as a recruiter. (we didn't use computers back then, and yes, I know I just aged myself, but there is a point here, I promise). I got so consistent at writing things down that I started to include what I needed to get done at home. I was also and still am, consistent at using a hard and soft calendar.

Consistency sounds easy, but can you imagine, as I know many of you have, having "the one great idea" and just telling yourself that you will remember it the next morning? And poof, your great idea is gone. You didn't write it down. If you were in the Habit and consistent about putting down your thoughts, ideas, and must do's daily, can you imagine where you might be now with that one great idea?

So, let me share this one Habit with you-be consistent in what you do, how you do it, and why you do it every day. I am not saying change is bad; on the contrary, I am saying in life, we get messy, we get lost, and we get busy. Writing down your thoughts and more is just one way of showing how consistency in your life can change you, as well as consistently make you more successful running your company the way you want it to run. I believe that if you are consistent with a few easy and much-needed Habits in your daily life, like writing it all down, you will find a bit more balance as well.

The Un-Habit: Stop using filler words when you speak

Why: Have you ever been so excited to see your favorite author come to read from his new book and talk about himself? Did you imagine that his voice was going to be just a smooth as in the book?

And then he starts to talk. At first, you don't hear it; you chalk it up to nerves or what have you. And then it starts. Every other word out of this man's mouth is a "filler" word. It gets so bad you begin to count how many times he uses, "and," "but," "like," "maybe," etc. You start to lose interest in what he is saying and find yourself thinking he is not as debonair as you hoped. He is not smooth; does he know what he is saying? What is he saying?

You lose confidence in a man you have always thought was the best at everything. It turns out; he is as normal as many out there who use "filler' words when they are not confident in what they are saying or don't know how to format the words they want to express.

Can this Habit of using "filler" words change? Yes. How? PRACTICE!

You are in charge of a small yet successful company. You talk on the phone; you make pitches to new investors and or you speak to an audience. How you speak and come across to everyone you touch will be how they measure you and trust you to invest in you.

So, what do you do? Practice in front of a mirror. Record yourself so you can listen back. How do you know if you use "filler" words? Ask someone. Ask the person you live with, your friend or colleague, even people you network with.

Make it a point to go slower in your speech, make a point to know that unless you have something to add to a conversation, you don't talk. But you want to contribute? PRACTICE your speech. Listen to yourself. Using filler words is a bad Habit that needs to be broken. How do you break it? PRACTICE.

Just like any Habit, practice makes it better, never perfect. But it will make you stand out; people will take you more seriously, you will have people listen to you, and your confidence will get stronger.

Why does this Habit of using filler words need to be broken? Because you want to sound like yourself, not like a person who doesn't care.

About Jennifer: Jennifer is a dedicated and performance-driven Professional Recruiter with a growth mindset and passion for reading people. She is valued for her stellar interpersonal communication skills, relationship building, and ability to recruit and manage resourceful, top-performing candidates. Jennifer has proven success in creating recruitment and networking strategies, employee referrals, complex industry research, and developing an extensive pipeline of passive candidates to fill potential needs.

As a Career Consultant, she specializes in listening first, offering suggestions second. She believes in helping in all areas of starting a new career. Jennifer has proven her ability, time after time to help in the areas of resume writing, reviewing job offers, the art of interviewing, and preparing others for what-ever comes next. She believes that everyone has a story, their story, and it should be heard. This goes with emotions, fears, and excitement. She guides others that ask for help on where they believe they should go. Mostly, it is her special way of giving them their confidence back. She understands that everyone has it, just at times they misplace it.

Jennifer has been a Professional Recruiter & Consultant for 28 years now and admits, she still hasn't seen it all! She is open that she is not perfect, but she offers common sense and reasoning skills along with every con, she gives a pro, and for every pro, she gives you the con. She wants to make sure you see the whole picture. She is known for being honest and direct and finds most people gravitate to that more than sweet words and soft touches.

Jennifer has always been a giver of her time. Whether it be volunteering her time at both her children's school for career days, speaking at the local Junior Colleges, or sitting on panels for soon to be college graduates. Jennifer has a "pay it forward" attitude when it comes to helping others. Her volunteer help with transitioning Veterans is no exception. "I have the time, the means and experience, why shouldn't I help?" You will also find Jennifer at every WBO (Woman Business Owners) event and she is presently the Awards Chair for this non-profit woman's group.

Jennifer has been involved in a few podcasts, was spotlighted in 425 Magazine, and is seen almost daily on LinkedIn with her "thought of the day" post. She is considered "old school" in her ways of recruiting and consulting, and her clients will say the same thing. She is incredibly proud of her loyal clients and never gets tired of consulting new people who ask for help.

Jennifer was born in sunny California, but calls Issaquah, WA her home. She has two amazing adult children; her son Athan, stationed in Kansas in the Air Force and her daughter, Raiya, loves being a professional Dog Groomer.

She is a very happy, positive, and real person who happens to love her career and what she does.

19 MINUTES OF MOVEMENT - HEATHER DENNISTON

Why: You may not realize it, but you are a perpetual motion machine.

Your body is designed to function best when it is in movement.

But movement is not just about staying fit, although that is important. Movement invigorates the brain by stimulating creativity, problem-solving, focus, happiness, and joy.

When working from a home office, it is easy to get tethered to your station and spend hours immobilized staring at a screen. Without movement, your brain battery starts to lose bars and become depleted. Without movement, we produce less, lack creativity, and grasp for energy, come the end of the day.

Consider an old crank flashlight. You are granted light by "moving" the crank faster and faster. The more cranking you do, the longer the glow lasts. Your brain works the same way! When you inject movement moments into your day, your brain lights up like a glorious beam of light.

So, now that we know that, one Habit that is essential for home-office success is to implement non-negotiable movement breaks. Every fifty minutes, take ten minutes to move your body – squat, reach, push, pull, and twist your body to engage all the motions with which we are capably blessed. Bonus points for movements such as dancing, Thai Chi, or jumping jacks because they incorporate coordinated whole-body movements.

I often use the phrase "every joint, every way, every day" to remind myself and clients to twist and turn all joints in as many ranges of motion as possible. Because of the activities most of us engage in, we tend to spend most of our time working directly in front of us eating, driving, keyboarding, and remote controlling. Performing plenty of opposing movements like arching your back and stretching your arms overhead counteract the devastating effects of a sedentary lifestyle.

Leave with this. Movement is your brain's kale. You need more kale.

The Un-Habit: Blurred Lines

Why: Separating working hours from the time spent in roles and responsibilities of our non-working lives can be tricky when holding down a home office. Many allow work-related tasks to leak into family time and mealtimes long after the workday was scheduled to end.

A blurry separation of work-life and home-life will take its toll on your well-being. Fatigue, burn-out, and anxiety are just a few of the issues we can welcome to the party if we fail to assign clear delineations between our work and the rest of our lives. Long-term effects of this imbalance can create more significant issues such as early cognitive decline and disease.

There is a simple practice you can use to sharpen the blurry lines and segment the end of the workday. This process is called the Office Closing Mantra.

The Office Closing Mantra is a three-part system you design to train your brain to release attention on work and shift to your other priorities like working out, prepping dinner, or connecting with your kids.

To develop your custom mantra, pick three specific things that you will do EVERY day at the time you intend to disconnect. Examples might include, closing all folders on your computer so that only the screen saver is viewable, closing the laptop with passion and a verbal "BAM!" and pushing back from the desk saying boisterously, "I am done for the day!! Awesome job!" Be sure to assign movements and verbalizations that are unique and not used in other parts of your day.

The end of the workday mantra needs to be both consistent and demonstrative. These strategic motions or verbalizations signal the brain it is time to let go of work. It can take some practice, but eventually, this simple method allows you to focus on what is essential and allows adequate time to recover for the following day.

About Dr. Denniston: Dr. Denniston is a seasoned chiropractor with a certification in Wellness Chiropractic (CCWP). She is also a NASM, trained Certified Personal Trainer. She is an avid athlete and health enthusiast who has a passion for inspiring action in people of all ages to ignite first steps toward their personal best.

As a writer, she has penned for publications such as Paleo Magazine and FIX.com and authored the book The Three Day Reset, a doable food plan for those wanting to transform their nutrition. (Available on Amazon). She has also been featured in Thrive Global and Authority Magazine.

She is the creator and producer of The Junk You Should Know Show, an episodic targeted primarily to women over forty. Topics range the wellness spectrum from mindset to menopause to meal prep. Weekly, she breaks down tricky wellness topics by going head to head with wellness thought-leaders from all over the world.

She is a Wellness Strategist for companies like Microsoft. She has spoken on topics of resilience, stress management, trust in the workplace, fitness and nutrition for professional success, Habit training, and more.

Her proprietary Wellness Amplifier Method helps executives and entrepreneurs bridge the connection between wellness and professional success for themselves and the leaders on their teams. Her engaging and practical consulting style is refreshing and impactful, and her results-oriented curriculum is transformative.

Dr. Heather also curates an inner-circle membership program called The Change Cave that is geared toward women over forty looking to up-level their wellness through bulletproof resources, unwavering accountability, and a cohesive community of wellness-seekers.

Through online content, public speaking, and coaching, Heather shares wellness, fitness, and nutrition expertise for those looking for profound change. Dr. Heather presents nationally in a format that is energetic and engaging. For rates and availability, you can contact her at

www.WELLFITandFED.com.

20

CULTIVATE CURIOSITY - TABITHA COLIE

Why: "The important thing is not to stop questioning; never lose a holy curiosity." – Albert Einstein

Curiosity is as much a Habit as brushing one's teeth. We are all born curious, and one needs only to spend 15 minutes with a child to see that. But over time, life experience and the fear of looking incompetent can instill in us a need to project an air of expertise, as we confuse confidence with presumptiveness. This mindset can close us off to new possibilities. Returning to the beginner's mindset that is at the core of curiosity allows us to remain open to new ways of being that can make the difference between surviving and thriving.

To thrive in your home office, practice curiosity like you would practice playing an instrument. Question everything that's working and especially question everything that isn't. For example, if you're having trouble focusing and completing tasks, pause and ask yourself why. Is it because you don't know the next step to move forward? Or because you don't have all the information you need to proceed? Or maybe it's that you don't have appropriate boundaries set around your work vs. playtime. Or you don't like the physical environment of your office.

Whatever the problem, get curious. Ask yourself the question and then stop, take a deep breath, and ... listen - the answer is already inside you. Write it down. Then, decide what the next actionable step that will move you to resolve the issue is. Perhaps your solution lies in developing a morning routine that firmly delineates work time vs. not work time. Or painting your office a more uplifting and energizing color. Or making that phone call/sending that email/scheduling that video call to obtain clarity on your project.

Get curious, and then stay curious. Treat it like a regular check-in conversation that you have with yourself, and curiosity just might lead you to your next productive Habit or your next big idea.

The Un-Habit: Set It and Forget It

Why:

> "When you're finished changing, you're finished."
>
> — Benjamin Franklin

To paraphrase the second law of thermodynamics, all systems eventually break down. What works today may not work next year or even next month. "Set it and forget it" might be a good strategy for your Ronco rotisserie chicken, but in the context of your productivity and your life satisfaction, it can be a total killer. The most successful organizations and individuals remain open to adapting to changing circumstances.

For example, when I was in college, I could eat all the fast (heavily processed) food I wanted with no perceived ill effects. My youthful metabolism was able to handle that high calorie, low nutrient input without a hiccup. Until I hit my late 20s. Suddenly, the old familiar ways of feeding myself no longer worked. I realized that I was gaining weight, feeling chronically run-down, and, to make matters worse, had no knowledge of how to prepare wholesome food that would help me feel and perform my best. I asked why.

Then I got curious about nutrition. I took cooking classes and kept a food journal where I recorded everything I ate and how it made me feel. Over time I learned to change everything about how I undertook the process of feeding myself. Had I simply "set it and forget it" when it came to my nutrition, my systems would indeed have broken down long ago. And even now, years later, this continues to be an ever-evolving process as other variables in my life change.

When you're in your home office, get curious about what systems you need to be productive and inspired. Notice which ones work and which are breaking down. Then, check in, reevaluate, and adapt as needed. If you find yourself drifting to a negative, unproductive place, return to your fundamental 'why' question. To set and forget is to risk remaining stuck and stagnant, but to stay curious is to give yourself the key to unlocking the door of your full potential.

About Tabitha: Tabitha Colie follows her curiosity wherever it leads, which has led her to some rather interesting places and a non-linear career path as a Multipotentialite. For the past seven years, she has evangelized remote workplace culture for Seeq Corporation, a global technology company, from the comfort of her home office.

Before joining Seeq, she held roles in marketing management for technology companies, including Schoolnet and Insitu, Inc. Additionally, she has worked as a Productivity Consultant, Professional Organizer, Copywriter, Graphic Designer, Television Segment Producer, Fashion Stylist, Salon Coordinator, Massage Therapist, Waitress ... and more. She believes that one's work should support one's personal development and vice versa.

Tabitha holds a degree in Psychology from the University of California at Santa Cruz and countless certifications on various topics from institutions ranging from the Thunderbird School of Global Management, Institute for Integrative Nutrition, the New York Open Center, and Barre3. She is a licensed Private Pilot, Esthetician, and Realtor.

As an enthusiastic traveler, Tabitha has explored 12 countries, visited all 50 states, and lived in 10 of those states, including New York, Florida, California, and Washington. She currently resides in Hood River, Oregon, with her husband and dog. In her "free" time, her curiosity leads her mostly out of doors where she can be found hiking or riding her mountain bike on forested trails near her home.

An avid hobbyist, she enjoys learning new handicrafts such as knitting, sewing, and jewelry-making. She also sings in a cover band and serves on the Committee for the Music Festival of the Gorge, a fundraiser to showcase local musical talent to supports arts experiences in Hood River area schools and community.

In 2017 she followed yet another thread of curiosity and started a side hustle makeup artistry business. You can find her at www.tabithacolie.com or on LinkedIn https://www.linkedin.com/in/tabithacolie/.

CONTINUE YOUR EDUCATION - REGINA F. LARK, PH.D.

Why: Many of us created a home office to generate income or ideas. In this space, we learn to maximize our productivity. It is here that we use our knowledge to get ahead of the curve, as well as our competitors. We know that knowledge is power, and what we do with the knowledge can surely empower us.

Acquiring knowledge is everything. As you pursue a successful and thriving home office, I encourage you to consider the importance of continuing education, workshops, and webinars. Education transforms you from someone who has a lot of information, to being a business owner or household manager who is a subject matter expert.

When I started my home-based business, I knew that I had a lot to learn. I established a relationship with a great woman at my local Small Business Association and learned a lot about recording and tracking numbers. I took workshops and webinars on building my website, networking best practices, and marketing.

My home-based business is all about clearing clutter. As I was starting, I realized that anyone who is relatively organized could be a professional organizer, making education a key component to my thriving home office. Having a thriving home office meant that I was generating a decent income. To generate a decent income, I needed clients. Generating clients meant that I had to have something that my competitors did not: an education in working with clients with ADHD, chronic disorganization, and hoarding disorder.

For over eleven years, I am known in my community as the hoarding expert (or, rather, the de-hoarding expert!). I grew a solid business with the understanding that I had to know more than my clients and to position myself as a leader and expert. It bears repeating: Knowledge is power, and what we do with the knowledge can surely empower us.

The Un-Habit: Stop it with the office supplies!

Why: I know. They are pretty and fun and colorful and plentiful. But a thriving home office needs to go light on the office supplies! What do we really need, anyway? In 3-5 years, we will probably go through a box of staples and five rolls of tape.

A thriving home office is an uncluttered space. I know this because I work in these spaces all the time. It's what I do for a living. People call me because their home office is a mess; they don't feel productive; they aren't thriving. They need help to declutter and organize their home office, and the biggest offender of clutter in a home office is office supplies!

Mon Dieu! Baskets, note cards, sticky notes of every size and shape (and some are huge!). Boxes of hanging file folders, and manila folders, and little plastic tabs. Boxes of pens and pencils, and also, bags of loose pens and pencils fill the drawers of most home offices. And envelopes. I come across an astonishing number of envelopes.

What do all of these office supplies have in common? They aren't being used, and the majority of these items will never be used. A thriving home office has some streamlining to it. It's efficient; it's clear of clutter, it's got open space for you to work your magic.

Suggestion: Grab an empty Amazon box and walk through every part of your office and fill the box with the majority of your office supplies. Go crazy. Don't think about anything except for getting these unused items out of your thriving home office. You will be fine. Trust me.

When you've filled a box (or boxes!) think about donation places – local schools, senior centers, community centers – they operate with low budgets and often can use the extra supplies.

You've just given your home office a chance to breathe and to thrive.

About Dr. Regina Lark: Dr. Lark earned a Ph.D. in U.S. History from the University of Southern California. Her dissertation focused on the relationships between Japanese women and American soldiers who met and married during the U.S. Occupation of Japan. After graduation, Dr. Lark served as an adjunct professor at a community college. In early 2000, Regina worked with UCLA Women's Studies program and then joined

UCLA Extension for adult learning. In 2008, two months after an unexpected lay-off from her position as a Program Director, Dr. Regina Lark founded her professional organizing company, A Clear Path: Professional Organizing and Productivity.

Regina is a Certified Professional Organizer (CPO) and a Certified Professional Organizer in Chronic Disorganization (CPO-CD). She is a graduate of the Organizer Coach Foundation Training Program, and is a Professional Member of the National Speakers' Association.

Regina specializes in working with chronic disorganization, ADHD, and hoarding.

In 2017, Dr. Lark released the 3rd edition of the first book, Psychic Debris, Crowded Closets: The Relationship between the Stuff in your Head and What's Under Your Bed (now available on Audible). She is also the author of Before the Big O: Professional Organizers Talk about Life Before Organizing.

Worth noting is Regina's two other companies. Silk Touch Moves offers expert move and relocation services helping families upsize or downsize from one home to the next, and recently earned her industry's highest designation as an Accredited Senior Move Manager.

Dr. Lark is a speaker and trainer on issues ranging from hoarding, time management and productivity, women's leadership, and the power of positive thinking.

For more information visit, Speaking of Clutter. Her current project is a book, tentatively titled, Unmasking the Invisible: A Professional Woman's Guide to Organizing their Mental Load, Physical Clutter, and Emotional Well-Being – is in process.

Regina was named one of Top 10 Organizers in Los Angeles by CBS/KCAL Channel 2 and was also awarded NAPO-LA's Most Innovative Organizer.

For fun, she plays golf and tennis and writes goofy songs about clutter.

22

USE YOUR PHONE TO HELP BUILD A ROUTINE - SCOTT SCHWEIGER

Why: Working from a home office is liberating and exciting, but it does come with its own set of challenges; the biggest for me is maintaining a proper routine. Routine has never come naturally to me. As a child, I was always one to wake up late, miss the school bus, and end up biking to school. In my adult life, nothing really has changed, but I have learned that my phone can be my best friend when it comes to maintaining a routine.

First, it's important to separate your personal and professional life! This day and age it's so hard to maintain this separation, so you've got to be proactive about creating it for yourself. In my business, I've set up two 'virtual' phone lines to the same phone, one for clients and the other for personal calls. The same goes for texting, messaging, emails, and all other apps. Having them separated helps me to focus while working and relax while not working.

Secondly, ditch the notifications. Now that you've got your phone set up to separate your calls, you've got to make sure to turn off personal notifications during work hours. Remember, any 'urgent' personal calls can be added to your favorites list so that you do not miss them. Go through your list of apps and turn off anything not essential to your workday. Also, close any browser windows on your computer that are not related to the work at hand. Yes, that includes Netflix.

Third, voicemail is your secret weapon. You don't need to answer every phone call or message immediately. It's often better to let calls go to voicemail and return them with focus and intention, rather than answer them immediately while distracted and stressed. When you're done with your workday, turn off your work notifications. Set up an 'out of office' email and text reply, which directs your clients to contact you with urgent matters via voicemail. Better yet, forward urgent calls to an employee or answering service to help in filtering out the most pressing after-hours matters.

Lastly, wake up to make up time. Are you having trouble falling asleep? Set the phone alarm to get up earlier. You'll be guaranteed to be tired by the following night. Need to finish a big project? Get up early and start it with a fresh mind and a sense of calm and purpose. If you need to add hours to your day, it's so much easier to add these hours first thing in the morning.

The Un-Habit: If I work more I will get more done

Why: The strange paradox of productivity is that less is truly more. When it comes to working from a home office, it can be so easy to get pulled back into answering emails, responding to texts, and taking care of projects in off-hours. And when things get stressful, it can be nearly impossible to step away from those looming deadlines. So, what is the key to managing a stressful workload and allowing yourself time to step away? Organization.

First, make a checklist of everything that needs to be accomplished. Be detailed about each task and break it down into smaller action items if necessary. I find that writing everything down is therapeutic and helps me to declutter my stressed mind.

Second, prioritize the list of tasks by their importance or urgency. If the first few items seem too daunting, then continue to break them down into smaller action items. Seeing your tasks listed out will help you to come up with a strategy to tackle them.

Third, schedule an ample amount of time for yourself to start on the action items. Set the alarm or reminder for yourself and stick to it. I find it most helpful to wake up early and jump straight into my highest priority task. Since I've already gone through and organized my tasks, I don't need to spend the beginning of my day deciding what to start with. If possible, give yourself more time than you think you'd need so that you can work mindfully and methodically to accomplish your tasks without feeling rushed for time.

Four, don't stress. It may take a few trial runs with this new process to develop some faith in it. But know that you've got this. Organization and intentional effort are the keys to solving your tasks, and you've already taken the first steps, so have some faith in yourself! Now go out and enjoy your life. Take a walk, read a book, go on a weekend trip, enjoy one of your favorite activities, and build some excitement, confidence, and energy for the work that lies ahead. And then go to bed and get some rest. Know that you've allotted yourself plenty of time to take care of these items, so there is no need to stress. And, if you need more time, you can always use this same method to create more time for yourself.

About Scott: Scott Schweiger started tinkering with computers at a young age. His passion for technology led him to enroll in the Management of Information Systems at Washington State University, where he honed his skills in computer networking and business management. After the completion of his bachelor's degree, he began work in Seattle as a technology consultant for T-Mobile.

After his time at T-Moblie, Scott began work at a small managed services firm in Bellevue, WA, where he learned the intricacies of running a small business. He gained valuable knowledge in server support and maintenance as well as network architecture. He worked as sales and marketing manager and spent much of his time promoting the business **at** trade shows and networking events.

In 2018, Scott started Cascade Computing, a computer support and consulting firm where he helps hundreds of business owners and professionals with their technology needs. His focus on reliability and customer service has helped his business to grow rapidly through referrals and networking. Cascade Computing specializes in server maintenance, network architecture and security, workstation support, and managed services. Cascade Computing is set to expand to new markets this year, with a focus on providing remote support to clients working from a home office.

Scott also writes and performs music under the artist name, Scott Clay. He has recorded four full-length studio albums and toured extensively throughout the Pacific Northwest and Hawaii. His latest release gained the attention of American Songwriter magazine, and his music video was nominated as a finalist by American Tracks Music Awards and Canadian Cinematography Awards. He is currently in production on his fifth studio project, where he is working on releasing a music video series in conjunction with the National Parks Service.

Scott enjoys hiking and backpacking in the mountains of Washington State. He has spent many summer weekends hiking in the Cascade and Olympic ranges and is preparing to complete the Wonderland Trail hike, a 100-mile trail encircling Mount Rainier, this September.

23

MAKE YOUR SPACE BEAUTIFUL AND INSPIRING - MELINDA SLATER

Why: In today's world (especially during this pandemic, but let's call it a global retreat, that sounds less scary), everyone is home. This might potentially include your spouse, who, oh, by the way, is also working from home, your kids who are "attending school" are at home, not to mention any furry critters you might have living under your roof. And they all assume since you're home that you're available 24/7! Am I right?

Never in our history has this happened, and it's creating a lot of challenges for a lot of people. So ... how do you break the monotony of living and working in the same place when you are just steps away from "home" and all of the things that need tending to?

I wholeheartedly believe that creating an environment that is beautiful and inspiring will help you be more creative and more productive in your work. Anything that makes your workspace feel less like an office, and more of a haven is essential.

This can happen in several different ways, but here are just a few that can have a considerable impact:

- Hang inspiring, meaningful artwork: typically, scenes of nature and photography will be more relaxing than abstract art.
- Create different layers of lighting: task lighting at your desk, overhead lights that can dim, and the more natural light, the better, whether it's from a window or skylights.
- Create a spot for a comfortable chair and small side table: this will give you a space to start your day, take a break when you are finding yourself in a rut or blocked mentally, and a place to take a break without having to go out into the hall where everyone is anxiously awaiting your return "home."
- Provide closed storage for all of the books, binders, supplies, etc. that don't need to be accessed regularly so that when they aren't in use, they are out of sight. This will help your space feel less cluttered and more beautiful.
- Paint a wall a beautiful, fun color, something you might not put in your home but something that feels less boring or monotone.

All of these little touches will help to diminish distractions, create inspiration, deflect from boredom, and ultimately create a sense of peace and calm.

THE UN-HABIT: STOP SITTING AT YOUR DESK AND EXPECTING CREATIVITY AND INSPIRATION TO FLOW

Why: Likely you are sitting at your desk in front of a computer. And that computer is a source of distraction. Emails are flowing in. You just remembered that "thing" you needed to buy, and suddenly you're on Amazon making a purchase. You decide that you should check Facebook because hey you need your 15-minute break anyway and no one's watching and 15 minutes turn into 30 minutes! Or worse yet, there is that review you need to write, that next chapter of your book, and what are you doing? Staring at a white screen with nothing on it and you can't even think of the first word to write, and then you remember that it's due Friday morning, and it's already Wednesday. And you still have nothing written and not a clue where to start!

Sitting at your desk and expecting a genius thought to manifest is like staring into your empty refrigerator and waiting for a four-course meal to materialize. But you couldn't possibly take a break right now because you already spent 30 minutes hanging out on Facebook, texting back and forth with your friend, checking email incessantly. All of this because you don't know where to start.

And this, my friend, is the reason you created that beautiful serene spot in the corner of your office. The one that looks out the window onto a lovely landscape where you can have an afternoon cup of tea and sit and be still without expectation. This special spot allows you to step away from sitting in front of the computer and stop expecting inspiration to come flowing in and out of you from nowhere. Get up, move around, move to a new location, brain dump, meditate. Perhaps you need to grab a notebook and write longhand, curled up on your comfy chair. This simple repositioning might allow new ideas to enter your brain so you can regroup, refresh, and finish that project!

About Melinda: Melinda Slater is the Principal Interior Designer and Owner of Slater Interiors in Mill Creek, Washington. She specializes in helping clients fall in love with the home they already have. As well as helping boutique healthcare businesses bring that extra personal touch to the office, employees, and their clients.

Through her interior architectural space planning and design work, she helps clients discover the potential hiding in their home and work – no matter how cramped, outdated, and non-functional it may feel right now. With a combination of values-driven creative thinking, collaborative planning, and an emphasis on sustainability, she can help transform any space into a sanctuary.

She doesn't believe in a magic design bullet or quick fixes. What she does believe in is listening, learning, and encouraging her clients to dream big – so they can finally uncover the solution they have spent so much time searching for!

Melinda has 15 years of design experience and an AA in Interior Design from Bellevue College. Her previous career was working as a licensed massage therapist for 12 years, the last two years of which were helping hospice patients find comfort and relaxation through touch, at a time when touch either meant pain or very little comforting, positive touch. It is here, working with clients at the end of their life, that it became clear how important and impactful our environment is upon our wellbeing, both as we live on a daily basis and as we die (hopefully in the comfort of our home). Our environment has a direct impact on how we feel and our overall health and wellbeing. This is what she brings into her interior design business working with clients – providing spaces that are representative of who lives there, and how they want to express themselves in their space.

Melinda grew up on a small farm in Moscow, Idaho. Her motto is 'a girl can always dream' and her love for animals and the health of our planet runs deep.

24

TAKE YOUR EYES OFF THE CLOCK - JIM HESSLER

Why: In many traditional office or plant environments, there is an almost constant focus on the clock. There are start times and end times for the workday, and expectations that "40 hours means 40 hours." How many of us who've worked in these traditional environments would admit that much of the work we did there was done with one of our eyes on the clock? How many of us felt pressured to put in a certain number of hours to meet some artificial and external expectations of "time spent" that often had little to do with actual productivity?

In the home office environment, there can be an opportunity for many of us to free ourselves from keeping track of our work hours and to get into the Habit of thinking first about production and secondly about time.

I've worked out of a home office for almost 20 years. I work hard, but I work more thoughtfully than I did when I worked in a traditional environment. It's a smarter workday for me now because whether it's noon, or 5:00 PM, or 10:00 PM, I'm only working because there's something that needs doing, not because I want to prove that I put in the time. There are days when I knock off at 3:00 PM, knowing that I've achieved my most important goals. There are still other days when I go back and put in another hour or two after dinner, but only because my to-do list wasn't sufficiently emptied. Either way, I've formed the Habit of working my list and working to completion rather than to a target time on the clock.

In modern society, you hear a lot of bragging from some people about how hard they work. I think and hope that we will all soon have the courage to go to a dinner party with friends and say, "you know, I only worked 30 hours this week, and it was productive." Working from home presents this possibility for many of us – the possibility of judging for ourselves whether or not we've had a good day of work.

I believe that the average person's work experience in many offices and plants is less than fully productive. I wonder what would happen if all employees were expected to complete a certain set of tasks rather than work a certain number of hours. "Working hours" creates bad Habits – working your to-do list created better Habits.

The Un-Habit: Constant availability

Why: Working from home can help us break the bad Habit of being too available to one's co-workers.

"Wait a minute!" you say. "Isn't it a good thing to be available whenever people need you?"

Well, sorry, but probably not, unless you're an emergency room nurse or a member of a SWAT team. Our personal availability has to be more carefully managed when we're working in a distributed work environment. We don't have the luxury of strolling down the hallway for quick approval or turning our swivel chair around and verbalizing a question to the person nearest us. And surprisingly to many, while getting immediate answers and assistance from the people in close physical or technology-aided proximity seems like a good thing over the short term, it probably doesn't serve your organization or even your clients over the long-term.

As you set up your work environment at home, pro-actively break whatever Habits you have, either behaviorally accommodated or emotionally driven, to "respond at a moment's notice" or "always be there when I'm needed."

This is accomplished mostly through the analysis and development of processes and systems that enable information and accountability to flow through the organization and the hierarchy. In a highly reactive environment in which people are always doing their best for one another, the system is often the casualty – heroism replaces and even subverts solid business practices. The desire to do well overrides the study of how to do better.

Keep in mind that this also applies to your relationship with your customers and suppliers, even if you are self-employed. Of course, we are all essential at times, and I don't suggest tossing your smartphone out the window. But think about why your customers and co-workers need you right now, and if this way you have of always being there is making them dependent on you, and covering up holes in your business processes that should be fixed.

ABOUT JIM: Jim Hessler is the Founder and President of Path Forward Leadership Development. Jim founded Path Forward in 2001 after an extensive career as a business leader, reaching the level of Vice President in a Fortune 150 company before the age of 40. He specialized in the turnaround of struggling businesses, and leadership of large-scale change management programs.

The mission of Path Forward is to reduce human suffering and improve organizational performance through the development of more effective and human-centered leadership cultures.

Path Forward accomplishes this through the facilitation of powerful learning experiences that take place over many months, and in which experiential learning occurs in a community of challenge and support.

Jim is the author of Land On Your Feet, Not On Your Face, A Guide to Building Your Leadership Platform. The Leadership Platform is a proprietary Path Forward framework that helps develop a deep understanding of key leadership principles, called Planks. It then connects these Planks into a solid foundation for personal and organizational growth.

Path Forward believes that Leadership Development is best accomplished through a commitment to these principles:

- The entire organization, up to and including top leadership, is learning together every day. Even Senior and Executive Leaders are seen as works in progress.

- The development of positive cultural norms and values along with effective structural foundations, is given equal weight along with the development of individual leadership skills.

- Learning occurs in a structured and sustainable way, over substantial periods, using the learner's own experiences as the core of the learning process.

- The structure of learning is circular and continuous.

- The participants in leadership development programs are given significant feedback and coaching over time for them to create positive Habits of leadership.

- A solid conceptual framework for understanding leadership must be shared throughout the organization. The metaphors, concepts, and language of The Leadership Platform are an example of how leadership culture can be established in part by a shared vision of enlightened leadership.

Jim is the co-host of The Boss Show, and podcast versions of this show can be heard by going to…

www.PathForwardLeadership.com.

25

CREATE A CURATED WRITTEN TO-DO LIST FOR THE NEXT DAY - LIZ JENKINS

Why: Wrapping it up at the end of each day in your hone office to prepare for the next is critical in terms of being able to shut things off in your head. Our brains are so busy these days with everything we have to do that it can often impact sleep and health.

I recommend a written list for the day's activities rather than a digital list. I absolutely love a digital list for holding all of my tasks and for documentation on a more global level, but find it sometimes challenging in terms of what I need to do on a particular day.

Curating a written list that is do-able, timely, and detailed is the key to being productive.

Do-able meaning that you can do that thing on the day it is on your list. Don't add things to the list that have no chance of happening that day.

Timely meaning that this item needs to be done by the day you have it on the list. Ideally, you'll have lead time and aren't waiting until the last minute.

Detailed meaning that you have all of the info you need to complete the task. Collecting any documents, jotting down phone numbers and notes, etc. to make sure you are ready to go.

Tip 1: Keep an ongoing 'brain dump' to-do list where everything that needs to get done lives. Task or project management apps are great for this because you can group them by type of task with due dates and details. Then pull out your daily tasks for what you can accomplish for each day. You can always go back for more if you finish everything.

Tip 2: Bullet journals are a great way to make this system work. Having sections for the different types of tasks you need to do is super helpful. Chunking tasks such as phone calls or bill payments make it easier to get in the rhythm of getting things done.

Tip 3: Include phone numbers, keywords, and steps for each to do when you create your list.

Tip 4: If something wasn't completed, reflect on why that is. It may not be relevant, or more info may be needed to complete it.

Curating your list for the next day at the end of each day in your home office gives your brain a chance to reflect on that day's accomplishments. It also means that you've set down your goals for the following day, which puts your mind at ease that things aren't being forgotten and that you are prepared for the next.

The Un-Habit: Flying by the seat of your pants when it comes to systems, policies, and procedures

Why: Not a single business owner I know wants to spend time dealing with the creation, implementation, or updating of their company systems, policies, and procedures. However, not doing this means that when something happens within your company where you needed a particular bit of information for legal reasons, an issue with a client that you need to address, or an insurance claim, you may not have what you need because you don't have your systems in place.

Each person in the company must know what they are supposed to document and where the information is supposed to live.

And this includes you. Even (especially) if it is just you, working from your home office. It is really easy to slack off on this part of your business when it is only you. Unfortunately, this means there is nowhere to pass the buck when a situation happens. And it means that your company is not scalable or sustainable if you want to grow since you don't have much to share with new team members except what you can verbally explain.

Policies and procedures mean that you have your systems in place for growth, for reference, for documentation, and for the future.

I'm not just talking about a handbook that no one looks at again. I'm talking about really laying out how you do everything in the company and making sure that everyone, including you, does each step every time.

Systems can include tracking your time, how you keep notes on customers or templates for setting up new projects.

Policies can include what you do if there is a customer complaint, how you handle time off for an employee, or company dress codes.

Procedures can include the 'how-to's' for all of your systems, onboarding new team members, or steps to take when documenting transactions.

Having all of your ducks in a row not only makes your work easier since there is a definite way to do everything, but it also eases your mind because you don't have to hold everything in your head or rely on others to remember.

I often imagine someone coming in from the outside and looking at how we do things. If there is something that isn't clear to an outsider, then that's my kick in the pants to make it so.

About Liz: Liz Jenkins, Certified Professional Organizer and owner of A Fresh Space in Nashville, TN, specializes in helping people in their homes, home offices, and small businesses get organized so they can be more effective, productive and functional since 2005.

Liz and her amazing team of organizers provide high-level professional organizing as well as move management services with decluttering, home styling, and full-service unpacking.

A Certified Professional Organizer, Liz is an expert at identifying inefficiencies and ineffective systems. Her work with home office dwellers includes space planning, paper management, and supply storage in addition to her thriving consulting practice involving analysis, creation, and implementation of effective project management systems. She is quite passionate about her clients having their ducks in a row when it comes to systems, policies, and procedures and feels that when your systems are in place, they free you up to be the amazingly creative and entrepreneurial soul you are meant to be.

Liz speaks nationally about managing a business in an organized fashion, primarily in the areas of project management, documentation, tracking, and system creation, including at the National Association of Productivity and Organizing Professionals (NAPO) national conferences. She is the current Chair of Special Interest Groups for NAPO and acts as a mentor to new members of her profession.

Liz has been featured online and in print publications such as Martha Stewart, Sophisticated Living, Nashville Lifestyles, Rachael Ray, Working Mother, Real Producers, Franklin Lifestyles, The Tennessean, Pottery Barn, Good Housekeeping, and more.

Her background as a small business owner several times over, and as a special education teacher, brings empathy and understanding to her work as she fully understands the challenges of working from a home office and managing a thriving, multi-faceted business.

A passionate animal advocate, Liz has been involved in animal rescue and fostering for decades and is a current kitten foster mom. She has been married for 25+ years and has a college-age daughter.

Learn more at: www.afreshspace.com

26

CREATE A TRIGGER FOR YOUR WORK DAY - KELLY SMITH

Why: Because I work from home exclusively and have young kids at home as well, my workday is broken up into "work sessions." I produce my best work in sessions, kind of like a HIIT (high-intensity-interval-training) workout for my productivity.

Before each "session," I always prepare a cup of coffee or tea and fill my water bottle. For some reason, having a delicious cup of something adds to the fun factor and makes my office feel cozy. Next, I tidy up the office from the previous work session. I'll file away papers, put books away, organize my notes, find any materials I need for my current work session, etc. A messy office impedes my concentration, so I do my best to get a quiet and organized space before I start to work.

I never realized this until I started intentionally paying attention to my daily Habits a few years ago. Still, I have done this "beverage-then-tidy" Habit for years, and I do it before every single work session. It takes me all of ten minutes, and it is the ramp-up time for my brain to switch from whatever I had been doing previously, into work mode.

The making of the drink, the tidying up of the office - it's the process, or trigger, which alerts my brain to the fact that we're about to produce our best work. It's a "clearing of the decks," and it allows me to set the stage for what's about to happen next: productivity.

Once my environment is "just so," I feel primed to produce my best work; it's as if I've eliminated any excuses that could deter my focus away from the most important thing for the next few hours: creating my best work.

Creating a trigger to start your workday (or session) is a gift for your mind that allows for smooth shifting of the gears: It's the buffer between moving from one task to the next, one area of focus to another, with ease and fluidity rather than slamming the brakes and making a hard left into work mode.

Working from home can be a blessing or a curse depending on how you look at it, but starting your workday with a trigger that you get excited about will truly set you up for success and be something that you look forward to.

The Un-Habit: Letting work infiltrate your entire home & headspace

Why: No matter if you exclusively work from home or commute to an office each day, letting your work "bleed" into your home is one ugly Habit of being mindful of and then letting go of work.

When I started working from home, I had zero boundaries. I felt so fortunate to work from home that I overcompensated with my availability.

I quickly learned that just because you can work anywhere in your home, doesn't mean you should. The subconscious patterns we create when we work anywhere throughout our home remind us that we really can't physically "get away from the office."

At first, it seems like no big deal; what's the harm in checking a few emails while the pasta is boiling in the kitchen, or quick before bed? You may think, "Sure, I can take a client call on my way to pick up my kids from school," and the truth is that, Yes! You absolutely can. Sometimes, you must.

But regularly, it's a recipe for burnout. These open moments, the moments of white space, are the margin of our day. Allowing work to infiltrate any open space in your home and, more importantly, in your mind, will leave you exhausted but unsure of what you accomplished.

If "everywhere" and "anytime" is fair game for working, then you will always feel obligated to work, no matter where you are, who you are with, or what you're doing. Intentionally creating boundaries around where you work in your home will help to compartmentalize business and personal.

This is a hard Habit to break, and here are some tips to un-Habit this ugly Habit:

1. Create a space where you perform your work function, complete with physical and time boundaries.

2. Leave your phone in said space when your workday is over.

3. Set specific times of the day when you check email (and honor it).

4. Use the Do Not Disturb feature on your phone for extra Habit protection.

By being intentional about where and when you work, you will use your allotted work time and space wiser, which sets you up to do your very best work. Your brain now knows that "this is when and where we work." You will maximize your productivity, have better focus, and be able to leave your work session knowing, proudly, that you can leave work at the office, in this case the home office.

About Kelly: Kelly Smith is the Owner of Willow & Oak Business Solutions, and provides content marketing and administrative support to business owners who want to empower and improve the lives of others.

Placing the highest value on authenticity, integrity and relentlessly seeking improvement, Kelly's definition of success means meeting a need, improving the lives of others, and empowering the marginalized. Her company values are rooted in leading by example and in the betterment of the greater good.

Kelly teaches service-based business owners how discover their ideal clients, define their unique value, craft thoughtful and honest messaging, and deliver engaging thought leadership on the most relevant platforms. By creating authentic content marketing strategy, then executing it for her clients, Kelly invites engaged audiences to participate in her clients' services. Her work elevates her clients' brand in the marketplace, and develops them into sought after thought leaders in their field.

Prior to entrepreneurship, Kelly was an Executive Assistant at a global manufacturing company where she excelled in identifying and resolving communication gaps. She created international communication strategies and promotion plans to ensure consistent and accurate information flowed throughout the 3,800 employees worldwide. She developed and led collaborative and diverse teams ensuring all departments' needs were represented and their message was heard.

Kelly has 20 years of Operational, Marketing, & Administrative experience, as well as a Bachelor of Arts in English Literature from Seattle University and an Associate of Arts in Marketing Management from Bellevue College. She is an active volunteer in her local community and serves as the Membership Co-Chair for Women Business Owners. Kelly has been nominated for the "Solopreneur Business Owner of the Year" award (2020).

Born and raised in the Pacific Northwest, Kelly and her husband, two boys, and their yellow lab enjoy the bounty of outdoor fun that the region offers (rain or shine).

27

STICK TO A WORKDAY SCHEDULE - LAUREN BURGON

Why: When I started working from home in 2008, I commuted three days each week and worked from home the other two days. Working from home was relatively rare back then. It was sometimes considered to be less than professional, so my boss preferred that we not make it obvious to our clients that sometimes I was physically in our office, and sometimes I was at home. One of the most important Habits that I developed at that time was to keep the same work hours, whether I was physically at my firm's office or working from home.

I cultivated a mindset that I was at work on regular weekdays between 8:00 am and 5:00 pm, regardless of where I was physically located. This approach helped me in numerous ways.

First, it was predictable for my clients. Regardless of the day and where I might be located, I was available to them the same hours every workday. It didn't matter to them one bit where I was sitting; they wanted predictability of access.

Second, it helped me negotiate the challenges of working from home with small children. If it was a school day for them, it was a workday for me, and that meant that after school, Mom was still working and wasn't immediately available to them. Whether I was in my "real" office or my home office, I was still working after school got out, which meant no slamming into the house after school yelling, "I'm home!" or charging into my home office already in a mid-snack request.

Third, having a set schedule helped me manage my work and personal time. One of the biggest problems that I hear about from other home-workers is that work time and personal time bleed together.

Blurring the lines between work and personal can mean that work time becomes all the time, and that's exhausting. Having set work hours helps you to turn off the work side of your brain and fully focus on your personal life, which is a necessary mental break that we all need.

In the years since I first started working from home, it has become much more commonplace and accepted. Cultivating good Habits will help you make it successful as well.

The Un-Habit: Don't have a Plan B

Why: When I first started working from home, it wasn't by choice. Our two-attorney firm was so new and small that our office was too small for both of us to be physically working in the office at the same time. My then-boss hired me with the expectation that I would work from home two or three days a week, and that she and I would work alternate days in the official office. I was newly divorced and newly returning to a profession I had left a decade earlier, and I had to make it work.

As I was figuring out how to make it work, I remembered a radio interview I had heard many years earlier with one of NPR's founding mothers about being a successful professional woman in a time when professional women were relatively rare. My memory was that she attributed at least part of her success to not having a plan B. Huh? This way of thinking was inconceivable to me, and going forward without a backup plan seemed crazy. But it made sense, and it works.

Not having a plan B means that you can't give up. You don't have a fallback. And while it's scary, it's also incredibly motivating. It requires you to commit to your course of action completely.

In the years since I started working from home, I've seen the wisdom of this approach numerous times. I've seen people "try" to work from home and then give up and go back to working from a traditional office. I've seen people "try" at a new business venture while not letting go of their regular job, resulting in overwork and burnout. And I've seen people paralyzed by choices fail in the end to make any choice at all.

Determine your course. Don't make a fallback plan. Go for it.

About Lauren: I have a solo law practice based in West Seattle, where I have lived for more than 25 years. My practice focuses on business law and the needs of small business owners. I enjoy developing long-term relationships with my clients, so they know that they can depend on me to provide reliable, timely, and affordable assistance.

My prior work experience gives me useful insight into the needs of business owners, having worked in a variety of small businesses, including restaurants, a personal services business, veterinary clinics, and nonprofit organizations.

I help with small business's legal needs, including setting up and maintaining business entities, advising on employment matters, drafting strong and easily understood contracts, reviewing and advising on commercial leases, assisting with the purchase or sale of a business, filing and maintaining trademark registrations, drafting website policies, and basic estate planning for business owners.

I grew up in Massachusetts and graduated with a degree in English from Middlebury College in Vermont. After a summer of working two jobs on Cape Cod, I hopped on I-90 in Boston and drove across the country to Seattle. I graduated from the University of Washington School of Law in 1991 and settled down in the wonderful small-town-within-a-city that is West Seattle.

I have had a lifelong passion for animals. I have worked as a veterinary assistant, a dog walker, and a volunteer keeper assistant at the Woodland Park Zoo, as well as serving as a Woodland Park Zoo docent and a volunteer with Animal Services of King County. In addition, I live with an ever-shifting menagerie that currently includes an elderly labrador, an adolescent pit bull, two tuxedo cats, and a corn snake. I have two fabulous kids who are almost grown and enjoy close relationships with my extended family, who have all migrated to West Seattle over the years.

THE RIGHT DAILY TASK LIST - SILVIA PETERSON

Why: The Right Daily Task List moves you forward and focuses you on the right tasks to accomplish each day. It provides a list that you can check off and get a sense of completion and satisfaction. It gives you something to do when you have unexpected time on your hands, such as when a planned call or meeting is suddenly canceled. Focus on the next step needed to move a project or a customer forward to the next logical step. You do not need every step listed on your daily task list that represents all the activities in the life of the project or customer engagement.

Your daily task list should not have more items on it than you can accomplish; if it does, move the tasks with less priority to another day. Also, create a Must Do list for each day. Both lists are targeted and focused. Your Must-Do list should be small – 2 to 3 items max, depending on how much time they will take. Must-Do lists include time-sensitive items that have been promised or are super important for your business, such as: sending a proposal to a potential client, sending an invoice, or following up on any invoice payments that are over 30 days.

Sometimes, Must Do items are done at the very end of the day, and that is okay. Equally important to creating these lists is where you keep them. Whether you do it electronically or on paper is up to you and is a personal preference. The key is to have it in one place and that it is portable as you never know where you will have sudden free time. I prefer to see my calendar and my task list in one place and use the old fashioned paper planner. Find something that works for you and stick to it. Sometimes volume changes our methods. Pay attention when you feel something no longer works; you may have outgrown the method due to size.

The Un-Habit: Over-scheduling

Why: There is a myth about being back to back in meetings and calls, and how that correlates directly to success, how we must work 60 hours or more per week to be successful. Being super busy is considered a badge of honor, and we are happy to share this news with others. Sometimes this happens, and it is unavoidable – it should be the exception and not the rule.

My challenge to you is to create space in your day to make sure you are taking care of yourself and giving yourself time to show up to whatever is on your calendar that day, including any creative time. I find that after 45 minutes of focused work, I need to get up and take a break. My favorite breaks include going outside to take in the sunshine or fresh air. Sometimes the best next thing for me is to take a nap or to make a cup of tea. I give myself plenty of time if I am driving somewhere so that I get there on time and will be ready for the meeting. I exercise every day and drink lots of water. I do not work excessive hours, and I am hesitant to put in a specific number of hours - which will be different for everyone. Working too much and not taking care of yourself is not a sustainable practice. Being a workaholic is a form of addiction, just one that is socially acceptable.

How do you know if you are over-scheduled? You are not sleeping well. You have trouble focusing on tasks that require creativity. You make simple mistakes. You do not have time to go to the bathroom. You are not eating well or exercising at all because you do not have time. The rest of your life is out of balance.

About Silvia: Silvia Peterson is a productivity expert who has focused her 35-year career in helping restaurants operate better.

After corporate stints at Burger King Corporation in Miami, FL, and Denny's Restaurants in Spartanburg, SC, Silvia moved her family to Seattle to start the Operations Engineering department at Starbucks Coffee in Seattle, WA, in 2000. When Silvia started, Starbucks had 2000 locations and had just begun in the Drive-thru business. While at Starbucks, Silvia was featured in two articles: WSJ "Coffee on the Double" by Steven Gray on April 12, 2005, and TIME Magazine "The Big Gulp at Starbucks" by Barbara Kiviat on December 10, 2006, for her and her team's work on Starbucks operations which was enabling innovation while making sure customers got their coffee in a reasonable amount of time. The team was focused on designing stations and tools as well as making sure the labor model met the customer demand.

In 2010 Silvia started her own consulting business and has been happily working from home ever since. During this time, Silvia has worked with over 34 brands in the restaurant, fitness, and convenience store businesses. Projects focus on new prototype designs, retrofit designs, or labor-management projects that enable brands to deliver growth and profitability.

Silvia has been a member of WBO – a women's business owners networking group – since 2013 and served on the Board of Directors as Membership Chair (2014) as well as President (2015). Under her leadership, WBO saw its largest single-year growth in membership and event attendance since the 2008 downturn of the economy.

Silvia is happily married to Dan for 28 years and is the mother of two adult sons, AJ and Brandon. Hobbies include reading, Zumba, cooking, hiking, and volunteering at the local community center serving hot meals for the needy.

FINISH YOUR KEY PRIORITIES BY NOON, EVERY DAY - DAN FAULKNER

Why: Make a highly focused list of your most essential items for the day, and get those tasks completed (no matter what) by noon. I suggest one to three tasks that would be of high impact if they were completed. Most of the time, these are what Stephen Covey would call Quadrant Two activities.

Days don't always go as we plan them, and the only way to ensure a successful day is to focus on the vital few (leveraging the 80/20 Rule) and make sure you execute on them. For me, examples of these would be to make ten calls to clients, write five notes, negotiate a contract for a specific client, or to get a piece of a project complete that could be the bottleneck for the rest of my team (this happens surprisingly often). By thinking through these priorities, and keeping the list short (one, two or three items), you make it very achievable to execute this Habit. If you have ten high priorities, then you have none. If you have two, you have an effective day.

Getting these done by noon is important because it guarantees that no matter what happens with your day, your vital few are complete. The rest of the day could go completely sideways, but if you can get your one to three items complete, it still guarantees a really good day.

This does require some advance thought, as you should choose the one to three very carefully and strategically. But once you've done the advance thinking on it, it becomes quite easy to narrow down what makes the list. Save the Twitter feed and the ESPN updates until the afternoon, once the vital few are complete. I mean this quite literally, save the non-essential emails, calls to return, and less important tasks until after 12 PM. They'll still be there in the afternoon.

Archimedes said: "give me a lever long enough and a fulcrum on which to place it, and I shall move the world." Your focused list is your lever, and the noon deadline is the fulcrum. Once I realized all of this I was able to get way more done in way less time. And isn't that the ultimate goal?

If you do this, you will win. And you'll have more peace of mind because you'll have a system for getting the really important things done.

THE UN-HABIT: LETTING YOUR PHONE START YOUR DAY

Why: There's a routine I follow, and I've followed for a long time. It's putting your phone on airplane mode before you go to sleep, and not taking it off of airplane mode for at least 30 minutes (at least) after you wake up. Most distractions I can completely understand (and I even partake in from time to time), but the distraction of checking your email in bed, or catching up on social media first thing in the morning... I can't wrap my mind around that. How your morning goes will dictate the rest of your day. It sets the tone from a productivity

Finish Your Key Priorities by Noon, Every Day - Dan Faulkner | 189

standpoint and also from a mental, emotional, and spiritual standpoint.

My mornings usually start with my alarm going off (on my phone, which is on airplane mode), getting up, and letting the dog out. I let the dog back in, make some coffee in a French press, and then I feed the dog. I then go upstairs, meditate for 30 minutes using the Insight Timer app (while my phone is on airplane mode), and then when I'm finished, I flip the magical switch (the airplane switch) and let the messages flow in. Sometimes these messages and notifications stress me out a little bit, but that's the exception. More often than not, I get caught up and then move on with planning my day.

Compare this with waking up, opening up your Instagram, and diving into your email. It sets your day off on a different trajectory.

I'm not perfect, and sometimes sneak an early news story, or look at the weather for the week. But it's not about chasing perfection. It's about getting it right more often than not. And it's about forming Habits.

Use airplane mode, and use it often. Your mind will get clearer, your days will be better, and you will be happier and more proud of the life you lead.

About Dan: Born in Redmond, Washington, Dan is a Pacific Northwest native. Attending local schools, including the University of Washington, he formed a fondness and knowledge of the greater Seattle area that he uses in his professional life every day.

Graduating from the University of Washington in 2005, Dan initially planned to go to law school. However, the real estate business pulled him in and starting straight out of college; he's never looked back. His favorite part of being in real estate is building relationships with his clients. He loves getting to know his clients and their families and seeing them grow into their homes, as well as using his local knowledge to help people find the right area and the right fit.

Dan prides himself on having a 100% referral-based business, which is truly unique in today's day and age. This means he needs to do such a great job that his clients evangelize him and tell their friends and family. It also means he is focused exclusively on serving his people, as opposed to spending time marketing to try to find new clients.

While most Realtors spend most of their time advertising, chasing down Zillow leads, or using discounts as their value proposition, Dan and his team provide a Nordstrom caliber level of service that has created raving fans who come back year after year and refer their friends and family.

As his business grew, Dan started to build a team, to serve his clients' needs at a higher level. Each team member specializes in a different part of the real estate experience, so transactions go as smoothly as possible. Instead of running a solo practice, where he would have to negotiate deals, create flyers, show homes, and install key boxes (all varied activities), a team allows him to serve clients in a tailored, specialized way, where each team member focuses on their strengths.

In his spare time, Dan enjoys reading, exercising, yoga, and being in the woods with his wife Mallory and his dog Dave.

30

PROMOTE YOUR HIGHER SELF TO CEO - JESSICA RIVERSON

Why: This Habit will never lead you wrong. It's the absolute key to manifesting and creating the work-at-home success you desire and require to enjoy your most fulfilled life. When I started working from home at age 19, I constantly looked outward to find the answer.

Sure, I got some results by following the leader and learning from people who knew more than me. But more often than not, it got me into bouts of panic, anxiety, and overwhelm.

Most of the time, I was reactionary to customers, clients, vendors, and whether my sales were up or down that week. I didn't truly trust myself to lead my own business. Heck, I didn't even trust myself to run my own life truly.

I wish I could say it was a lot sooner that I learned this. Still, after 21 years now being a work-from-home entrepreneur--my entire adult life, I've learned that your Higher Self provides clues and answers and direction for where your next clients will come, whether your next marketing move is a good one, and even which Habits to grasp onto and which ones to ditch.

Your Higher Self knows ALL the answers.

Case in point: A private client of mine wanted to land a Microsoft corporate training contract and wasn't sure about her next step. Of course, we covered all the logical things like networking and reaching out to HR managers, etc.

She was doing those things. And still the results weren't coming fast enough. I reminded her to listen to her Higher Self. She heard, "go have a glass of wine at your friend's restaurant." So she left her home office, went on down there and proceeded to enjoy her glass of merlot, and chatted with her friend.

After confiding her dream of having a corporate contract at Microsoft, her friend promptly said: "oh, well, you need to meet with my friend so-and-so."

Not only did "so-and-so" become a personal client, but she also hooked her up with a $7500 half-day corporate workshop at Microsoft...all within a few weeks.

And that's exactly what I mean by listening to your Higher Self. Those little nudges or random thoughts are NOT random. Start trusting and following where they go...you'll be surprised how good you get at manifesting through the wisdom of your Higher Self.

The Un-Habit: Stop Following the Rules

Why: Never have I gotten anywhere by just toeing the line. Your most magical, productive, and creative think-outside-the-box self will never thrive here, and the longer you cramp your sassy style by following all the rules...the sooner you'll be dead in the water and burn out.

Remember when I said I was always stressed out? It was because I cared about what other people thought about me. I know this feels super counter-intuitive to the slogan "the customer is always right," but in my opinion, if you don't create a business or a career that feels completely aligned with who you are and how you operate...you're not permitting yourself to access your full power.

Rules were made to be broken. They're guidelines on how to be successful, not prison bars!

Powerful brands and power players aren't vanilla. They are chocolate chip mint mixed with Oreos (dairy-free, of course).

You can't stand out if you're totally focused on blending in.

I remember when I started my online coaching business, I thought I had to look professional all the time. So even though I worked at home, I'd always wear blazers in my marketing videos. As much as I love a good structured blazer, I don't wear them at home ever!

As I started letting go of needing to look or sound perfect on my videos, I started dressing in a way that felt more comfortable to me---and I discovered people were more interested in buying from the "real" me than the "professional" one.

I got so confident and in my power that even when one online hater said I was "unprofessional" for doing a livestream in a hot tub...I laughed it off—knowing that my soul mate clients thought it was pretty epic!

What unspoken rules are you following in your work-at-home routine right now? In what ways are you being inauthentic and keeping yourself playing small when you could be unleashing your true nature, true essence, and style on the world?

Decide today to release one rule you've been blindly following because you care what other people think, or because someone told you that you "had to do" to be successful.

You might realize there is a rule-breaker in you who's been waiting to be set free.

Free to be ten times more successful, that is!

About Jessica: Jessica Riverson loves to joke that she's never had a "real" job, and she isn't a "normal" person because she's worked at home since she was 19 years old, as a single mom and a college drop out at that time. It was that young that she become a professional at getting work done, changing diapers, and managing to stay sane. However, some things work out for the best.

Today she's known in the online coaching and consulting industry as the founder of the international coaching company, Permission to Charge®, where she and her team help female experts and coaches to confidently price, package, and sell their expertise from 10K to 100K using leveraged, scalable business models. In fewer than five years, she's scaled up her 1:1 coaching practice to a leveraged model, creating an opportunity for her husband to retire from corporate to work in the business, built a team and created the Academy, The Expansion Mastermind and a host of other programs serving women in coaching.

After a decade in the online coaching and leadership space, she is known among her premier clients as a conduit for allowing them to open their channel to serve and receive at their highest level. She teaches coaches how to step into what she calls their "Feminine CEO" and create highly successful businesses on their terms. And while she shows her clients how to create unthinkable amounts of money each month, what she truly does is enable them to access a space of infinite possibility within themselves—where there's no excuses, no apologies, and no shrinking to fit other's ideals. In this space is where women fully give themselves permission to charge and permission to receive—BIG.

She lives in the greater Seattle area with her husband, sassy 6-year-old daughter, and 22-year-old son. At one point or another, she has homeschooled both of her kids for short stints, and thanks working from home for the opportunity to be at every school appointment and chaperone field trips.

31

MAKE A DAILY "RESULTS" LIST - AUBREY ARMES

Why: Make a daily "Results" list to identify what results you want to produce instead of making a "to-do" list of activities that need to be done.

Our mindset is the single most important tool we have to achieve success. Staying consistently focused on what results are being produced instead of what activities need to be done will allow you to rise to the top of your field and achieve greatness status.

When was the last time that you left work with everything on your to-do list complete and crossed off your list? Rarely, if ever, does this happen. Given that there is always more to do than what can be done, does it not make sense to only focus on the tasks that will yield the most significant results? Yet, many workdays are filled with activities that produce little to no results.

When employees work from home, the biggest concern that managers have is, "Is my team member working or watching Netflix all afternoon?" If you make it a Habit to produce results consistently, you will win the trust of your manager and admiration of your team. This will alleviate stresses that come from being micromanaged as well as anxiety from an overwhelming to-do list.

If you are an entrepreneur, it means being able to do more in less time, giving you the freedom you crave.

What does this look like in practical application?

1. Instead of looking at all the items on your "to-do" list, reframe and ask yourself, "What do I need to accomplish today, this week, this month, this quarter?".
2. Make a list of accomplishments that you are working towards, including the due date.
3. Focus on today's Top 3 results to be accomplished.
4. Ask yourself, "What action can I take that will accomplish X in the fewest steps as possible and still deliver high-quality results?"
5. Get into action!

When you are more focused on results than activities, you will do what it takes to move the project forward rather than being satisfied with sending emails, leaving voicemails, and making the perfect PowerPoint deck.

Stand out from the rest and develop a reputation for excellence by focusing on producing results consistently.

THE UN-HABIT: CHAINING YOURSELF TO YOUR LAPTOP FOR THE ENTIRE WORKDAY

Why: How most people work, being chained to their computer for 8, 10, 12+ hours a day is not conducive to creativity, innovation, problem-solving, or high productivity. Many people are often too busy with back-to-back meetings and heavy workloads that they eat at their desks and can barely find time in their day for much-needed bio breaks.

It certainly is not good for their health either, which also decreases work effectiveness. Experts recommend moving at least every 30 minutes. Those who sit for long periods are more likely to suffer from a whole host of medical issues; most are guaranteed to decrease your quality of life and even shorten your life span.

Einstein said, "We cannot solve problems by using the same kind of thinking we used when we created them."

The next time you have a task that requires brainpower and creativity, try getting away from your desk and doing something physical while you think about the solution or which direction to go.

By getting your body moving, you are also getting your energy flowing. This helps to clear the cobwebs and allows new ideas to flow.

This could include going for a walk, run, hike in nature, having a 2-song dance party, or doing a set of squats. Not only will you reap the benefits of greater creativity and higher productivity, but you will also receive the rewards of the physical activity physically, mentally, and emotionally.

You can also employ this tactic when you have been interrupted (by others or your compulsions), and you need to switch tasks. Instead of jumping from one task to another, get up and move your body and then switch tasks.

Research shows it takes over 23 minutes to get back to an activity after being interrupted and is accompanied by increased levels of stress and frustration. By getting up, moving your body, and getting your heart rate up, you will be able to process the stress and frustration while allowing your mind to prepare for the upcoming task in less time.

By unchaining yourself from your desk and getting your body moving, not only will you be more productive and benefit from the positive side effects, but you will also have a lot more fun and increase your quality of life significantly.

About Aubrey: Aubrey Armes is a woman on a mission: To change how business is done.

Passionate about doing business differently, Aubrey brings her 20 years of Business Leadership, Human Resources, Professional Coaching, and Spiritual Leadership experience to the modern business leader.

By teaching leaders and employees to shift away from the old command and control business model and how to authentically own and embrace the highs and lows of being human in the business world, Aubrey is leveling up leaders all over town.

She's giving leadership teams the right tools and teaching them "how to" elicit high performance, set appropriate expectations, hold their team and themselves accountable for greatness, and have some fun along the way.

Her leadership produces empowered and engaged leaders who lead effectively and empathetically, producing great results from their teams and from themselves.

Aubrey takes disengaged and mediocre business teams, and transforms them in to energized, high-performing, collaborative teams by creating cultures that value transparency over secrecy, authenticity over posturing, progress over perfection, and accountability over blame.

Aubrey works with leaders in one-on-one in private coaching sessions, mastermind groups, and by working with the entire business team.

You can also book her to speak at your company event, facilitate your next corporate retreat or lead one of her popular Crunchy Conversations training and workshop for your team. Other popular trainings include Women in Leadership, Accountability & Blame Culture, Emotional Intelligence, Mindfulness in the Workplace, and Management 101.

Aubrey lives in the beautiful Pacific Northwest outside of Seattle with her husband of 20 years and her dog, Lucy, the pug. She enjoys gardening, hiking, searching for beach glass on local shores, Friday night fires with friends in her backyard firepit, traveling, and all that sparkles.

Aubrey's volunteer service includes leadership roles within the non-profit organizations of Women Business Owners and Woman's Way Red Lodge.

32

GET YOUR DAILY "DOSE OF HAPPY" - LAURIE NICHOLS

Why: "Knowing yourself is the beginning of wisdom." - Aristotle

Now more than ever, I know with absolute clarity, what it means to thrive truly. It's personal! The official definition includes two primary elements: prospering and flourishing. To be candid, the notion of flourishing never occurred to me. It's all about being healthy, happy, and successful. Working from home proved to be the perfect opportunity for experimenting with the "Goldilocks Principle"; to find my sweet spot for prospering and flourishing. I discovered that, for me, daily doses of happy are non-negotiable.

I launched my home-office based practice as a business coach six years ago. I dragged some heavy baggage along for the ride: old notions about hard work, sacrifice, and constant striving as necessary elements of success. At first, it was easy to slip right back into the old pattern of long hours with over-scheduled days. It felt familiar and given my lifelong struggle with ADHD, normal. Yet, I reached a point where I was feeling anxious and fearful that I was failing. Thankfully, I heeded the inner voice that said, "You. Must. Stop." I gave myself the gift of time to reflect on what I needed to be successful AND feel happy.

Over two years, I set a conscious intention to be successful and not burn myself out. Two particularly helpful exercises were Darren Hardy's Values Assessment and Gallup Strengths Finders. Both contributed significantly to my process of experimentation with a work schedule that allowed me to leverage my strengths to focus on what mattered and enjoy the process.

I discovered daily; simple pleasures were not only permissible; they were necessary for my well-being and succeeding on my terms. A workspace that inspires with pretty paint and fresh flowers. Breaks in the day to putter, get outside for a walk, or maybe a nap! Face-to-face connections with like-minded people to share and learn. These are all on my "happy" menu.

Just like Goldilocks, I discovered what was just right for me. Enjoying my daily "dose of happy" is now a daily Habit. It's how I harness my energy to focus on what matters and is core to loving my work. As a result, my business has exceeded my original goals using all my traditional metrics. How about you? What "dose of happy" might inspire you to thrive?

The Un-Habit: Going it alone

Why: "Life (and work) is not a solo act. It's a huge collaboration, and we all need to assemble around us the people who care about us and support us." Tim Gunn

When first launching a home-based business, it may feel necessary to "go it alone." In this context. I'm talking about getting started and how you operate day-to-day. This could include getting business licenses, writing a business strategy, setting up a website, writing marketing copy, figuring out technology, where you set yourself up to work. In the beginning, I was excited to start, and it felt super productive, checking all these items off my to-do list. Also, this saved money, which contributed to feelings of self-satisfaction over how resourceful I was.

The problem was, as time passed, I was unknowingly being "pennywise and pound foolish." I was stingy with smaller amounts and wasteful with larger amounts. Reflecting back, this was so true for me financially and in terms of my physical energy. I found myself spending hours and hours on tasks—large and small—that not only made me miserable; I was terrible at them! This left me drained and anxious and, not surprisingly, limited my success in those first years.

My perspective changed as my network of like-minded solopreneurs grew. It was such an eye-opener to realize the breadth of affordable support that was available for the asking. I took baby steps at first, starting with a hiring a copywriter for my website, which was followed by a virtual assistant to help with creating a professional presentation. As my business grew, so did my delegation muscles—and my budget for support.

I now assess my needs regularly around support for my business and my home life. Currently on my team: a sales coach, website administrator, virtual assistant, CPA, and housekeeping service. These amazing professionals have freed me to grow my business, leverage my strengths, and, importantly, enjoy more free time. As a result, my business and I thrive.

HABIT 1

About Laurie: Laurie Nichols' mission is to guide and nurture a successful and fruitful succession experience for business owners and their successors. She's a coach, confidante, and catalyst for clients firing up a vision so powerful it moves them to action, taking ownership of their legacy—now and in the future.

What lights her up about this work, is she's been there as an entrepreneur building a business. She knows how daunting it can feel when you recognize the moment when it's time to move on. She also understands how isolating it can be to create and execute a real plan for a succession event that aligns with an owner's vision for themselves, their team, and clients. This experience inspired her to follow her passion for working with other professionals to bring heart to the process of creating vision-centered succession plans so that everyone involved feels empowered and engaged for the journey ahead.

Laurie created the Triple-Win Formula for Succession Success to support her clients in this important work. This proven process is the framework clients need to confidently move on a clear path forward so that their successors can confidently lead and grow their company now and in the future.

She brings 30 years of experience to her work:

- CPA and bank auditor

- 20+ years as a Managing Partner in a money management firm

- Lead role in a management buy-out, founder succession, and sale of a registered investment advisor business

- Certified Professional Coach

- Confidential Intelligence Certified Coach

- Succession Planning Workshop facilitator

In her personal time, Laurie enjoys "daily doses of happy," including getting out on her bike to explore local beaches, logging in the miles with her Fitbit, and trying new recipes on her ever-patient husband. She's also active in the community serving as a board member for Big Brothers Big Sisters of Puget Sound, Financial Planners Association, and past president of Women Business Owners in Seattle.

33

60 SECOND MORNING MIRROR - ERIK "MR. AWESOME" SWANSON

Why: I call this my "Habitude Warrior 60 Second Morning Mirror." It has been a game-changer for me. It allows you to start your day off in the correct fashion for ultimate success throughout the day! Here's how it works. Every morning right before you are ready to start your workday, head over to what I call the mirror of success. Take at least 60 seconds to give yourself an awesome pep talk. Some people refer to this as 'affirmations.' You should stare right into the mirror and see yourself in the reflection. Make sure you are 'dressed for success,' rather than just heading over there in your sweat pants since you are working from home. The most successful people I know all dress up for success no matter where they are and no matter who is really going to see them that day. One of the most important people who will see you every day is YOU!

As you are staring right into your own eyes, repeat an amazing and inspiring mantra or affirmation repeatedly so that you start to believe it. Say it with conviction in your voice. Say it with an inspired and strong stance. Say it so that it seeps deep into your subconscious for your brain to work and give you an amazing feeling of accomplishment throughout the day.

Your affirmations may sound a little like this:

I am the best! I am focused. I will succeed. I believe in myself. I have the will to win. I set high expectations. I surround myself with winners. I visualize my awesome future. I don't let others bring me down. I will learn and grow every day! I will be super productive all day long!

Repeat your 60-second mantra about ten times. After about the tenth or twelfth time saying it, your subconscious mind will start truly believing it. You need to pump yourself up in the morning (every morning) to make it an awesome day. I even write it on my mirror, so I see it every morning. Who else better to pump yourself up than **YOU**!

Do one more thing right before you leave the mirror, high five the mirror! Have you ever high fived a mirror before... it's AWESOME !!! You never fail.

The Un-Habit: Stop taking constant and distracting breaks throughout the day!

Why: By taking constant breaks throughout the workday, it creates a huge distraction in your focus. It's very easy to allow things to distract you when you are in your home environment that generally would not be there had you been in a regular office setting. Vow to not allow these distractions to get in your way. It takes a full 80% of effort to get back on track on to your task at hand once you get distracted away from that task. Use what we call "single-handling," in which you single handle a task to completion ... and then take your break. You will feel a huge sense of accomplishment by doing so.

About Erik: 5 TIME #1 BESTSELLER & SPEAKER ERIK "MR. AWESOME" SWANSON

As an award winning International Keynote Speaker, #1 National Best- Selling Author in 5 different categories of success & a Habits & Behavioral Coach, Erik Swanson is in great demand around the world!

Speaking on average to more than one million people per year, and honored to be invited to speak to Business and Entrepreneurial school of Harvard University as well as joining the Ted Talk Family with his latest Tedx speech called "A Dose of Awesome," Erik is both versatile in his approach and effective in a wide array of training topics.

You can easily find Erik sharing stages with some of the most talented and famous speakers of the world, such as Brian Tracy, Nasa's Performance Coach Dr. Denis Waitley, from the book & movie 'The Secret,' Bob Proctor, Jack Canfield, John Assaraf, Millionaire Maker Loral Langemeier, Co-Author of 'Rich Dad Poor Dad' Sharon Lechter, Legendary Motivator Les Brown, among many others!

Mr. Swanson has created and developed the super popular Habitude Warrior Conference which has a 2-year waiting list and includes 33 top named speakers, all in a 'Ted Talk' style event which has quickly climbed as one of the top 10 events not to miss in the United States! Erik's motto is clear: "NDSO!" No Drama – Serve Others!

34

CREATE YOUR WORK FROM HOME ROUTINE - BROOKS DUNCAN

Why: Create your work from home routine, even if you're not a "routine person".

When I decided to leave my downtown office job, I knew that I wanted to work from home. I wanted flexibility, and I wanted to be able to take my kids to school and be here when they came home.

On my last day in the office, one of my soon-to-be-former coworkers pulled me aside with a concerned look on her face.

She said, "my boyfriend works from home, and he does NOTHING all day. Make sure if you're going to work from home, you treat it seriously. If you don't, you'll end up being lazy like him."

I realized that I needed to come up with a way to work from home successfully. It doesn't just happen.

I found this out the hard way once I was on my own in my home office. All the usual triggers to work were gone — there was no commute, no walking into the office building, no 17-floor elevator ride, no putting my bag away at my desk. There wasn't a manager in her office across the hallway, and if I wanted to spend all day on Twitter, no one would know.

The answer was to create rituals and routines to do every single day. This provides the missing triggers and cues but also ensures that important-but-not-urgent tasks are taken care of.

Here's an example of what a routine might look like:

- Wake up (ideally, earlier than the rest of your family if you have one)
- Exercise
- Read
- Make breakfast
- Review the previous day, your calendar, & plan your most important tasks (if you haven't done that the night before)
- Take kids to school
- Work (ideally on one of your identified most important tasks)
- Have lunch/family time
- Work
- Afternoon break/welcome kids home
- Work
- Wrap up - leave space at the end of the day for admin tasks & the unexpected that had popped up throughout the day

Your day will likely be very different depending on your goals, but the key is to make it a routine — to do the activities at roughly the same time every day, so you know what you should be doing at any time.

Once I adopted this practice, I became much more effective at home, and I was able to focus on my work without feeling stressed out and behind. Even if you are creative and aren't a "routine person," putting some structure into your day will give you the scaffolding to apply that creativity even at home.

The Un-Habit: The "I Just Want To Finish This Up" Mindset

Why: Perseverance and dedication are great qualities that will help you be successful in work and life.

However, when your partner has to call you upstairs to dinner four times every night, or when your family goes out on an evening walk, and you'll "try to catch up later," or when you stumble from your laptop to bed, that might be a sign of too much of a good thing.

Similar to how the lack of typical office triggers makes it hard to *start* work, the lack of those same triggers makes it difficult to *stop* working.

When your co-workers start packing up to go home, that is a good sign that it is time for you to go home too. When you have a train you need to catch, or you want to beat rush hour traffic, you are likely going to shut down at a predictable time.

When you work from home, there's no commute and no physical co-workers, so all of those cues go out the window.

This becomes a problem when you are in the middle of a task or a project. The "I just want to finish this up" mindset leads to work-life bleeding into home life.

If one does this consistently, it will lead to tiredness and lack of energy, which leads to lower effectiveness throughout the day, which leads to having tasks take longer, which leads to more "I just want to finish this up."

You can see how this becomes a vicious circle!

The solution? Have a defined stop time when you work from home. Even if you're in the middle of something, make your best effort to wrap it up. Take note of where you left off, put action items in your task manager, and block out time the next day to finish it off. Tasks rarely MUST be finished that night, and your energy levels and ability to be present in the evening will thank you.

About Brooks: Brooks Duncan is the COO of Asian Efficiency, where we help people become more productive at work and in life. He is the co-host of The Productivity Show, a top productivity podcast with more than 8 million downloads and counting.

He has been working from home full-time for more than a decade and has worked at home alone, with toddlers, with loud teenagers, and as part of a very productive remote team spanning multiple timezones across the world.

Brooks has been featured in The Globe and Mail, the BBC, and Country Life Magazine. The Productivity Show podcast has been featured in Fast Company, Forbes, The Guardian, and many more publications.

Brooks is an experienced speaker, speaking at events such as the American Bar Association TECHSHOW, the National Association of Productivity & Organizing, the Institute of

Professional Bookkeepers of Canada, the Real Estate Board of Greater Vancouver, and many more.

In addition to his productivity work with Asian Efficiency, Brooks helps individuals and small businesses go paperless with DocumentSnap, where he writes about tools, workflows, and taking action.

He is a Chartered Professional Accountant (CPA, CMA). He has worked in roles such as a software developer in a small startup and Director of Client Services for a large multinational firm.

Brooks has loved technology ever since he was a kid in northern Canada typing away on a used Apple][+, and has gained an international reputation for translating technical topics in ways that people can understand and use. He firmly believes that using technology to be more productive is something anyone can do, and they can have fun while doing it.

Brooks lives in Vancouver, Canada, with his wife and two teenage sons. If he is not typing on a keyboard, he is probably taking them to soccer practice or traveling around the world to different soccer stadiums.

35

FIND WHAT WORKS FOR YOU - KIRSTEN SANDOVAL

Why: "Get showered, dressed, get your makeup on, and hair done, have breakfast, then start your day." "Have your day planned out before you start working." "Work out first thing in the morning, so you're more productive." "Work from your office." You know what? None of that works for me, my schedule, my business, or my life, and I finally feel okay about it! I spent years being less-than-productive as I tried to do what we're "supposed to do" or felt as if I must not be a professional for not working from home the "right way."

That is okay because I have found what works best for ME, and I encourage you to do so, also.

Here is how I have found I'm most productive: I get up a bit before everyone else, take my laptop down to the kitchen table, pour myself a pot of coffee, and get straight to work. That's right; I am most productive in my pajamas. I find that quiet one to two hours in the morning, fresh from a night of sleep is when I work best. It allows me to focus intently, accomplishing a ton of the more right-brain type of work (my least favorite) that needs to be done. When that is complete, I have the mental clarity to create the list of creative tasks I'll be doing the rest of the day.

From there, my perfect day involves seeing my son off to school, my husband off to work, and then I work out, get showered and dressed, have some breakfast, then continue my day. The next 6 hours or so are devoted to creative work, planning, and breaks to answer urgent emails. By then, my son is generally home again, I do any deliveries or work errands, and then it's dinner time. Sometime between dinner and bed is when I sit down to go over non-urgent emails and jot down a list of anything urgent to work on the next day.

Find what works for you, makes you the most productive, and go with it! It may not be what works for everyone else, and that's okay, as long as it works for you.

The Un-Habit: Feeling like this has to be hard

Why: What if it's not so hard? What if you find a way for work/life to mesh perfectly? What if sales/customers/solutions come to you easily? What if you're not always so busy and stressed out? What if everything you're doing IS enough?

The glorification of busy, and the tendency to feel as if you're not stressed out that you're not doing enough, these are common threads I observe among fellow business owners. I've felt this way myself, but it didn't serve me very well, so I changed my Habit of thinking it always needs to be hard.

We need to tell ourselves a new narrative. This doesn't mean we don't work hard, challenge ourselves, or have a strong work drive. This means we offer ourselves some grace. We would not be a failure if a project didn't get done because our child was sick, or you took a little longer than expected on something else.

Instead of stressing out, try taking some time to slow down and reflect. I find this allows my mind to be clearer, and I come up with ideas and strategies that really drive the business forward, instead of always just feeling like I'm trudging through the weeds.

Write down what a successful life means for you. Does being stressed out and constant busy with work fit into that vision? Likely not. Being a great mom, a great partner, having the people important to you know that you love them, having your employees look up to you as a source of strength and stability, those are markers of success for me. I also love being able to cook a meal for my family, make sure the house is well stocked with groceries, and have a clean and healthy home. These things help me feel successful, and help my mind be clearer when I work. Instead of looking at these things as a chore, as something that takes time away from my work, I value them and realize how important they are to my life in the grand scheme of things.

Start telling yourself, "it can be easy" and see how that changes your work, and life, and redefine what success means to you.

About Kirsten: Kirsten Helle Sandoval is a mom, wife, chef, and founder/CEO of Mesa de Vida, a line of global gourmet cooking and seasoning sauces available at Whole Foods Markets nationwide. She is a former private chef to professional athletes and high profile clients, and chef ambassador for real food brands and food commissions. Kirsten has been seen on the Food Network, the cover of Women's Day, Women's World, and heard on radio commercials across the country.

At the age of 25, Kirsten was diagnosed with high blood pressure, high cholesterol, and was pre-diabetic. She had a family history of heart disease and early death due to lifestyle-related issues, and she knew she had to write a new story, and

Photo by Audra Mulkern

create a healthy new family legacy. She started by studying the Blue Zones across the globe, the areas of the world where people live the longest, and the healthiest. She found there was one common thread: real food. So, instead of following another diet, or eating more chemically processed diet food, she began by making a commitment to only eat real food. This led to a 100-pound weight loss, but more importantly, a clean bill of health. It also led to discovering a passion for cooking and developed into a career as a private chef, where she could directly have an impact on helping others live a healthier life.

It was in the kitchens of her private clients where Mesa de Vida's blends were originally developed. Fruits, vegetables, spices, and herbs, all tailored to her client's heritage, culture, and preferences, blended up together, became the base for an endless assortment of delicious meals. She could bring them a taste of home and honor their culture while continually meeting their health needs.

After a day of cooking for others, she longed for these healthy cooking sauces and flavor bases in her own cupboard. How amazing would it be to have something quick, healthy, and flavorful on hand to make dinner for her own family? She knew she couldn't be the only one with this need. And thus, Mesa de Vida was born.

Kirsten is also a mom to two children with a rare genetic health condition and is a living kidney donor herself. She is a fierce believer that food is medicine, and her personal journey is now her professional mission to help others live better through cooking with whole foods.

Kirsten lives with her family in Oceanside, California, and you can find her working at her kitchen table, and often, the beach.

You can find more about Mesa de Vida and Chef Kirsten at MesadeVida.com.

SET EXPECTATIONS WITH FAMILY ABOUT YOUR HOME OFFICE - JEN TAYLOR

Why: When you think about working from home, you think about the space for your office, filing, and what technology you need for your business. Still, it's important to create boundaries and expectations for your home office to keep the peace and let the household know how you intend to work from home.

Expectations - what should your family and clients expect from you, and what you should expect from your family and clients. Then what do you expect from yourself by working from home? You could create a contract of sorts with the family and yourself or a a simple note on the home office door.

So, what are the areas that you should be setting boundaries around and what are the specific expectations to consider?

Days & Hours – Do you work five days a week? Or somewhat flexible days? What are your office hours? Do you take a lunch break? Do you have set days and time for working on your business versus working with clients? If you have set hours, make a sign for your office door with your hours. What is your expectation about your work day or hours if someone is sick in the house?

Interruptions – what are your rules for your family when they are home and have a need or something to share with you? Do you put on a Do Not Disturb sign on the door handle of a closed door? What are the expectations on when they can break that boundary? Think about the age range you have in your house; younger children may not be aware of the difference in interrupting for a snack versus interrupting because they are bleeding and need your immediate attention. With older children, give them tasks they can perform independently without your supervision and have a place for approved snacks for after school.

Meetings – what are the boundaries and expectations for meetings? Do you hold them on certain days? Do you use Zoom or other video conference software? If you meet in person, do you have a set location to meet with clients, or do you leave it up to them? Having these set will help in streamlining your time as well as being in control of your business.

Housework & Personal time – this is more a personal boundary and expectation, but how will you address the distractions of working from home? Will you let it play itself out or will you work the hours and then do what needs to be done around the house?

Setting boundaries and expectations with your family in the above areas will help with productivity, well-being and give your family a guideline on what they should expect from you during the workweek.

THE UN-HABIT: NOT SETTING BOUNDARIES

Why: What becomes of you and your business if you do not implement some boundaries and expectations in your business?

I won't necessarily say chaos, but you are juggling and struggling with everything, and nothing is scheduled. You're working when you can; instead of planning your work, your work, and the projects are working you.

You could be working late at night or early in the morning, and you become more stressed, and that takes its toll on your family and clients.

You could be taking phone calls during dinner, working through the weekend or other family time, missing events in your family because you have to get something done for a client.

Not taking vacations or working through vacation, so instead of spending time with your family, you are stuck inside a hotel room taking calls or working on an important project.

Your family won't know what to expect from you as a spouse or as a parent; this, in turn, causes family friction and possibly more arguments with everyone involved.

Your health becomes more of an issue, due to the stress of work and family, because of working too much.

Your clients are walking all over you; you are meeting all over town, running from meeting to meeting or call to call. They are demanding things that may or may not be in their contract, but you are so stressed you don't know, so you are doing more work for them, and you may not be getting paid for it. If you calculated your hourly rate, you might be making pennies, because you are spending so much time appeasing them.

All of that leads to resentment of your clients, of the work you are doing, and resenting your family for getting in the way of the work you want to get done.

Set boundaries. You'll be glad you did.

About Jennifer: Jennifer Taylor is an award-winning wedding planner; she carries over 15 years of wedding planning experience and has earned a wealth of knowledge throughout her career. While running her own business, Taylor'd Events Group, she had the pleasure of working alongside highly innovative and talented creatives throughout the industry and beyond.

She noticed that many creatives are predominantly right-brained—wildly imaginative and expressive, but missing the necessary structure to create logical systems in their companies. In launching Jen Taylor Consulting, she made it her mission to help creatives build streamlined workflows, processes, and procedures so they can grow their business and spend their time on what they love most — their craft, their family, and their life.

Jen's systematic knowledge of the inner workings of creative businesses has brought her to national stages and major industry publications. She has spoken at conferences like The Special Event, NACE Experience, and ILEA, as well as chapter-based events for NACE, The Wedding Network, ABC, and Western Washington University. Her expertise has also graced the pages of WeddingWire EDU, Special Events, Catersource, Book More Brides, Honeybook, and Wedding Planner Magazine.

Also, an author, she's written content for both to-be-married couples and small business owners. She has contributed to "Planning the Perfect Seattle Wedding: Featuring 15 Interviews with Top Wedding Professionals", written "Six-Word Lessons for a Stress-Free Wedding: 100 Lessons to Plan Your Wedding Without Worry and Enjoy Your Day" and for a small business she created workbooks that help you start and grow your business: "Sexy Startup Business Startup Guide" and "Ops Boss: Business Planning & Operations."

Outside of work, you can typically find her traveling throughout the West Coast or in Maui — the two markets her company serves for destination events. She also has a penchant for cooking and can often be found sipping on a refreshing glass of wine in the many tasting rooms from Woodinville, Washington to Napa, California, and everywhere in between.

CHOOSE THE RIGHT TOOLS - LORI VANDE KROL

Why: Have you ever purchased a new product or used a new system expecting it would solve your disorganization and time management problems, only to find it was not the magic solution you hoped for? Using a simple process to choose the *right* tools and systems for increased productivity in your home office is a Habit that will save you time, money, and frustration. Below are five steps you can use to ensure you are implementing the best solutions for your specific needs.

1. Make a list

Grab a notebook and create a list of obstacles to your productivity and organization. In other words, what is keeping you from a thriving home office? You might categorize your list into the following three areas:

(a) Space – Consider both your working area and the space around you.

(b) Information - Include the challenges you face in managing physical and digital forms of documents, contacts, email, and any other information you use regularly.

(c) Time – Do you struggle with management of your time, including weekly and daily planning, projects and tasks, procrastination, or distractions?

2. Prioritize

Using *your* list, prioritize the obstacles that, if addressed, will most impact your organization and productivity. Choose three to tackle first.

3. Complete a simple needs analysis

For each obstacle, analyze your unique needs by asking a few simple questions: What isn't working? What would a new tool or system need to do? How does an ideal outcome look and feel?

4. Research

With a clear idea of your vision and needs, you can then search for tools or systems that best fit that vision. Look online, ask friends and colleagues what works for them, or reach out to a Productivity Consultant to assist. Just be sure to find the best match for *your* needs.

5. Implement and maintain

After completing steps 1-4, you are much more likely to have chosen a tool or system that will be effective going forward - saving time and money and eliminating the frustration that occurs when systems *don't* meet your needs. But new systems often require new Habits, which take time to develop. Use your new solution regularly for a month, and then review what is and is not working.

Once you have implemented solutions for your top three obstacles, move to your next three priorities. Step through the process until it becomes a natural way for you to make decisions and choices. In other words, until it becomes a Habit.

The Un-Habit: Delaying Decisions

Why: A disorganized office, workspace, computer, or even a cluttered mind is often the result of delayed decisions. For various reasons, we put off making choices or decisions about what to do with a piece of paper, email, thought, or idea. Regarding time, procrastination can be a form of delayed decisions. The result is piles of paper, full email inboxes, long lists of to-dos, and feelings of overwhelm and lack of control. The good news is we can address this "un-Habit" by creating a better process, and eventually better Habits, for decision-making.

Every item that comes into our home office (or anywhere else for that matter) - whether it be paper, digital, or intangible items like thoughts or ideas - fits into one of three categories. It is either:

1. actionable, requiring current or future action by you or someone else,
2. an item to hold on to for future reference, or
3. something that can be tossed, deleted, or forgotten.

To remember this, think of the acronym ART™ - Action, Reference, or Toss.

Having the appropriate tools and systems readily available for these three choices will make your decision-making process quicker and easier. As a simple example, for paper that needs to be tossed, you will need readily accessible locations for this: a trash can, recycle bin, and a shredder. Be diligent in what you decide to keep and get rid of.

For those items that are not tossed or deleted, the simple step of separating what is actionable from what is not can make a big difference in the way that you work. For those items that require action, the most valuable question you can ask yourself is simple but very powerful, "What is the next action?" Answering this question will guide you in deciding where this item belongs in your working environment (e.g., a paper or digital project file, an email folder for actionable items, a task list, calendar, or even delegated and transferred to someone else.)

As you work on the "un-Habit" of delayed decisions, it is important to be purposeful about your choices throughout the day. By practicing intentional decisions consistently, with systems in place to capture them, you will find that decision-making becomes simpler, less overwhelming, and maybe even fun!

About Lori: Lori Vande Krol is a productivity consultant, speaker, and trainer who helps busy professionals and growing businesses around the world implement systems to increase efficiency and success. Lori has developed programs that help her clients tackle their overwhelm by better managing time, space, and information. Her work has resulted in savings of thousands of dollars and hundreds of hours for her clients, in addition to a considerable reduction in stress and frustration.

After receiving a BS in Mathematics from Iowa State University, Lori worked 13 years as an Actuary and Risk Manager in a Fortune 500 company. During this time, she spent ten years studying for and passing the rigorous series of actuarial exams. But eventually, she realized being an actuary was not her true passion. Lori saw there was a need to help those that, like herself, often feel overwhelmed with work and life. She chose to use her organizational and analytical skills to help people get clear on their goals and implement more efficient systems to achieve those goals. In 2005, Life Made Simple LLC was born with the mission of helping others live more productively, feel less stressed, and have more time for what matters most.

Lori works with clients both in-person and virtually. She offers services, including productivity assessments, strategic planning, tool and software training, monthly coaching, and system implementation. Her presentations and webinars on topics such as "Time Management Techniques to Manage Your Day and Sleep Better at Night," "Taming the Technology Tiger," and "Finding Balance in An Ever-Connected World" have been highly praised by attendees, companies, and associations around the country.

In addition, Lori's expertise has been shared around the world through various publications, tv, and radio, such as Bloomberg Business, The Sydney Morning Herald, Des Moines Living Magazine, FedEx.com, AmericanExpress.com, WHOtv, ScanSnapWorld, CentralJersey.com, Des Moines Amplified, and Blog Talk Radio.

Active in her industry, Lori is a Golden Circle member of the National Association of Productivity and Organizing Professionals (NAPO) and served on its Board of Directors from 2015-2018. She was honored with the NAPO President's Award in

2019. Lori received her Fellowship in the Society of Actuaries in 2000 and graduated from the Greater Des Moines Leadership Institute Class of 2015.

Lori lives in Des Moines, Iowa, with her husband, three beautiful daughters, and two cats. When she isn't working on new ways to find and help clients, Lori enjoys doing BODYPUMP™, working on puzzles, reading, lounging by the pool, traveling with her family, and anything Disney.

TREAT YOUR HOME OFFICE AS A SACRED SPACE - JILL NICHOLS-HICKS

Why: How important is it we get a good night's sleep? Do you make efforts to find the right mattress, bedding, surroundings, and other touches to assist for better sleep and to create a sacred space? We know the value of having a good night's sleep and the difference it can make in our productivity. The same can be said for creating a Habit of treating your home office as a sacred space. We treat our sacred spaces differently, with more reverence and respect. Walking into a room where it is imperative for you to make money needs to reflect that same importance. We smartly invest in having an organizer, business coach, and interior office decorator to help us create the sacred space in which we do the business that creates us an income for the life we desire.

Jan Marie Dore, Professional Certified Life Coach, Speaker, and Writer, says:

"Creating Sacred Space in your home office... your emotions and energy are affected by your home office. If your office or workspace is humane, loving, and sacred, then what you produce there will have a sense of humanity and integrity. The challenge is not to change yourself to fit the space but to seek a way to occupy your office space in a way that harmonizes with your personality and energy. Also, it is important to see your work in the greater context...You must know that your work can make a contribution to the world and that your office space can reflect this intention. Think about what changes you can make to the layout and design of your workspace to create an environment that inspires your best work, and what objects you will place in your ideal workspace to give you a sense of the sacred."

The Habit of keeping our home office flowing in the rhythms that serve our goals will trickle down in other aspects of our life.

HOW: When we treat our home office as a sacred place, our energy changes, and we can be more productive, creative, and organized. This assists in helping us release anxiety and stress over important lost items, with less scramble, and a smoother easing into the necessary transitions. The office will be inviting, gravitating towards a deeper satisfaction, and improving the quality of the work done. If it is our Habit and mindset to treat our home office as a sacred space, an abundance is waiting there; an inner peace and joy that creates a juiciest and delicious professional fruit.

The Un-Habit: Eating lunch at your desk

Why: In the drive and urgency of owning a business or staying employed, when working from a home office, many people are working with no or little breaks; this includes eating lunch at the desk. Studies have shown that this is more harmful to our overall health and steals from our necessary self-care. In an article shared by the company Rise, September 25, 2018, called "7

Reasons Eating Lunch at Your Desk is a Bad Idea," the author writes, "Staying at your desk all day can decrease your productivity and increase stress levels. Furthermore, sitting for long periods can cause a whole host of health issues, including back pain, leg disorders, and increased risk of heart disease." The author is correct to highlight the effects on long term health such as heart health and sore joints. It also actually brings on more stress, brain fog, less productivity, fatigue, and less inspiration. In the long run, the simple act of "just eating lunch at the desk to catch up on emails" does more harm than good. We may think that's counterintuitive in our fast-paced, multi-role, long list day; that we need to use every moment of the work- (and beyond) day checking off boxes or making that must-call not to waste valuable time eating ANYWHERE else but at the desk. However, we have seen or even personally experienced that pushing through our workday comes with a cost payable at the expense of our physical, emotional, and spiritual wellbeing.

Imagine what retirement looks and feels like. Are there fun activities like travel on the list? Spending more time with family and friends? These with other hopes and dreams will need a healthy mind and body to enjoy the benefits of a life post-work truly. Much like a daily whack of an ax to a tree, eating lunch at the desk is just one more hit to your only body. If we want a richer life, then self-care health steps are prerequisites for maximizing the outcome. Visualize that retirement dream again; better yet, do it while eating lunch on your patio or kitchen table.

When I broke my Habit of eating lunch at my desk, I found I wasn't missing opportunities to get more business done. Instead, I gained a greater and more profound renewal in the life I envisioned stemming from joy to contentment; a life better lived.

About Jill: Jill Nichols-Hicks is very passionate about women's needs and concerns, believing in the importance of health and wellness for physical, spiritual, and mental self-care in helping to strengthen women. Born and raised in Walla Walla, Washington, a graduate of Western Washington University, Jill has for many years been active in her communities advocating for social justice, special needs children, animal rescue, and environmental concerns.

In 2014, Jill had the vision to bring women together by building a community for connection, education, and empowerment, helping women have more enlightened lives through encouragement and support. Illuminating Women was born and raised with the help of many women, and it continues to grow throughout the Puget Sound area with a community of over 1,500 women providing quality programming, supportive community, and fun engagement.

Through Jill's leadership, Illuminating Women hosts a yearly women's empowerment conference bridging the woman entrepreneur, to the woman working in corporate, to the woman in transition. Jill's passion is to provide a safe place for women to gather for personal development and professional growth. They are bringing together a variety of esteemed speakers, in-depth programming, and a fulfilling sisterhood.

Jill also created an avenue to showcase women-owned businesses, getting into the raw and gritty details of what it takes to be a business owner. Women get inspiration and fulfillment while lifting up businesswomen through the support of their goods and services and using their social media platform to bring greater attention to these amazing businesswomen.

Jill is an electric connector helping women find new avenues and networks to learn and grow while also helping to showcase their talents and expertise. An inspirational speaker driven to empower women to create a community for traverse, productive and unifying common goals serving the greater good.

What continues to drive Jill is the countless stories women tell her of their struggles, interpersonal pains, their hunger for greater opportunities, and the gifts they desperately want to grow with celebration. Watching women grow, exceeding through the difficult times, knowing that having a community to be there through the good and bad times keeps the vibrant community of Jill's vision.

Jill loves to travel, especially in Italy with her husband, have dinner parties, hike with her Great Dane, read, and serve her faith community at St. Andrews Lutheran Church in Bellevue, Washington. She has two adult children and many "sisters" who she loves to inspire and lift up.

CREATE STRUCTURE AND SPACE TO SUPPORT WORKING FROM HOME - YVONNE D. HALL

Why: Work is important. Our commitment to our clients, our work family and our professional colleagues matter. AND work is only one spoke on the wheel that makes us whole, complete human beings. As someone newer to working from home, in the beginning I found it easy to let work seep into all the corners of my day and time. This created an illusion of productivity---look, I can do analysis and return emails at 2 am! It is so easy to try to fit in just one more thing before logging off for the day. But in reality, I have realized that I am the most creative and productive for my work relationships when I take time to nurture the relationships with my family and friends and also to recharge my own batteries. Working from home still needs to provide time for self-care and relaxation. Now that our commute time and other bridges between work and home have been blurred or eliminated, it is more essential than ever to make these a priority.

Creating a dedicated space for work—both physical and/or mental space-- helps support these goals as well. A space away from the distractions of spouse, pets, children, or housework can create the opportunity for greater focus on people and projects for work. There is value in dedicated focus for specific blocks of time. This dedicated space—whether it is physical, mental, or both—creates a positive energy and momentum that makes it easier to accomplish the tasks at hand.

Transitioning from that space and returning "home" can create reminders to re-engage/re-connect with the family relationships. If physical separateness is not possible, then creating rituals to transition into and out of work mode can be helpful. A few minutes of yoga or meditation, preparing a cup of tea, or taking a walk with the dogs are all ones that work well for me. And do not underestimate the psychological impact of closing the laptop! Allow work to be finished.

The Un-Habit: Let go of judgment and self-criticism around all the times that good Habits and good intentions don't workout for you

Why: How often do we allow negative self-talk become our Habit? The way we communicate with ourselves can become a constant barrage of "shoulds" and feelings of inadequacy when we fail to get everything done the way we believe it is supposed to be accomplished. It is helpful to step back and cultivate perspective.

Some of the greatest obstacles to our productivity and peace of mind are our expectations. Everything about our work processes and interactions may be different now in our COVID-19 world, but somehow we expect our output and productivity to be the same. And when reality doesn't match our expectations we can quickly drop into self-criticism and frustration.

It is always a good time to set goals and intentions but it may also be a very good time to hold any expectations loosely and to develop acceptance for things as they are and not as we wish them to be.

We are in a time of massive change and uncertainty both globally and locally. We are each dealing with life experiences and stresses that are unique to our time and almost completely without a roadmap or guidebook. Unless you live alone, there are going to be children that need to be fed, laundry that has to be done, or a pet that needs to be cleaned up after. And even if you don't have any of these, there will be days when technology doesn't work right, a project goes badly, or an unexpectedly beautiful day calls you outside. Whatever the reason, it is important to cultivate grace and space for yourself and for others. We are each on an unexpected and challenging journey. The more we can stay grounded in our own kindness and compassion --starting with for ourselves—the better we can navigate the highs and lows and pivots that will doubtlessly be required of us.

About Yvonne: As a child, the expression "as long as you live under our roof, you must follow our rules" was heard frequently around Yvonne's home. Being somewhat independent by nature, these words were a catalyst for her life-long passion for personal empowerment.

This passion has fueled successful careers in both the information technology sector and the financial services industry. In both industries, Yvonne has enjoyed the educational and coaching aspects of supporting clients in their work to achieve their unique goals and objectives. As a veteran of the financial services industry since 1993, her work since then has been targeted less in support of corporations and more specifically toward the needs of individuals and their families. Collaboration and team building have also been important elements of her work in both client-facing and management level positions. All of her career emphasis has been high-contact, high-touch...both in the office with her team and their clients and out in the communities they serve.

In addition to Yvonne's primary vocation with the Hall Wealth Management Group of Wells Fargo Advisors, she is also a certified yoga instructor and has taught yoga in her local community for over 7 years.

COVID-19 has created challenges and opportunities as face-to-face contact has been eliminated and creativity to maintain and deepen relationships has become essential. 2020 has provided a crash course in the do's and don'ts of working from home and there has been no aspect of her life—be it yoga, financial services, book clubs, or community board work – that has not been affected. In Yvonne's view, COVID-19 has provided a great opportunity to practice yoga off the mat which is to explore flexibility and balance in the face of great change. Figuring out how to do this well is a work in progress. Habits (and non-Habits) presented here represent early lessons that have had a positive impact on the full range of her life events impacted by "working from home".

Yvonne and her husband Daniel have had their own roof in the Snoqualmie Valley for over 25 years. The "rules" under the roof are now set by two geriatric Brittany dogs who live with them and who are quite happy with the new work from home arrangements and by identical twin grandsons who used to visit often (and hopefully will again soon). Yoga, hiking, and dog walks allow Yvonne to relieve stress and enjoy nature as well.

Wells Fargo Advisors is a trade name used by Wells Fargo Clearing Services, LLC, Member SIPC.

Investment and Insurance Products are:

- Not Insured by the FDIC or Any Federal Government Agency
- Not a Deposit or Other Obligation of, or Guaranteed by, the Bank or Any Bank Affiliate
- Subject to Investment Risks, Including Possible Loss of the Principal Amount Invested

BE INTENTIONAL WHEN SETTING UP A HOME WORKSPACE - GAZALA URADNIK

Why: Some people find that working from home is a double-edged sword. My colleagues have told me: "I don't know how you can get work done in a home office." However, I consider myself lucky to have a home environment that makes it possible for me to work from home successfully. Working from home can make it challenging to stay focused, and it does take discipline and an important key Habit: a dedicated, well thought out and well-equipped workspace.

One of the most important ways to increase my productivity is to have a dedicated space set up and stocked intentionally as my home office. Your home office space should ONLY be used for your business and your work. It is important to keep your home office and the work you do in the office separate from the rest of your home. Do not work from the couch one day and then the kitchen table the next. Keep your office space, whatever that is, consistent and clutter-free.

Make sure your workspace at home is well appointed. Don't just assume you can "get by" with your laptop alone. You will be more productive by having the right set-up and the right tools at your disposal. My office space is a separate room in my home. I have good lighting, a printer, dual computer monitors, file cabinets, and complete office supplies. I used to share that space with my entire family when it functioned as a playroom for my kids. It was during that time in my life when I realized the importance of organizing your workspace the best you can to remain focused and productive. Being intentional about the way you set up your workspace, and ensuring that it is provisioned with the right supplies will help you have what you need at hand and be productive throughout your workday.

Over the years, I have found keeping my home office separate and to complete all work in that home office to be the most important factor in maintaining productivity. Don't bring work "home" and take files, materials or other work-related items into other parts of your home to work on in the evening. When you shut your door to your office or get up from your space, plan to go "home" for the day, both physically and mentally. Conversely, there should not be personal papers, kid's school items, personal bills or other items that are not related to your business in your home office space. You would not bring personal papers to your office if it were off-site, so treat your home office the same way. You should also not have to leave your home office to get a supply from elsewhere in the house (this leads to distraction), so if that means having a double set of staplers, scissors, etc. so that one set can "live" permanently in the home office, then that's best.

It is important to be intentional when setting up your home office so that you can keep home and work separate so that you have what you need for your work when you enter your office, and can "leave it all behind" at the end of your workday.

THE UN-HABIT: NOT GETTING DRESSED FOR WORK EACH DAY

Why: I started my company eight years ago and have been working from home from the very first day. During the first year or two of business, I would not get dressed for my home office day, unless I had to go out to meet a client or see a colleague. If I was in my home office all day, I would not worry or care about my appearance, and I didn't necessarily "dress" for my work day.

Breaking this Habit has been an incredible boost to both my productivity as well as how I feel about my day. I can't stress enough how important it is to get dressed for your day, as if you were headed to an outside office or seeing a client each day. You don't necessarily need to wear a suit or high heels into your home office, but it is important to dress for work. How you look during the day can affect how you feel, and makes an important difference in your day and the work you are able to complete.

I make it a point to only step into my office after I have gotten dressed for work. I work for nonprofit clients, and my normal dress code with clients is business casual. I get dressed like this for work, even if no one will see me all day. There are a couple of reasons for this. First, getting dressed and looking your best, makes you feel more confident and energized for the day. If you decide to stay in your pajamas until noon, you will find that you are just not in the same frame of mind and in a business mode as if you had gotten dressed for your work day.

A second and more practical reason to get dressed for your day is to bring the same professionalism that you would have in an off-site office into your home office. If a client or colleague calls for an impromptu meeting that you cannot miss, you want to present yourself with confidence and professionalism, and be available to them at a moment's notice. If you are already dressed for your day as if you were meeting a client in person, you will have the confidence to tackle any workplace meetings or issues that come up.

About Gazala: Gazala Uradnik was initially drawn to the development and nonprofit field because of her interest in the health care field. This interest eventually led her to pursue a master's degree in Healthcare Management from the University of Michigan School of Public Health. Years of working in strategic planning and business development for hospitals and healthcare organizations gained her the analytical skills, organizational expertise, and compassion that she now brings to the field of nonprofit fundraising and event management.

Gazala started GFS Events in 2012 because she knew that nonprofits needed help through her own nonprofit board and volunteer experience. She is an entrepreneur by nature, and starting her own businesses was a natural progression of her goals and skills. GFS Events provides strategic event planning expertise to nonprofits through focused event strategy, logistics coordination, mission/messaging, and audience and donor development. Over the last eight years, her team has helped countless nonprofits raise millions of dollars throughout the Pacific Northwest. GFS Events has received numerous awards for the best nonprofit event and best public event through the International Live Events Association. Gazala also serves as a board member for the International Live Events Association

Seattle Chapter and has served as President and Vice-President for the Business Network International.

As a wife and mother to three wonderful children, it is important to Gazala to teach her kids the importance of nonprofit work. Her family regularly supports and volunteers at many of the GFS events each year. Gazala enjoys helping her clients plan a successful event so that they can reach their fundraising goals. She listens to her clients to understand their needs. She loves fundraising and working with nonprofits to help them to reach their goals. She has been able to double and sometimes triple the fundraising goals for her nonprofit clients. It makes what she does every day a privilege and not just a job.

41

BE LIKE PHINEAS: SPEAK YOUR PLAN ALOUD! - RON RAEL

Why: Imagine that you wake up one day and find yourself in a city that you don't recognize. (This is a common occurrence for a professional speaker, but that is a story for another time).

You leave an unrecognizable room and wander, trying to figure out 'what is what?' and 'why am I here?' Intimidating, right?

When you decide to establish an office in your home, you will have these "Where am I?" and "Why am I here?" moments often, especially if you come into this from a structured work environment.

Finding success in your Home Office (HO) requires a mental adjustment - a new attitude. My first home office launched in 1984, so my perspective is based on experience.

Once Phineas Flynn (a Disney cartoon character) has a plan, there is nothing that stops him from accomplishing it. I believe your new HO attitude must include a desire to plan out each day and then speak your plan. For certain people, this is hard. You tell yourself: "I'm motivated by spur-of-the-moment impulses. I don't like being boxed in. I want to be flexible. I don't want a boss telling me what to do."

Yet, having detailed ideas for specific outcomes, and affirming them out loud will reduce your stress and result in less time-wasting.

First thing, Monday morning, I make a list of my Top Priorities for the week – no more than 10. Next, I select two or three for each workday and add goals/outcomes for that day. Ten minutes later, I hit the ground running. A shiny, attractive journal is where I record these, and I look at it several times a day. I'm old school and love doing this manually. If you are like me or prefer digital tools, please get into a Habit of starting each day with a plan. Speak your plan aloud, and your priority becomes your mantra until it's done.

You may be shocked to know that I do not like structure! Yet, if I did not have this structure in place, my Home Office 'career' would have ended years ago.

You've heard this: When you fail to plan, you plan to fail. I want you to feel and be successful. Please, as you start each day in your HO, be like the irrepressible Phineas, and say to the mirror, "I know what I am going to do today!" Then, make it happen.

The Un-Habit: Only You Can Prevent Boundary Wars!

Why: I confess... I have a problem. Whenever I enter a room, I spread out. This occurs in hotel rooms, kitchens whenever I cook, and my wife, Ann's sacred space: our bedroom. Yes, I even accomplish this in my Home Office.

This message is not about me – it's about a Habit you must break!

Finding success in your HO requires a mental adjustment - a new attitude. My first home office launched in 1984, so my perspective is based upon experience.

Close your eyes, say "home," and pay attention to your feelings. Then close them again, say "corporate office," paying attention to your feelings. Did you sense a difference? You felt that emotional difference that leads to Boundary Wars, once you decide to establish an office in your home.

A HO needs to be a sacred place where you can be productive and effective. Your home is a safe place where you – and others – relax and live. Yet all too often, people who work in their residence ignore the boundaries. This leads to Boundary Wars, where home and work blend into one environment, and they both lose their sacredness.

Want an example? Employees work in my HO. One week, not long ago, a male relative came for a long visit staying in a bedroom located on the same floor as my HO. One morning he walked out of the room in his skivvies startling a female employee, who had just arrived. I forgot to inform him about the need for boundaries. Doh!

Here is what works to instill the mindset: "This is my office, not my home." Set office hours. Use storage and furniture that is "office only." Close the door when working. Do not share office supplies with family. Install a separate landline (if you need one). Acquire an office copier, printer, and WIFI. Set and use a separate bank account and credit card.

The family peace and goodwill you foster by maintaining these boundaries far exceed the cost!

My best advice to help you break the Habit of letting the office and home meld into one space comes from my uber-organized spouse. When Ann leaves her office, everything is put away, so clean, neat, and joyful that you'd swear Marie Kondo just left.

I confess... for over 40 years, I've tried to end my sin of spreading out and creating chaos.

Perhaps one day...

About Ron: I develop leaders worth following™. There is an alarming lack of high-quality leaders in today's global economy. We need more of them, especially in the workplace!

As an authority on the art of leading and influencing people, I'm able to transform the professional who cannot lead into an influencer who is caring, empathetic, courageous, and committed to their employees' success. Over 14,000 technical experts have experienced a revitalization of their impact, as a result of my virtual programs, coaching, mentoring, and tools. I authored 14 books on leadership in business, including: "The Reluctant Leader™: Own Your Responsibility with Courage" and "Leadership: the Key Ingredient to a Good Budget."

I work with organizations that need their technical experts to step up and lead better. Working together, we create a custom Leadership Development Program which delivers leadership experience that every emerging leader needs.

My highly interactive virtual and live presentations on leadership remove people's fears and reluctance and then instill the confidence and courage to make tough decisions and deal with workplace challenges. I concentrate on people's growth in personal & corporate accountability, culture-shifting, and attitudes.

My journey to becoming a good leader is typical of most Reluctant Leaders™ - being thrust into a leadership role without training or guidance. In fact, "I learned how to lead the wrong way!" Learning to lead is mostly trial and error and can take five or more years. Together, we can accelerate the time it takes to transform a novice into a person who has a positive impact and beneficial influence.

I've been in the role of a leader since the age of 11, but it took me 30 years to realize this was an honor and privilege instead of a burden.

There is a less serious side to me – I am usually irreverent, sometimes satirical, and always provocative. I am addicted to exercise, good health, chocolate, and good sangria. Two of my 'grands' love to tease me saying, "You're Grumpy Gramps!" A true misnomer. I don't know what my four other 'grands' think of me. But they do like using me as their scratching post... that's because they are cats.

My awesome sense of humor is the result of a steady diet of sitcoms, comix, and YouTube videos. No one ever guesses my true age because I am not young or old; I am simply backdated.

Do your employees say, "Our leaders don't know how to lead?" Let me help you to ignite the improvements in your leadership landscape!

42

STOP WORRYING AND MAKE A DECISION!
- KRISTIN BERTILSON

Why? Every day when working from home, we are faced with thousands of decisions, and many can stop us in our tracks. For many of us, different from working in a commercial office space with other people, we need to decide to move forward on something by ourselves. Without someone else to run a decision by if we are unsure, we worry and overthink these decisions, both big and small, to the point where they are not completed effectively, in a timely manner, or perhaps not made at all.

We can make decisions on our own in our home office (or call a colleague, advisor, partner, or friend for their thoughts). The bottom line – deciding is a productive step forward. My father has always told me that the best decision is the one that we make. That even if the decision made turns out to be a bad decision, you could always change your path, but you will never know until you try! Staying stuck in the unknown allows doubt to grow, frustration to take over, and fears to intrude. When you are working from home and feel like you are not sure what to do next with your day, how to answer an email, what project to start on next, what to call your new business, or any of the other large or small decisions we make in the workplace every day... take a deep breath, make the decision and check back in with yourself after a little bit of time and see how it feels. If it still feels right, and that you are on the right track, continue going down that path until a new decision pops in to detour you.

As the quote by Peter Drucker states, "Whenever you see a successful business, someone once made a courageous decision."

Decisions are hard, maybe even more so when we need to make them on our own working from home, but don't let them take over! You have got this! So change your furniture around in the home office, if you don't like it, change it again. Start on a project. Not the right one? Set it aside and move on. Not sure whether to email or call, do both! Whatever the decision is, just make sure that you make it. The outcome that follows will not only guide you and your future decisions but will also allow you more time to complete work from home by not staying in the unknown place.

Good luck, and happy decision making!

The UnHabit: STOP underestimating your time!

Why? Sitting at your home office and the timer goes off, and you think, how did eight hours just go by. This home office doesn't seem to be working for me; I don't feel productive. Are you feeling like you are continually running out of time, running late, or not knowing where the day goes? It could be because you are underestimating your time. Time is valuable, it controls our days, and lots of people are in a position that someone else controls much of what they do with their time, even when not working actually in the office space. So you might be asking, how do I control my time? How does estimating time help?

Let's start with a household example most people can relate to... grocery shopping. We put it on a to-do list, tell ourselves it will take lets say an hour, but is that all the time it really takes? We have to make a list, go to the store, shop, load the car, unload the car, put items away... and the kicker is, open packages to put items away entirely, and perhaps even throw out old stuff from the fridge! So grocery shopping has many steps and lots of time involved that you may not have accounted for.

Back to working from home... let's take answering an email. If you are in the middle of an emailed conversation with someone, and your estimation is just a few minutes to send off an email, but you know that you will get a reply that you then have to reply to, (that then will get another reply, and so on) make sure to not just count a few minutes into your day for that email exchange. It really will end up taking a half hour with all the back and forth. Say you have a meeting, the meeting should take 45 minutes via zoom. However, after the meeting, you will have meeting notes that need to be typed up, put away, and dealt with. You will have new to-do's from that meeting, and you will have to follow up with those to do's by the end of the day. You need to estimate more time than just the 45-minute meeting.

Underestimating our time makes us rush, flustered, and frustrated by the end of the day. Yes, we all need more hours in the day, but knowing how to manage the hours you have and the time it will take you to do the complete tasks in those hours will help you feel successful at filling your calendar up successfully.

About Kristin: Kristin Bertilson, owner of Queen B Organizing in Corvallis, OR truly believes there is no limit to what you can achieve if you do the work you love. She has appeared on four episodes of the TLC network's Hoarding Buried Alive and one episode of A&E: Hoarders. She started Queen B Organizing ten years ago, on her own. It has grown into a business that employs 16 people and has various focuses, including residential organizing, hoarding, senior downsizing, packing/unpacking, and move management, large home cleanouts, and estate sales.

Queen B Organizing's goal is to help people, one clutter-free space at a time. They want individuals to love their space, to find joy in their surroundings and find the peace they seek in their space.

Kristin is honored to have given back to her community at home as well as her community of organizers in various ways. She has been Vice-Chair on the Historic Resource Commission, Chaired multiple auctions for Zonta, and Chaired the National Association of Professional Organizing and Productivity Consultants (NAPO) Conference and volunteered on multiple committees for NAPO, and many other various board positions locally.

START YOUR DAY STRONG WITH MOVEMENT - STACEY SORGEN

Why: In all my years as a Personal Trainer and Health Coach, there is one Habit that I've learned over time to help create a more prosperous and thriving experience while working from home. I've tried to cheat my system and deviate from the "plan," but each time, I come up short.

The Habit I'm talking about is getting out of bed on time and taking action, with movement. You might be thinking, "of course, the personal trainer would suggest movement." I agree, it's a little cliche, but it's the truth. This is about *starting* your day with a step to be successful. Doing so shapes the rest of the day.

Now, I want to clarify that movement can be so many things. A 20-minute timer and a swift clean up of your kitchen and living room might keep you from thinking about the chaos that looms outside your home office. It might lighten the load on your shoulders of "things to do," allowing you to focus more time and energy on the things that matter most. A 40-minute walk in nature might enable you to let go of the rough night's sleep that you had, letting go of stress, and help to energize you and your body. The act of clearing your mind and relieving stress and anxiety through movement is pretty miraculous, and I haven't found any worthy substitute for what some movement can produce.

Anecdotally, I've found that in the last ten years, the majority of people view movement as "all or nothing," meaning that they feel they have to complete a certain amount of time or exert a certain amount of effort or achieve a certain level of sweat to feel accomplished. Anything less that this ideal they've built in their mind, and they'd rather skip movement because it may not feel complete. I want to assure you that every bit of movement counts. A mellow yoga flow to your favorite music for 10 minutes. A dance party-of-one in your living room for the length of three songs.

We can decide how to move and how long to move by evaluating our energy level when we awake and listening to our bodies. When we have more energy, we can do more; when we have less, we do less. It all counts, and it all makes a difference in how we approach our work and our productivity before we ever even sit down in front of a computer or a client. Movement anytime, but especially first thing as you start your day works to calm the mind and body, allowing you to focus your energy and attention on making your home office thrive.

The Un-Habit: Starting the day on the defense

Why: So, this talk of movement and bright starts to the morning in the home office lead me to think about how starting your day on the defense, or in reactive mode as you start work at home can quickly squash hopes for a productive morning and day.

Start Your Day Strong With Movement - Stacey Sorgen

Everything falls apart when we lack intention and just "launch" into our day defensively. I think every human has experienced a morning where they overslept and arrived into the day like Cosmo Kramer crashing through Jerry Seinfeld's front door on "Seinfeld." Disheveled, confused, arriving in body - but maybe not in mind. Do you ever roll out of your bed right before you need to start working and show up in your chair, feeling a little out of control and off-center? I don't know about you, but these days often result in me feeling like the day is happening "to me" or "at me," and I'm on the defensive as things pop up and surprise me. A meeting? What phone call? As I write about this, can you feel the drain of energy and how days like this feel like we're pushing a boulder up a hill? When started on the defensive, the entire day feels like a game of catch-up or tag, and we're starting with a significant disadvantage.

Want the opposite? A proactive approach to the day begins not only that morning, but the night before. Setting the alarm, setting up the coffee pot, laying out clothes that are comfortable for your activity (or even sleeping in them), going to bed on time, and setting an intention are what make all the difference. Unfortunately, this is where we can fall short - because we are optimistic people, and we want to believe that we'll wake up, spring happily out of bed, and begin the day with ease. In reality, it isn't about willpower or muscle, but intention, and it's hard to muster intention while in a warm bed, on a cold day, with rain falling outside. To succeed, we do all we can to lessen resistance and make it a smooth path to success. Smelling the coffee brewing in the kitchen, knowing you're already in the clothes, having gotten enough sleep; you've put yourself in the best possible position to succeed.

Now, it only takes movement, which leads to focus and success in working from home. A clear and defined start to the day begins with a level head, a boost in energy, and confidence in your ability to meet your own goals and intentions. Start your day offensively instead of defensively and watch your productivity soar.

About Stacey: Stacey Sorgen is a certified personal trainer, holistic lifestyle coach, and yoga teacher based in Seattle, Washington. She owns ModBody Fitness and Stacey Sorgen Coaching and offers compassionate Life, Wellness, and Business coaching. Stacey received a B.A. in English from the University of California, Riverside, where she served as Academic Coordinator of Omega Zeta Chi Service Sorority, as an ALLIES volunteer- speaking at local high schools, a UCR Resident Advisor and Editor of Opinions for the Highlander Student Newspaper.

After college, she went on to work in healthcare and maintains certification as a phlebotomist, professional rescuer, CPR, AED, and first aid. As a Team Coordinator at a major cancer center, Stacey worked to integrate all facets of the patient care delivery system to facilitate chemotherapy, radiation, transfusion, physical therapy, and surgical appointments from within a team of physicians. Deciding that rather than only working in treatment, she wanted to have a more active role in rehabilitation, wellness, and prevention was a driving force in a career change. As a result, Stacey sought training in STOTT Pilates and earned certification with the American College of Sports Medicine as a Certified Personal Trainer to bring holistic movement and exercise to all clients and patients.

A graduate of the Institute for Integrative Nutrition Health Coaching Program, she is a Certified Holistic Health Coach. She

Start Your Day Strong With Movement - Stacey Sorgen

received training in more than one hundred dietary theories and studied a variety of practical lifestyle coaching methods. Drawing on this knowledge, Stacey creates a completely personalized "roadmap to health" that suits the unique body, lifestyle, preferences, and goals of each individual.

She loves paddleboarding on Lake Washington, trail running, triathlons, and spending time with her wife, Heather, and their two tiny dogs. Stacey started in the wellness/coaching field 10+ years ago and continues to push the field forward with movement offered for all body types, a belief in health at every size, and a general spirit of joy in movement. She believes in the importance of strength, balance, power, stability, and flexibility - and the wisdom of our bodies. Stacey also works to holistically and compassionately support like-minded entrepreneurs with developing business practices that protect their personal wellness, success, and longevity.

www.StaceySorgenCoaching.com www.ModBodyFitness.com

5-10 MINUTE MORNING MEDITATION TO START THE DAY AND GET CENTERED - JACKIE RAMIREZ

Why: Stress, anxiety, and fear are common responses in this unprecedented environment of staying home and staying safe (written during the Covid-19 pandemic). With this said, I am very grateful to have the opportunity to work from home and have found the need to find ways to be more mindful, organized, and structured. I have recognized this is not an easy process as my mind wanders, and I find myself losing a little motivation and focus.

What I have been able to rely on during this time is meditation. The process of meditation did and sometimes still does not always come easy. Many lifestyles, including mine, are so busy and crammed with appointments, meetings, family needs, etc. that it becomes difficult to be mindful or present and be able to focus on day-to-day activities and productiveness.

I have attended many classes, seminars, and workshops on meditation. I am certainly not an expert, but have found in my practice of meditation; I can help control my ability to be present and purposeful. For me, this process has helped me "turn-off" my brain and focus on my breathing and the slow rhythmic flow of a mantra (a few short, repetitive words) that reflect how I am feeling.

Finding a quiet place where I can sit comfortably with my feet planted on the ground, my back and spine supported but relaxed, I close my eyes. Breathing in several deep breaths and letting my shoulders release from my ears is such a conscious process, and it feels so relaxing. When and if my brain starts to wonder, I do repeat a short mantra to focus myself again and concentrate on the breath.

Meditating 5-10 minutes a day has been such a calm, clarifying process to start my day that it has helped me focus on letting go of some of the stresses and anxieties that can envelop us each day. It is an easy process, and I highly recommend it to anyone who would like not to wear their shoulders as earrings.

The Un-Habit: My Love-Hate Relationship with Social Media

Why: Technology is amazing and life-changing in so many ways, especially in my profession as a Realtor working from home. Everything is now so accessible on my computer, my smartphone, or tablet. The ability to pull up listings on your phone in the middle of a showing to set an appointment. Driving directions are easy and convenient that I don't have to pull a map out of my glove compartment and fumble around to find a "close enough destination". Searching for homes online through the multiple listing service vs. having to open a thousand-page paper binder to search for listings that fit your client's criteria. Yes, I know this is showing my age.

What I also do love is the technology of social media and all of the platforms i.e., FaceBook, Instagram, Twitter, Snapchat,

TikTok, etc. All of which I enjoy scrolling through and seeing friends and family from the past and present and all of their beautiful pictures, stories, and comments.

What I hate is my lack of self-control. I could completely get sucked in. I used to be able to scroll and scroll and comment and research and scroll some more to find out that I have been on social media for an hour or more and first of all, did not even think it was that long and secondly realize that maybe I am getting information overload and then feel a little more anxiety and stress about current events social opinions that neither help me or better me in any way. Which leads to more meditation...

What I have found to help me with this overwhelming feeling is to limit myself and find self-control. By allowing myself just a few minutes a day either at lunchtime or in the evening when things are settling down a bit from the day, to do a quick scroll and only allow myself to view specific things such as Instagram for inspirational pictures or if I need to research something to only allow myself the time to do just that and to avoid scrolling all the platforms. I have found this to be very helpful in my overall outlook on social media and have found my time is well spent elsewhere and a sense of accomplishment with a little less anxiety and stress.

About Jackie: Jackie Ramirez began her real estate career 18 years ago, following her passion for the diverse Puget Sound region and her interest in home design. She has distinguished herself as a leading professional in the area by providing platinum level service to clients interested in buying, selling, building, or investing in real estate. Her commitment, honesty, integrity, and knowledge are the skills that are the core of her business practice. Focusing on goals that help educate, facilitate, and advocate the needs and aspirations of her clients to achieve the common goal of completing the real estate transaction with the utmost professionalism possible.

As local builders noticed her expertise and dedication, they began to enlist her partnership to locate and develop land into premiere homes. Today, she regularly collaborates with architects and designers from inception, ultimately listing and selling their final new development communities.

To bolster her already extensive real estate knowledge, Jackie is an Accredited Buyer's Agent, a Certified New Home Specialist, and a member of the New Home Council.

A proud Broker affiliated with Windermere Real Estate, dedication, integrity, and market expertise are the core skills that drive her business. She strives daily to meet and exceed her clients' aspirations and bring their real estate dreams to fruition. Known for her friendly, helpful approach and transparent communication, Jackie considers the referrals her clients make to their friends and family her most significant career achievement and the finest compliment.

When she isn't helping clients find their perfect Washington home, Jackie owns and operates a girl's youth lacrosse club with her husband. It's an amazing opportunity to be involved with the community and connect with players and their families. She is also an active member of the Junior League of Seattle, a women's organization committed to promoting voluntarism for education and charities.

Jackie and her husband first came to the Seattle area in 1993, having fallen in love with the scenic beauty of the Puget Sound. She enjoys traveling to explore and have fun in new places. Having successfully launched her child off to college, she now enjoys reading, volunteering, finding and dining at new local restaurants, long walks with her husband and their English Bulldog, Tyson, and spending leisurely time with family and friends.

Home is Where Your Heart Is.

45

BE CLEAR ON HOW YOU SPEND YOUR TIME
- NICOLE MANGINA

Why: Working from home is a fantastic opportunity to improve your work/life balance. In what seems like a universal quest to get more done, it appears to be the perfect answer. The average American spends 60 minutes a day commuting, according to the US Census Bureau. I would much rather give up an hour sitting in traffic than an hour of sleep if it provides the time to work out or attend a baseball game for one of my boys.

As with most things, though, working from home has its challenges. One of the trickiest adjustments is managing the blurred lines between personal and professional time. After all, isn't it efficient to hop on email first thing in the morning while making coffee, and switch out the laundry in between conference calls, or mow the lawn on your lunch hour?

In theory, the answer is yes, we've been taught that multi-tasking is where it's at. However, in reality, we often end up trading effective activities for busy activities. It can feel like we are always on the go, but not getting anything done work-wise.

When the going gets tough at work, or there is a phone call you would rather avoid, it's easy to "take a break" and shift your focus to something that offers less resistance but still allows you to feel productive. Doing your laundry in the middle of the day will enable you to say that you were busy and got something done, but it doesn't move you forward in your business or help you generate more income.

You still need office hours, where the focus is on work. Which means, the laundry is done outside of office hours. Admittedly spending more time at home means the to-do list is never-ending. But it's still important to have those tasks wait until later.

With each thing that you do during the day, it's important to ask yourself, "Is this a work activity or a personal activity"?

Creating boundaries around your activities, and being clear and honest with yourself about which activities are income-producing will help you stay on track, get more done, and make working from home more enjoyable.

The Un-Habit: Stop going with the flow

Why: For those of us that resist structure, and I'm right there with you, one of the appeals of working from home is the ability to have your day be more free-flowing. After all, no one knows if you duck out in the middle of the day to get your hair done or chaperone a field trip for your child's class. No one monitors the time you spend at your desk. You can get the work done just as easily at 6 am or 10 pm as you can during a traditional 9-5 workday.

The ability to "go with the flow" and have a different schedule based on your personal life is a seductive one. It often feels like it's working in the short term, but about six months in, most people are off track and struggling to right the ship.

Two things happen when we throw structure out and decide to "let things come to us."

First, we start to confuse action for productivity. All of a sudden, you are going non-stop from the time you get up to the time you go to bed. You've put in a full day, and yet things aren't getting done and work. Instead of being more productive, you're falling behind.

Part of this is because of multi-tasking and continuously shifting gears wastes time. Each time you take a break during the day to do something non-work related, it takes a little longer to refocus. Suddenly your 11 am hair cut has turned into an entire day off.

The second is that working all of the time puts a strain on family relationships when you aren't fully present. Interrupting dinner because you need to send a last-minute email that you forgot to send earlier gets old for everyone.

It starts to feel like there isn't an off button.

Working from home doesn't mean you suddenly have time for everything. Stop trying to fit work into your personal life, and create structure around when certain things happen in a day.

About Nicole: Nicole Mangina is a real estate agent in Kirkland, Washington, a suburb of Seattle. With over 20 years of experience, she is a consistent top producer and mentor to many of her peers.

Deeply involved in the real estate community, Nicole is a past president of the local Women's Council of Realtors and helped to double it's membership during her tenure. She also teaches continuing education for her company and was recently awarded one of their top instructor awards.

With a business built on repeat and referral clients, Nicole is continuously focused on building relationships and finding fun and unique ways to serve her clients and support her community.

Part of this includes hosting a weekly radio show, where she features local people, businesses, and events. The inspiration was that buying and selling homes is about more than bedrooms and baths. It's about the businesses and events that create the community surrounding the home. Helping clients find not just the perfect home, but the ideal community has long been one of her passions, and so the radio, which was a natural addition. It has also been a great way to give small businesses some much needed and well-deserved exposure and has earned Nicole the unofficial title of one of the best-connected people in the area.

When not selling real estate, teaching a class, or hosting the radio show, Nicole is out and about with her husband and spending time at the baseball field with their two teenage boys. And somewhere in the midst of it all, Nicole also finds time for her joys with including walking, yoga, and travel.

Be Clear on How You Spend Your Time - Nicole Mangina

Life is meant to be lived fully and richly on all levels. It is one of Nicole's main beliefs and noble pursuits that she strives for daily.

UPROOT YOUR BOOT(Y) - REISHA HOLTON

Why: My current commute is 62 steps. What's yours? Take the time to count it. That shift in mental awareness could increase your productivity.

From the first foot I put on the floor when I swivel out of bed to the final one I place under my desk inside my outdoor workspace, I count 62 paces. During the trudge to my beloved outbuilding, with socked feet stuffed in Birkenstocks or toes dangling out of flip flops grazing the wet grass along the brick path between my house and my hut, I allow my body to embrace the morning mist and my mind to transition from the sink full of dishes or the sofa scattered with laundry needing folding.

This one shift in location – both physical and mental - has been the Habit that has helped me focus more, write more, and feel better about my new work-from-home experience.

As I think about it, this is the same Habit I embraced eight years ago when I began working with high school students who were writing college essays. My house was and is too lived in to invite students and families into, so I started meeting students in the cafeteria of our local hospital. Always open? Check. Starbucks available? Check. Enough background noise to be comforting during personal conversations? Check.

When a new grocery store opened between the local high schools, I decided to switch to meeting students in the dining area there. Tables and good lighting? Check. Grub to go? Check. Incidental noise level? Check.

Even though my work could have been home-based, I needed to be somewhere other than where I could see all my messes. When I began to transition out of working with students and into my writing, I struggled to get going. My upstairs "office" was going to be my go-to space, but it was cluttered with too many distractions – bills to pay, birthday cards to send, magazines to read.

Too much of my life was staring me in the face.

When I ventured the 62 steps "out" to the hut, I left all that behind. I have a desk, a pencil cup, and somewhere I can plug in my computer and phone. The change in location loosened the grip that home held on my creativity and productivity. "Sixty-two steps" isn't the magic formula. It's making a Habit of going to a location where you can leave behind life and get down to business.

The Un-Habit: Don't Fill That Cup

Why: Scattered around my otherwise barren work surface are remnants of my breaks in productivity. One glistening white Glacier National Park mug snuggles my left elbow, so close that there have been accidents involving spilled hot liquid and my MacBook keypad. You'd think I'd learn.

In an attempt to change the always-have-a- beverage-handy Habit, I have placed my tall metal Christmas to-go carafe directly in front of me so that I have to reach over my laptop screen to take a swig. A long stretched out sleeve of a University of Washington sweatshirt most often snags on the cracked computer cover, resulting in more messes and spills.

What ensues is chaos. I jerk the computer off the desk, ripping the charging cord out of the wall socket where it clangs on the wooden floor. I quickly shove my rickety wooden folding chair back and away from my work surface to create space for the flowing liquid to fall. I break out in a cold sweat for fear that I haven't saved the 1,000 words I'd worked so hard that morning to craft. I dash inside the house to grab a towel to sop up the messes. After all that, all I want is something else to wet my whistle while I get back to work. Is this all worth it?

Juggling food and drink at my desk creates a circus out of my work area. While it's important to stay hydrated throughout the day if I separate the two activities – working and sipping – I gain productivity threefold: I can give myself a real break when I get up and walk to the kitchen to source something to eat or drink. I can keep my work area clutter-free and can focus better. I can protect my equipment, thus saving time and money in the long run.

So, the next time you consider taking a soothing, steamy cup of love to your work area, remember the clumsy clown who wrote this and take her advice: don't fill that cup.

About Reisha: I threw a book at my fourth-grade teacher, Mrs. Sellers. I landed on a hard, cold chair in Mr. Moore's office.

This is the story I wish I had written for my college essay. What Mr. Moore said to me, showing I had a temper, facing my unorthodox behavior, what throwing that book taught me.

What I would have written in a college essay years ago doesn't matter, but the idea of the story still does.

On long road trips across Georgia to visit grandmothers in houses that spoke their own tales to me, I crafted stories that found their way to composition books or were pecked out on a dusty Remington typewriter kept around for the sole purpose of typing envelopes. Stories are how I have communicated my whole life.

To get to a student's story, I turn into the journalist who graduated from the University of Georgia. I quiz her about her adventures. We talk about road trips and rough relationships. I ask the hard questions. We talk like we are sitting around a campfire. We sip coffee and take walks, and we get to the real stuff.

Being a youth leader, a writer, and a mother has helped me coach students, to find the story they need to tell. Not the one that makes them look good to admission counselors. Not the one they think someone wants to read.

During the years of leading writing workshops and classes, I have learned that there are different types of written stories. There are the stories students write initially, the ones that don't take much effort, the ones that don't tell much about them.

And then there are the other ones. The ones where students grapple with what their story means or the ones that so clearly define them bell starts ringing. These are the ones that have students tossing a pile of rough drafts to the trash can and onto the floor.

These are the ones that college admissions officers want to read.

For the past eight years, I've been focusing my passion for storytelling and self-discovery on college-bound students. I think we've had a lot of fun, belly laughed, and passed out Kleenex. I'm addicted to watching students grow in self-awareness and confidence. And oh yeah, to see them get into the colleges of their choice.

Moving forward, I'll be exploring the stories of my past in search of new truths for today.

Come along @ www.reishabehrholton.com

BE PROFOUND - DAPHNE MICHAELS

Why: Thrive is a profound word, and to thrive in your home office, you'll need to integrate your work and personal life at a profound level.

This depth of integration is beyond mindset. It is beyond wearing multiple hats. It is beyond playing roles. It is about broadening the poles of your inner universe to breakthrough to higher perspectives, elevated reasoning, and expanded visions.

Prior to working from home, many professionals made a mind-shift from their personal world to their work-life while traveling to an outside office. However, shifting between disparate parts of your life is very different from integrating your life.

While shifting keeps parts of your life separated, integration combines parts of your life into a unified whole.

This is an important distinction because shifting between parts of your life divides your energy and focus, while integrating combines your energy and focus so that it can be more powerfully channeled.

Weaving various focuses in your life together at a deep level — such as your personal and work life — has always been the goal of human potential work. Why? Because integration brings about greater creativity. So imagine how this works, think of the difference between an egg carton and a web. By building a web, integration allows you to run broad and diverse wisdom through the deepest parts of your subconscious. And this is where your most brilliant thinking comes from!

As you can imagine, developing this web also reduces confusion, overwhelm, and self-doubt. It increases focus, efficiency, and productivity.

If you are thinking this sounds great, but it's too complex to put into practice, wait! It is very simple to integrate your work and personal life while working from home.

All you need is a simple mental technology.

When it comes to shifting your inner landscape, simple yet dialed-in mental technologies are the only ones that will work.

Here's a simple mental exercise to adopt each time you embark on the trip within your home to your home office: BE PROFOUND. Take a moment to connect to why your work mission is important to both you and the world. Think about how you will move your mission forward. Make a mental commitment to move your mission forward through the tasks you identify to accomplish in your home office today.

Remember, thrive is a profound word. It means to grow vigorously. Being profound opens pathways in your inner universe for continuous personal and professional growth.

THE UN-HABIT: ISOLATION

Why: One of the most significant challenges of working from home continuously is a tendency to feel isolated. This comes from a mental Habit of retreating from others when we are not in their physical presence.

When it comes to working from home, you must master shifting your inner lens away from retreat and toward engagement to experience an unbroken connection with others — even when they are not in your physical presence.

The risk of not mastering what I call your Connections Experience is quite severe. Not only will it leave you feeling empty, miserable, and lonely, but it can cost you much more. Loss of ambition, purpose, structure, accountability, joy, creativity, and momentum are just a few of the endless consequences of isolation.

The truth is that a disabling experience of isolation comes much more from your mental state than from the solo activity you are engaged in. You can feel isolated with a group of people all around you as you can feel connected to others when you are alone.

To "UnHabit" isolation and master your Connections Experience, spend time thinking about your personal and professional connections. Create a Connections Experience Diagram. Then complete the suggested practice regularly and especially when you feel the slighted ping of isolation.

Connections Experience Diagram

1. Begin by drawing five concentric circles.
2. In the center, write "My Expanded Self." This is the part

of you that never feels isolated because it is has a deep connection to all that is.
3. In the next layer, write the names of the people you feel closest to in your personal life.
4. In the next layer, write the names of your closest work colleagues and associates.
5. In the next layer, write your "potentials" — people you want to be connected with both personally and professionally.
6. In the outer layer of your Connections Experience Diagram, write your role models — people you most aspire to emulate.

Practice Your Connections Experience

Every morning and evening, review your Connection Experience Diagram to develop a strong mental, emotional, and energetic connection to every person. Experience your connections throughout the day!

About Daphne: Daphne Michaels is a leading expert in human potential and the creator of a 21st Century model for success. As an author, speaker, trainer, and consultant, she has guided thousands of people to their highest potential for over 25 years. She is author of the Amazon #1 bestselling book, Mountaintop Prosperity: Move Quickly to New Heights in Life, Work, and Money, and The Gifted: Free Your Inner Gifts for a Brand-New Life.

Daphne's lifelong journey includes earning a masters degree in the behavioral sciences with an emphasis on leading, consulting, and advanced formal study in integral psychology. Her work has included a rewarding longterm practice as a licensed psychotherapist, executive consultant, and the founder of an institute dedicated to the development of human potential.

Endorsed by New York Times bestselling authors and the national media, Daphne is a regular guest on nationally syndicated radio programs and a content contributor for the national media.

Through the Daphne Michaels Institute, founded in 2001, Daphne has designed and facilitated transformational programs that utilize Energetics-of-Success™ methods to access creative flow. As such, participants are guided to connect with powerful, catalyzing, and life-changing potential.

Daphne's life's mission is to bring the wisdom of her journey to others through her books and human potential training programs.

This includes her Profound Success Mastermind Program - a comprehensive, energetically based LIVE Online program for the development of human potential. Daphne's 21st Century Model for Success offered through this program addresses both inner and outer success. It helps people develop a bridge in the deepest part of their psyche to consciously connect their inner and outer worlds for greater success in both.

Daphne is passionate about offering Profound Leader training, which utilizes a flywheel model to broaden awareness of all experiences within and beyond an organization and to increase creative flow throughout.

Seasoned and emerging leaders are encouraged to consider The Profound Leader training, which is offered LIVE virtually and may be arranged in-person.

The Profound Success Mastermind Program is offered LIVE Online and includes a complete program HUB with unrestricted 24/7 access to powerful resources that affect deep changes to support ongoing transformation between LIVE sessions.

DIVERSIFY YOUR END MARKET AND/OR YOUR CUSTOMER BASE - ASHOK S. RAMJI

Why: There was a time when work and leisure were distinct spheres of physical activity. With socio-economic changes and technological advances, the home and office have become more intertwined. According to U.S. Census data, the percentage of Americans working from home has steadily increased from 3.3% in the year 2000. In the year 2020, the COVID-19 pandemic has made working from home a necessity. Authorities have even classified some businesses as either essential or non-essential.

Against this backdrop, it is essential to create a diversified home office. There should be some variety in the client base and end markets. If you are making auxiliary lighting products intended for cars and hospitals, for example, sales to first responders could keep the top-line growing. In my financial services business, we serve a diverse base of retail clientele. We focus on both insurance and investment planning.

There are going to be some practical limits to diversification. For starters, the home office is likely to be a service business since you are not likely to have enough space for a manufacturing plant. The end markets may also have to be adjacent and have some relationship to one another. For example, in my financial planning business, investments and insurance are different end markets -- but both are part of the overall financial planning universe.

Marketing to clients and prospects should be clear and comprehensive but not confusing. The key is to show how your home office can add value in a variety of contexts and settings. From our own experience, spending on research and development (R&D) today brings in revenue tomorrow. R&D provides one with confidence, and the requisite skill sets to work with different types of clients across multiple end markets.

Technology makes it possible to work from home. Government regulation may make it necessary too. For your home office venture to be commercially successful, you must go further. Hopefully, a Habit of diversification will make for a positive difference.

The Un-Habit: As you diversify, do not get distracted or have indigestion

Why: Hewlett-Packard co-founder David Packard is quoted as having said that "more businesses die from indigestion than starvation." As we diversify, we have to be wary about going down the wrong rabbit holes and making the most of the precious resource that is our time.

As we work on projects, we continuously look at scalability. Can we develop a template so that this report, or more generally this output, can be configured to serve more than one client easily?

Sometimes we have to work on saying 'no' if a task does not get us to fulfilling our vision. That project may seem appealing, or may we have a desire not to disappoint another. Still, we have to ask, will this work take us down our beaten path?

Many times, we can be distracted by people and things. Debbie Rosemont from Simply Placed is our Professional Organizer and Productivity Consultant, and she taught us the value of blocking off time on the calendar for appointments, even appointments we make with ourselves. Sometimes we need to block off time on our calendar for moving big rocks. Reviewing and previewing time blocks on a calendar is a good indication of where our priorities lie. We may need to allocate more time or other resources to a different priority if the accomplishment of that task gets us one step closer to achieving our vision and realizing our potential.

The busyness of running a home office can also leave behind a lot of debris. It may not seem urgent, but an important task that needs tending to daily is organization - regularly cleaning out e-mail inboxes, digital files, and paperwork.

Running a home office in the twenty-first century with all the multiple stimuli is no easy task. The best-laid plans can be easily disrupted by an unexpected professional or family obligation. Deal with these as they come up, but never lose sight of the vision of a diversified yet focused home office for your professional and personal development.

About Ashok: Ashok S. Ramji is a CERTIFIED FINANCIAL PLANNER™ (CFP®), Chartered Financial Consultant (ChFC®), Chartered Life Underwriter (CLU®), and a Certified Annuity Specialist (CAS®). He leads TOP Planning LLC, which is headquartered in Washington state and operates in several other states as well.

Ashok graduated with a BS in Mathematics/Applied Science from UCLA. He holds resident Life & Health and Property & Casualty licenses in Washington state. Ashok is also an investment adviser representative with Insight Folios Inc., which oversees managed portfolios of dividend-paying stocks for clients.

Ashok is a member of Ed Slott's Master Elite IRA Advisor group, with which he began his affiliation in 2018. Members of Ed Slott's Elite IRA Advisor Group train with Ed Slott, CPA, and his team of IRA Experts on a continuous basis to maintaining the most current education on advanced retirement strategies and tax law changes. Membership represents a dedicated, ongoing commitment to protecting clients' hard-earned retirement dollars from unnecessary taxes with the highest standard of care.

Ashok collaborates early on with his clients so as to best manage expectations and to provide the client with true ownership of the process. Banking, insurance, and investment products are all carefully considered as alternative courses of action to helping the client accomplish his or her end goal. If permanent life insurance is contemplated for the financial plan, for example, Ashok utilizes a patented, objective, and transparent evaluation process to screen across a wide universe of products to provide a recommendation that is in accordance with the clients' best interest.

Clients should be aware that insurance and investment planning services pay a commission and involve a conflict of interest, as commissionable products can conflict with the fiduciary duties of a registered investment adviser. Insight Folios always acts in the best interest of the client; including in the sale of commissionable products to advisory clients.

Learn more at www.topplanning.com.

49

START WORKING ITERATIVELY - ANDREW HINKELMAN

Why: Working from home can be fantastic when you have your space and some extended periods to do your work. Being alone can be a very creative time. You'll start thinking about what you need to do and how to do it, make an outline, and start capturing some notes. Left undisturbed, you'll think a little more about how great that project will be. And isn't it nice to be alone in a comfortable place where you can think about producing your very best work?

Stop it.

When working from home, we need to be even more aware of human nature and our tendencies to over-think an idea or project. Working alone, we miss the collaboration and social aspect of brainstorming that helps us understand when to move on. We can get bogged down in planning and analysis. "Analysis paralysis" is a real danger.

A great way to counter this tendency towards over-thinking and over-planning is to work quickly and iteratively purposely. This means placing a much higher value on finishing a project than making everything perfect first. Set a short amount of time for planning ("timeboxing"), honor that limit, and then move into action, execute on your plan, and launch your project.

A while back, much of the software industry moved to an "Agile" methodology, which prioritizes releasing usable software quickly over perfect software released at some later date. The core tenet is that finishing a project and putting it into action or making it available is the only way to get feedback on what works and what needs further refinement.

This works well because most of what we do is a work in progress. If a project or initiative is important, we'll understand how and where to improve only AFTER moving into action. The do-ing/publishing/launching/going live is the action that allows for the data and feedback we can use for further improvement.

Working iteratively in this way recognizes that causes and conditions will change, solutions will change, and the opportunity itself will change and evolve. In other words, that opportunity with a new client may look very different a month later when you finally get your slide deck perfected.

The Un-Habit: Stop Over-Zooming

Why: Remember when email was new, trivial, and fun? Me neither, but I'm told there were a lot of emails forwards with cute sayings coming from some faraway place called "AOL." Right now, we have Zoom, or your preferred video-conference platform, in a similar phase of popularity in our culture. Zoom call, Zoom meeting, Zoom happy hour, Zoom dog walk. We already use "Zoom" like we use "Google" as a universally understood verb.

Because we're so accustomed to email, we see it as just one of many communication tools—no big deal. Email is good for transmitting certain types of information in certain situations: maybe longer, non-urgent messages, that are a little more formal than texts or instant messages.

But there's another, more important factor for choosing your communication tool: Your audience.

You already use email, text, IM, or a phone call to connect with people differently. Friends via text, former co-workers via LinkedIn Messenger, extended family over email. Why? Because certain channels or tools are more effective for reaching different people. By keeping your audience in mind, you're more likely to get your message through to them. Or more likely to engage and connect.

In essence, you're meeting these contacts or friends where THEY are.

Just like with email, a Zoom call might be the most appropriate under certain conditions. Just because you work from home and want to see people does not mean everyone else does. More importantly, continually forcing your audience or contacts onto Zoom is simply ineffective and may even alienate certain people. Further, we're starting to see research about how constant video-conferencing adds additional mental fatigue compared to traditional face-to-face meetings. "Zoom Fatigue" is a thing. Google it.

Not sure which communication channel your audience prefers? Easy. Just ask.

I find that most 1:1 communication is much more effective over a phone call where I can listen more intently and not wonder about their beautiful bookshelf ("is that IKEA?") or if they've actually read any of those books... when I should be listening.

It's time to think of Zoom as having a time and place, rather than blanketing all our contacts with Zoom calls just because we work remotely. Yes, we all want connection in some form, but video conferencing is not the only answer. It's just another tool we need to learn to use appropriately. Until it gets AOL'd.

About Andrew: Andrew Hinkelman is the founder of Priority-1 Group, a Leadership Coaching, and Consulting organization.

Andrew has more than 25 years of experience in the Technology and Financial Services industries across roles in IT, Product Management, and Business Intelligence, along with consulting and advisory roles. Most recently, in the role of Chief Technology Officer, he focused on building strong, high-performing teams while solving complex, company-wide challenges and driving strategic goals.

In addition to core infrastructure and proprietary software development, Andrew has had responsibility for Information Security, Digital Transformation/UI/UX, Business Continuity, IT Compliance (SOC1/SSAE16), and Project Management. He is CISSP, and ITIL v3 certified.

In transitioning from executive roles to professional coaching, Andrew has brought together his skills and experience with both personal development and professional excellence. As a mid-career professional in his early 30's, Andrew figured out a formula for driving sustained success in his career: the more he focused on his personal development and interpersonal skills, the more he could use those skills to drive success in his professional life. A constant focus on forging the right mindset, staying curious about other people, and building strong relationships allowed his career to blossom, resulting in a C-Level role at the age of 42.

Along the way, Andrew realized the most meaningful part of his professional work was always helping others succeed. This meant always taking the time to mentor and guide others to look further, around the corner, to do the uncomfortable things, and to challenge themselves.

In his capacity as a Leadership Coach, Andrew is now focused on guiding driven, ambitious professionals to optimize their teams while building their own personal definition of success. This transformation is often a result of a renewed level of focus and energy that finally steers your professional life and aligns it with your values, vision, and goals.

Andrew lives in the Seattle area with his family, where he spends an enormous amount of time on a bike or paddleboard and watching college baseball.

CREATING SPACE ANYWHERE TO THINK AND LET GO! - LEONA THOMAS

Why: One of the most important tools in my "work from home," really my "work from anywhere," toolkit is my wireless Bose Noise Canceling Headphones. Even when I am home alone, I block at least 1-2 hours each day to work with them on. These headphones help in numerous ways, but most importantly, they help me create space for me to think and let go no matter where I am. This can take many forms, including:

• Blocking out distractions when I am trying to concentrate on critical tasks.

• Getting up and dancing to some of my favorite songs – both helping me relax and get some much-needed exercise.

• Forcing time when I am not on video chats and focus on my tasks rather than get pulled into everyone else's.

(No mic = No talking!)

• Listening to podcasts and audiobooks for new ideas and to learn about new things.

- Just sit and focus on my own thoughts, clearing out what is really important to me.

Creating space for me is critical for helping me focus, recharge, and get my priorities done. It also gives me time to explore new ideas and new opportunities. Using headphones helps minimize distractions and makes it possible to focus truly. I know my neighbors, and even a few office mates, have sometimes wondered what the heck was going on as I chair danced my way through writing critical presentations or proposals, but I can tell those presentations and proposals are much more effective when I wasn't interrupted 1000 times while I was trying to crank it out. And I know some of my best ideas have come from dancing behind my desk chair belting out some of my favorite songs.

I know it may sound silly - but I encourage you to try it; you might just find a new spark of inspiration!

The Un-Habit: Unlearning always saying "Yes"!

Why: My biggest challenge, the "Un-Habit" I'm still working on, is learning not to over commit. I was blessed with a constant thirst for learning as well as a wide and diverse set of friends, family, and interests. I was also blessed with the ability to overcome challenges, and a long track record of doing things I was told couldn't be done - meaning I rarely think something CAN'T be done! What I was NOT blessed with is more than 24 hours in a day!

Do you know that old saying "Sometimes your greatest strengths can be your greatest weaknesses"?... Well, this is definitely mine.

I've had to learn to say, "No", almost tricking myself into believing I'm already booked. And of course, since I'm good at overcoming challenges, I've had to use multiple techniques to do this. The first is blocking out time for specific tasks AND blocking out unstructured time for me. Something about my calendar being blocked makes me think I'm busy, and it takes me really wanting to do something, or it being critical for me to go in and schedule over the "me time." This also helps when I send someone a "Calendly invite," or they are looking at my calendar because they can't see why something is blocked – just that I'm not available. They have to reach out and convince me to move something, giving me a chance to say, "No", or even, find a better way!

I've also gotten better about blocking social time on my calendar – and it takes a lot for me to move it. My Saturday morning dance party (yes, you read that right) is just as crucial as that sales meeting or meeting with my team. You are welcome to join me, but I will not reschedule or cancel. Bring your dancing shoes and have some fun!

I still need to watch that endless voice in my head saying, "Sure I can do that..."! Thankfully I have a collection of friends who hip check me if I get too far off course, but I think I'm finally getting the hang of not assuming I can or have to "do it all"!

Funny after decades of managing teams where I've always been conscious of trying not to overload anyone else, I finally am learning to do it for me!

And I am much happier and healthier for it!!!

ABOUT LEONA: Leona Thomas is President & Founder of Enabling Investments, LLC providing Strategic Management and Business Advisory Services. Leona is a Business Transformation Expert with over 25 years in building and reshaping organizations. Throughout her career, Leona has led and advised companies from startups to Global Fortune 500 corporations through major transformations involving innovation, high growth, emerging technologies, emerging industries, corporate repositioning, new product creation, turnarounds, regulatory and industry changes, mergers & acquisitions, and operational improvements.

Before Enabling Investments, Leona was Chief Operating Officer (COO) and SVP of Product and Technology for Wylei, Inc., an AI and Machine Learning Digital Marketing Solution Provider where she led their transition out of incubation - building out the end-to-end operations, eventually leading the Product and Technology teams, and finally, guiding Wylie through reacquisition.

Before joining Wylei, Leona was the Global Transformation Director at Hibu, leading critical Digital Transformation and Globalization initiatives. She also spent ten years with CSC's Strategic Management and Consulting Practices, where she launched CSC's Global Practice on European REACH Chemical Regulations, enabling companies worldwide to strategically negotiate sweeping chemical regulations and transforming the practice into CSC's Global Chemical Compliance and Sustainability Practice. Leona has also successfully led strategic transformation and turnarounds for companies such as SEI Investments, Norm Thompson Outfitters, Nautilus, Inc. (Bowflex), and State Street Bank.

Leona has BSE in Electrical and Computer Engineering as well as an Executive MBA from Drexel University and is a member of Beta Gamma Sigma.

Beyond her professional initiatives, Leona has always committed to serving her community. In addition to being on the SIM (Society for Information Management) Women's Executive Leadership Summit Council, Leona is a long-standing Board Member and Strategic Planning Chairperson for the William Way Community Center - Philadelphia's LGBTQIA Community Center directly serving over 60,000 people a year. Leona also built WITI Portland Chapter's Professional Development and Mentoring Programs and continually mentors both young kids and adults within her communities.

51

SET & HONOR TIME BOUNDARIES - SARAH FRINK

Why: Setting and honoring boundaries around your time and working hours is one of the most important things you can do when working from home. When I first started working from home, there were no boundaries around my time. I worked all the time, morning, noon, and night and took meetings whenever someone asked for one. Three years later, I found myself 20 pounds heavier, burnt out, and resentful that I hadn't made myself and my family more of a priority.

Working from home has some major pros, but there are also cons that you may not realize until you're a couple of months, or years, into it. One of those is the ability to work non-stop.

So, what changed for me? Last summer, my bonus son was coming to stay with us for an extended period, and both my husband and I wanted and needed to spend as much time as possible with him. I refused to miss out on time with him because of work, and we didn't have daycare, so it forced us both to figure out our working schedules. For the first time in 4 years of business, I set a non-negotiable schedule—Monday–

Thursday, 9:00 am–2:30 pm, with Fridays off. My team and clients were notified of my new office hours, and I set up my calendar accordingly. No one even blinked an eye. I was so focused during the new working hours that I was often able to complete my to-do list, do a couple more tasks, and check out early occasionally.

Ultimately, I decided to adopt this as a permanent schedule, adding in a mandatory lunch break and leaving Friday as an optional half-day to work on my business with a hard stop time that allows me to run errands and do something for myself each week.

Let me tell you; it's been a game-changer. It has allowed me space in my day to create, to take care of myself mentally and physically, and it has improved my quality of life and work performance.

When you have a set schedule and boundaries around your time, your work becomes more focused and intentional. Setting boundaries around my time has allowed me to make big shifts in my business operations and given me back so much time that I can use in areas where I shine the most.

The Un-Habit: Digital Distractions

Why: With setting and honoring time boundaries and a firm work schedule comes minimizing distractions. On average, how many times do you check your Facebook page or email and respond to notifications or text messages on your phone? If you don't know, you might want to start paying attention. According to a study done by Gloria Mark at the University of California, Irvine, it takes an average of about 25 minutes (23 minutes and 15 seconds, to be exact) to return to the original task after an interruption. Twenty-five minutes, my friends! Think about it—four distractions in a day could cost you an hour of productive work time!

As a digital marketer, my phone, email, and social media notifications are going off all day, every day. If I were to read and respond to each of them as they come in, I'd be the least-productive human being on this planet, no joke. Depending on how many times a day digital distractions take you away from your work, you may be able to add HOURS back to your day.

When I left my 9-to-5 corporate job, I realized how much time was wasted each day working in an office. With co-workers stopping by my office to chat and tell me about their weekend and me doing the same, plus emails, phone calls, etc., it's actually shocking that any work got done. In hindsight, I could have worked half as much and had the same result. When I started my own business, those distractions became digital, and they took up just as much time.

When I implemented strict working hours, I got really firm about when and how often email, social media, and my phone would get checked in a day. My routine is as follows: I check my phone and social media each morning before I start working and before the day ends. I respond, comment, and return calls and text during this time. My email is different because it's where most of my team and client correspondence takes place, and it gets checked every two to three hours between work projects.

Silencing my digital distractions throughout the day has made a HUGE difference in my daily productivity and has also allowed me to stick to firm working hours. If I had to guess, it's given me at least 8–10 hours back per week.

About Sarah: Sarah Frink is the CEO and Founder of Real Marketing Solutions, an acknowledged Digital Marketing Expert and sought-after industry speaker. Her peers describe Sarah as a creative, driven, and radically authentic digital marketing strategist with a head for marketing and the heart of an entrepreneur. She has a unique talent for taking big picture ideas and creating a one-of-a-kind marketing strategy to get your business results.

Sarah's professional experience lies in the mortgage industry, where she spent nine years building two highly successful businesses, consistently acknowledged as a top producer in her field. During her time in the industry, she realized the gap between marketing and digital marketing that companies didn't know how to adapt to. In 2014, Sarah said farewell to life as a loan originator. She founded Real Marketing Solutions, a creative digital marketing agency specializing in supporting businesses in restricted industries, including mortgage, finance, and real estate.

Sarah and her team help companies create an online presence that consistently builds brand awareness in combination with lead generation and sales funnel strategies to help convert strangers to followers, followers to leads and leads to paying clients. Real Marketing Solutions' client portfolio also includes a variety of service-based businesses with a strong focus on real estate and mortgage specialists and companies. Real Marketing Solutions offers end-to-end social media management, digital advertising and lead generation services, copywriting and graphic design, and social media training and coaching for DIY marketers and business owners.

In her off time, Sarah is a wife, mom, writer, avid outdoors enthusiast, hiker, and lover of travel. She has over 33 stamps on her passport and looks forward to adding more each year.

To connect or learn more about Sarah Frink and the Real Marketing Solutions team, visit realmarketingsolutions.net or follow their journey on Facebook @TheRealMarketingSolutions and Instagram @realmarketingsolutions.

GET UP, DRESS UP, SHOW UP - LISA FISCHER

Why: The secret to building a strong self-image is created in your daily routine. The Get Up, Dress Up, and Show Up Habit helps develop a spirit of preparedness.

Preparation time is never wasted time.

What comes to mind when you think of a daily routine? What activities do you purposely engage in? In our home, we typically begin our mornings with a coffee and an hour of quiet time, reading, praying, reviewing goals, and affirming the day .

If you asked me five years ago, what my morning routine consisted of would be met with one word, "craziness." It was hurried, systematic, and busy getting kids to school while handling the morning logistics before diving into email and the schedule. Can you relate?

I was introduced to a morning routine by my business coach, who suggested successful CEO's rise and go to bed early. I hated this practice and resisted it for about a year before dipping my toe into the idea. That said, once I committed to an intentional morning routine an hour before my day officially started, my life changed, and yours can too.

As a wardrobe stylist, one of the many blessings is getting to work with a variety of women and being invited into a multitude of closets. The self-image stories are just as diverse as the women sharing them, yet one common theme repeats... the need to feel congruent from the inside-out.

Frumpy is a common description some clients use to describe their current image. Feeling invisible, boring, and overlooked can lead to a lack of motivation and decreased productivity.

Studies say 93% of our communication is non-verbal, with 55% of that is derived from wardrobe, grooming, and accessories.

Consider using the Get Up, Dress Up, and Show up as an effective Habit for preparedness. When we're prepared, we're productive.

A productive style tip to create confidence and feel pulled together is the Rule of 10.

Objective: Wear 10 points

Count the number of items you're wearing and set a goal for 10 points—one point for each item. High contrast pattern items receive 2 points.

Result: Feeling pulled together using wardrobe and accessories to communicate your personality, preferences, and style.

You're essentially creating a non-verbal representation of who you are, what you're up to, and how you want to be treated.

Studies say we see our reflection upwards of 50 times a day. Use this Get Up, Dress Up, Show up Habit to increase your productivity and effectiveness.

The Un-Habit: Sleep In, Dress Down, Don't Show Up

Why: Have you ever experienced a time when you've woken up late for work or school only to have moments before needing to walk out the door? How about waking up late and realizing you have 5 minutes until your zoom call!

Stressful right! We all know that feeling when we're unprepared and not our best.

I can recall this feeling when waking up late for school. I'd sit in the back of the class, hoping the teacher would not call on me.

Studies show there's a direct link between how we act and how we feel about ourselves. When we feel confident, we're more likely to be confident.

One way to boost productivity in our home office is to show up confident for the day. Being intentional with what we choose to wear and how we pull ourselves together visually is a major contributor to our level of confidence.

Can you think of a time you've worked from home and the doorbell rings? What are the first few things you consider? Often what we're wearing determines if we answer the door or not.

This may sound funny, but it's so true. What if that doorbell was an opportunity for creating new business? How many opportunities are we turning away because of unpreparedness?

Eliminating a "dress down" Habit while working from home may keep you more productive and prepared for opportunity. To have more, we must first become more.

Tips to consider when breaking the dress down Habit:

1. Decide to look and feel your best daily.

2. Commit time to visualize your work from home style.
3. Use Pinterest or LikeToKnowIt App to spur your creativity.
4. Schedule a time to clean out the closet of what no longer serves you. When it's scheduled, it's real.
5. Shop for a wardrobe that accentuates your style preferences. Consider complimenting your figure with well-fitting pieces in colors you love.

Have fun developing looks that best reflect you in work and play.

About Lisa: Lisa Fischer is a Personal Wardrobe Stylist, Image Consultant, and Speaker with 20 years of experience helping individuals achieve a confident self-image.

Lisa began her image journey when she was fired from her first job in high school due to excessive body odor. It was an embarrassment and lack of knowledge that became the catalyst for personal development and her interest in the beauty industry.

The majority of Lisa's experience comes from her time as an Instructor with a global etiquette and protocol school teaching youth and young adults the art of strong social skills. In addition to her etiquette training, Lisa is a Certified Wardrobe Stylist and Image Consultant serving women all across the nation.

In 2016, Lisa combined her love for teaching with her image background and began her own business, Lisa Fischer Styling. Lisa consults and trains on visual mastery skills for busy professional women. Lisa teaches how to show up being congruent in self-expression using wardrobe, accessories, and grooming practices. Knowing how to accentuate your personality through style, flatter your silhouette, and use color to enhance your personal beauty are critical to building a strong self-image.

Clients who work with Lisa feel seen, heard, and protected. There is no judgment, and perfection is never a part of the conversation.

Lisa's mission was to create a safe place for women to develop their image and appearance confidence by way of community programs and private services.

Image Strong VIP was created as a Mastery program for women seeking life long learning with transformational results. When we look good, we feel good.

If you want to grow your image and appearance confidence by learning some simple and effective strategies, I invite you to connect for a free consultation call.

www.LisaFischerStyling.com

Lisa@LisaFischerStyling.com

MAKE DAILY NATURE BREAKS PART OF YOUR SCHEDULE - ROSE HARROW

Why: Most people vacation someplace with great natural beauty. The ocean, the mountains, or the forest. There is an instinctive need to connect with nature, and it feels crazy that we limit it to a few weeks vacation a year. For me it is a daily necessity when working at home.

Since one of the greatest benefits of working from home is flexibility, why would you want to stay inside all day? Getting outside gives joy, aliveness, and variety to your day.

All your senses are fed by nature: feel the warmth of the sun on your skin, feel the air on your face, see the changing landscape, the colors, the light changing depending on the angle of the sun, watch the cloud shapes and movement, smell the fragrance of flowers, herbs, freshly cut grass, or even the smell after a rain storm. And listen: There is so much going on in the trees!

For me, it is a daily 'must do.'

Fresh air and sunlight clears my head, puts a smile on my face and lights me up. My brain is sharper, intuition is more keen, and I can be more present for my business clients.

Sometimes I can take a long lunch break and do some gardening. I don't mind adding an extra hour or two of work in the evening after dinner, because I feel so fed by my "nature" lunch.

A Daily Nature Break will change your life and improve your health.

If you want to read the research, take your laptop outside to read it!!

You could Google any of these benefits:

- Better sleep!
- Fresh air = oxygen to your brain and your body
- Sunlight is a nutrient which balances your body chemistry.
- Soil microbes are now known to increase health and happiness
- Everyone turns to nature to recharge.
- It's a great way to de-stresses
- Nature gives a sense of serenity and order in a chaotic world.
- Breathing changes into a more peaceful pattern.
- Nature is visually beautiful, and beauty makes happy chemicals!!
- Being in nature creates more coherent brain waves.

On some level, we've always known these things – it has shown up in every culture, and in common expressions and songs, "forever." It is worth singing about! "Here Comes the Sun."

So find your happy place – outside – make it an essential part of your work at home schedule.

And join me for tea in the garden.

The Un-Habit: Stop working "All the Time"

Why: Hard work is enshrined in our very competitive left brain culture. I grew up hearing that the way to success was to work hard, "take on more challenging projects," or "start an hour before everyone else." Some job announcements even state that they hope to hire a "workaholic," as if that is a great thing!

Now, as an executive coach, too many very successful clients have confided in me that their success came at a painful price. Even with a lot of money, or a prestigious position, if their kids have stopped talking to them or their marriage is falling apart, the cost is too high.

Overworking is not sustainable. Period. Burnout sneaks up on us, and sometimes the cost is our health. Overwork triggers the fear & survival part of our brain, and stresses our whole body.

And – it doesn't necessarily lead to success!

A thriving home office is a great chance to work in a way that makes us happy.

So, take a deep breath and remember true success does not require you to abandon or neglect yourself, well being, happiness, health. It does not require giving away bits of your soul, until you hardly know yourself anymore, and your family feels very far away.

When we identify *our* triggers to overworking, we can turn things around and start getting our life back.

Do you relate to any of these signs of overwork?

- Financial pressure

- Feeling like you are never doing enough
- Having vague goals, but never feeling "done"
- No clear sense of what your work hours are
- Exhausted but can't sleep
- General anxiety
- Family issues that you are avoiding
- Your friends have given up inviting you to social activities

What to do?

Be moderate, set work hours. Find a way to stay connected with your essence, and those you love. Practice yoga, meditation, paint, play music, or play with your kids. Or just make a regular practice of being outside.

A few more tips:

- Chunk your work down into manageable pieces, so you can have a sense of accomplishment, and a good stopping point for each day.
- Take regular days off (um, like a weekend?)
- Schedule fun things to look forward to every week.
- Laugh, sleep, exercise, dance

And here's a big secret: probably nothing bad will happen if you start taking time for yourself, though it may make you anxious at first. Don't do this perfectly – just ease yourself into it a little at a time.

About Rose: Rose Harrow is a ChangeMaker Catalyst, an executive coach, a business coach, and an international speaker

What's totally unique about Rose Harrow and her work is that she combines a very diverse background of training and experience so that she can meet people 'where they are' in a variety of industries, to help them not only build skills and strategies, but to answer their own heart's longing.

Her diverse professional background includes being executive director of an international non-profit, training and experience in brain science, group facilitation, transformational bodywork, and mind-body education.

As a coach for heart-based change-makers, she provides consultation to national and international leaders as a confidential sounding-board and mentor.

Always curious, and working globally, Rose has coordinated educational networks for North and South America, and been Faculty Chair of an International Faculty.

After coaching hundreds of people over the past 30 years Rose is convinced that the #1 ingredient for success is to build your business connected to the core of who you are..

Having worked on four continents she's distilled the essence of what helps people make the changes they want to make.

"Authentic Marketing from the Heart" is her business coaching program designed for Change-Makers – people who want to make a positive difference in the world through the services they provide, and the way they provide them.

Keen to accelerate results for her clients, Rose has combined the best tools, techniques and strategies from brain science, psychology, and coaching to create a laser-focused and powerful customized experience that will dramatically increase confidence, give results, and transform the way you think and feel about yourself.

For a sample of how Rose helps her clients leverage their resources, you can download her audio: **"The 5 Minute Miracle to Lighten Your Load"** at RoseHarrow.com/miracle

This 5 minute audio gives you a simple and profound process that dissolves the mental clutter that makes tasks harder than they need to be, so you can get on with the work you love.

PLAY THE RIGHT MUSIC - JEFF VANDENHOEK

Why: "Choose the right music to support your home office work, productivity, mindset, and attitude."

A significant part of getting to work from home is you get to play whatever you want, unlike the dentist's office, where you are trapped in a chair without an escape. Do you play music in your home office? At your home office, you get to do what you need to do to make it work for you.

Practicing this 1 Habit of using music to enhance your home office is extremely valuable.

As a solo-preneur, choosing the right music has helped me get through boring business details like paying bills and sending invoices. This is when I go to classic rock and fill the house with Queen, Boston, Fleetwood Mac - and crank through boring!

When I need to focus on writing client proposals, vlog posts (video blogging), client follow-thru reports - I play music without words because lyrics can result in mind-wandering. Listening to instrumental jazz or classical guitar adds focus and flow. Spotify, Pandora, and Apple Music make it easy to enjoy music. You can curate your playlist or have them do it for you. There are so many great tools to choose from.

I purchased a record player three years ago as a Christmas gift to myself. I needed to give away all the vinyl discs living in my basement storage or enjoy them again for the "first time." Playing vinyl throughout my day has provided me the beauty of "The Flip." It gets me out of my chair as I get to get up every 20 minutes (+/-) and flip the beautiful grooved disc to enjoy the other side.

Silence is music. Not all of life needs to be filled with sound. Silence can be beautiful. Beautiful for reflection. Beautiful for focus. Simply beautiful! Many find working in an environment without sound to be refreshing. As a musician and a distracted, curious soul, I sometimes need silence. Do you?

Tools for your ears. Earbuds? EarPods? Headphones? These tools help when you aren't the only one in the house when your office doesn't have a door or the neighbors are jackhammering their concrete patio. They help block out distractions.

Practice the 1 Habit of using music (or silence) to enhance your workday. You will experience great results. Do what you need to make it work for you. What are you listening to right now? Is it helping you? If not, get up and "flip it!"

The Un-Habit: Get Off Your A** (GOYA)

Why: "Staying stuck in our home office chair is a bad idea."

I recently discovered an acronym from Chester Elton called GOYA. Get Off Your A**. So simple. So difficult. When working in your home office (or work office), you can get so glued to your chair that it feels like someone pranked you with super glue.

Why do we do this? We want to be productive. In the name of productivity, we put off taking bathroom breaks. This can ultimately result in bad health outcomes (urinary tract infection). Believe me. I know. Staying "stuck" in one place for hours upon end can result in decreased inspiration, creativity, and oxygen flow to our brains, to name a few. "Don't just do something. Stand there!" GOYA!

Too often, we don't plan scheduled breaks into our home office workday. When working at a company office, we have meetings, bathroom breaks, coffee/snacks, and lunches to walk to. The distance for these walks at home is typically much shorter. Our GOYA is shortened. Scheduled breaks are not taken because we don't find them necessary. Is this because we want increased productivity? Because we are lazy? Because we are addicted to work? These questions have to be answered.

Put a walking break on your calendar and follow through. Add a lunch break and short walk on your calendar, as well, and show up. Easy can sometimes be so difficult yet completely necessary.

There are options for not staying stuck in our office chairs if we are willing to get creative. A Fast Company article (2020) says that "...using a standing desk, or simply placing your laptop on top of a high counter or bureau, so you can shift your weight as you work" can be great options. I am standing at a counter and shifting my weight as I type this. It's a great option.

The 1 Habit of practicing the GOYA is something you can proactively plan when your home office requires a lot of sitting. Maybe you should give it a try right now?

About Jeff: He is the owner and consultant for Intentionality; providing business teams, individuals, start-ups, and not-for-profits with strategic, creative, and collaborative input to build greater trust and business impact.

As a prior Director of Business Relations for the College of Business for a private University, Jeff worked with hundreds of senior administrators for corporate, not-for-profit and small business entities. He developed integrated, "real-time" projects with these entities to bring learning to life. These projects were all about blurring the world of business education with the world of business. He led Executive MBA, Part-time MBA, and Undergrad students through these important learning experiences.

Jeff has extensive training, corporate team-building, leadership coaching, and organizational health development consulting experience. Some of his training and leadership development consulting work has taken him to India, Iraq, Lebanon, and China.

He has worked with clients that include Columbia Sportswear of Beaverton, Ore., Mentor Graphics of Wilsonville, Ore., Nike of Beaverton, Ore., Rohde & Schwarz of Munich, Germany., Allied Waste of Portland, Ore., and Bigelow Tea, Boise, Idaho. He has also worked with 150 different non-profit organizations.

Jeff specializes in Team Development | Executive Leadership Development Coaching | Trust Development | Emotional Intelligence Assessment & Coaching | Business Start-ups

With a love for new ideas and ventures and a deep concern for the environment, Jeff helped launch a company that recycles sheetrock by diverting it from landfills, processing/grinding it, and selling the gypsum (90% of the sheetrock product) back into the agricultural market. This ultimately reduces carbon footprints for construction, landfill, and some agriculture industries.

As an entrepreneur with an ideation mindset, Jeff was an executive coach for Launch Mid-Valley and Oregon Entrepreneurs Network (OEN) for an entrepreneurial Start-Up Bootcamp Weekend in McMinnville, Oregon.

Jeff loves exploring the outdoors through backpacking, skiing, rock climbing, and just about any other outdoor activity that time and money allow.

He is passionate about music. He is in love with his wife and has three children, ages 29, 26, and 20.

For Jeff....Life is full. Life is good. Life is beautiful.

MOVE YOUR BODY DAILY - MINDY GARRETT

Why: For as long as I can remember, moving my body has been an important part of my daily life. As a child, moving my body offered me an outlet to reduce stress, boost mental clarity, problem-solve, and so much more. It came from a place of empowerment and self-preservation. You see, my parents divorced when I was young, and it was tempestuous. I needed a way to reduce stress, think creatively, and feel empowered. And it happened every time I moved my body. That was when I had my best ideas, came up with solutions, and was my happiest. It wasn't until I was an adult that I truly understood what a gift this was for my mind, body, and spirit.

As a small business owner who works from home, continuing this practice has been essential. Working from home can have its blessings and challenges. You might find yourself distracted by home-life interruptions or find it difficult to end your workday at a reasonable time as task piles onto your plate. Whenever I find myself feeling stuck, overwhelmed, or overextended, a simple walk around the block with my dog can do wonders!

Practicing this one healthy Habit enables me to be more productive by boosting mental clarity and increasing energy so that I can return to my task with renewed energy, focus, and productivity.

How often do you find yourself spinning your wheels, struggling to complete a task, racking your brain for solutions to challenges, or working long hours to meet deadlines and sacrificing healthy Habits to get it all done? To be your most efficient and effective self, you must give yourself the tools to perform at your best. When you take a break from work to move your body, you step away from the "problem" so you can return to your task with improved focus and increased energy, so you can keep moving forward in your business.

This might mean lacing up your shoes to go for a walk to boost energy rather than reaching for that third cup of coffee. It could be practicing 10-minutes of yoga to get the creative juices flowing before you jump on a conference call. It might look like hitting the gym in the middle of the day so you can eliminate distractions and return to your home office with renewed energy. Choosing to take an active break, even when it feels challenging, will provide a fresh perspective, renewed energy, and mental clarity, so you can thrive while working from home. Developing this daily Habit will help you work smarter, not harder.

The Un-Habit: Making your self-care negotiable

Why: "You cannot pour from an empty cup."

When asked the question, "Do you take care of yourself?" Most of us will answer, "Yes!"

Yet, if you were asked in what ways, the answer might be trickier to come by.

Self-care is defined as *"the practice of taking action to preserve or improve one's own health."* In essence, it is an act we do deliberately to support our mental, emotional, and physical health and wellbeing. And practicing self-care is essential for a thriving home office. Consider for a moment how often you put everyone and everything ahead of your own needs. Do you often find yourself feeling anxious, stressed, or overwhelmed? Self-care is the key to a good relationship with yourself and others, and it promotes a healthy balance between work and home life.

When practiced regularly, self-care can boost mood, reduce anxiety, support a healthy life balance, and improve overall wellbeing. By setting ground rules, creating a routine and making a schedule that includes breaks to eat healthily and move your body, you craft a healthy routine that serves you, so you can thrive working from home. Start by determining what you need to be your most productive self while living healthy and happy. This will enable you to prioritize tasks and implement practices that ensure you take action to support your needs regularly.

Setting boundaries, asking for help, and delegating tasks, will also help you to prioritize self-care so you can show up as your best self, both personally and professionally, feeling fulfilled. And as humans, we all need that. We thrive when we prioritize and meet our self-care needs regularly. Take a look around you, some of the healthiest and happiest people on the planet are those that regularly practice self-care.

My challenge to you is to make yourself a non-negotiable and craft a routine that supports your ability to feel and perform at your best. Because the gifts you bring to the world matter.

About Mindy: Mindy Garrett is a health & fitness coach, the founder of Mind & Body Elite, and the creator of Healthy Habits Game Plan, Eat, Treat, Repeat, and The Online Fitness Club, as well as a variety of other healthy living programs.

She uses her unique background in education, business management, and entrepreneurship to help busy women create healthy Habits that simplify eating well and exercise so they can transform their bodies, restore their confidence, achieve their goals and live their best lives.

Always an active and athletic person, Mindy's world was turned upside down about fifteen years ago after undergoing multiple back surgeries due to ruptured discs. She felt lost, discouraged, and frustrated, stuck in a body that didn't feel right. She decided to use her recovery time as an opportunity to improve her health and wellness, learning all she could about post-injury care, nutrition, and fitness training modalities. Over the next year, Mindy not only regained full mobility but surpassed doctor's expectations, running her first half marathon. It was through her life experiences that she was able to create a healthy lifestyle plan that works.

Passionate about health and fitness and realizing the powerful impact it has had throughout her life, she founded Mind & Body Elite in 2013 on a mission to empower other women to live their best lives. Mindy firmly believes that the three pillars to a healthy and happy life are to eat healthy, move daily and live happy. And by focusing on simple, satisfying, and sustainable daily Habits, she helps her clients ditch perfection so they can make real progress and achieve meaningful results that last.

Mindy walks the talk and backs it all up with a diverse knowledge base, with over two decades of experience in the education field, working with youth and families, in developmental and supportive nutrition, strength and mobility training, and healthy lifestyle program design.

A self-proclaimed "forever learner," Mindy is a certified Precision Nutrition Coach and Personal Trainer, with a Bachelors in Health Sciences and a Montessori certification in early childhood education. She is a youth and senior fitness specialist, TRX certified trainer, and a member of the National Education Association, National Wellness Institute, American Council on Exercise, and I.D.E.A. Health & Fitness Association.

Mindy lives in Washington state, where she enjoys an active lifestyle with her pup Pacey and her partner Kevin.

DRESS FOR THE OFFICE EVERY DAY! - CYNTHIA LINDSEY

Why: Working is a mindset, and when you dress for success you are ready to take on business conversations, you feel more powerful in your decision making, and you feel and play the part of a successful business owner, employee, or manager.

The home office can lend itself to a lazy approach, so get up, shower, and get dressed and go to work. This doesn't mean that some days you are not more casual, but the structure and routine are most important to accomplishing your daily, weekly, monthly and annual business, and personal goals.

There is something very powerful when you go into a space that you have created for being productive. That space should be sacred and used for just that sole purpose. Setting boundaries around that space will help in focusing on productivity, and then when you take that scheduled break, you leave the office space and go outside or to another part of your home that is relaxing and lets your mind rest for a few minutes.

Working from home requires a discipline that takes practice so give yourself the grace and time to develop a new Habit that will grow your business, your professional development and on the flip side, in the big picture working from home may allow for more quality time to do the things you love.

Just imagine not having to commute an hour or more each day. What will you do with that extra time, and isn't that what we all say," I don't have time"? This could be life-changing for you, so look at this as an opportunity, a gift to get your life back!

The Un-Habit: Procrastination!

Why: Procrastination comes in so many forms, and the trick is recognizing it when it is happening.

We get up from what we are doing to do something else that may be more pleasurable. A phone call comes in from a friend; we check our email and decide we will take an early lunch. There are all kinds of examples, and we are good at creating false "distractions" to take us off what we perceive to be a difficult or painful task, project, or conversation.

We all have our go-to Habits when avoiding something we don't want to do. Sometimes we feel overwhelmed, unsure where to start or worse, or we tell ourselves we don't have time while we play a game on our phone for two hours.

For example, its time to work on your business strategy for the coming year. That feels daunting to most, especially if what you are good at is execution but not necessarily coming up with a good strategy for say marketing or business development. You know you need a road map, so you don't flail and stumble around and make no progress. If you avoid working on your business strategy and do other things instead, you may get some work done, but it might not take you in the direction you want to go. Fighting procrastination and establishing the strategy will create a road map that makes all other work better defined.

The Habit of procrastination prevents you from moving forward in life, getting things done, and fully developing your problem-solving skills. If you can break down projects or to-dos in small bites, they eventually become manageable. A key element with procrastination is our relationship with time. Time is the same for us, but how we use it is what makes us different. We can waste so much time doing absolutely nothing, or we can look like we are using every bit of our available time and still accomplish nothing if we're not focused on the right things or procrastinating on what matters.

We all have heard Nike's phrase "Just do it". Well, it is what you must do to fight procrastination. Establish a plan by planning weekly and thinking about what you want to accomplish, when you want to accomplish it and how you can get it done. This one action takes time, but it is the best time you will ever spend when you set it aside to create your road map for the week. Start somewhere, and bit by bit, you will eliminate the bad Habit of procrastination.

About Cynthia: Cynthia Lindsey, Partner of Its ARRANGED, has been in the world of Professional Organizing, Move Management, and Life Management since 2007 with her former company Organizing Ease.

She recently partnered with another organizing company merging strengths and skillsets to create Its Arranged and continue the life of the business but with a new flair, look and feel.

Cynthia is a Business Development Professional having worked in Radio for 12 years before her entrepreneur life as a multi-person business and consultant facilitating life transitions with Move Management, Residential Organizing, Life Management, and Productivity. Currently serving on the NAPO National Board of Directors, Cynthia is also a NAPO Golden Circle member and has her REALTOR license in the state of Tennessee.

Cynthia acquired a Bachelor's Degree in BioDynamics (Exercise Physiology) from California State University. Having come from a military family that traveled around for the first part of her life, change has always been part of her makeup, leading to her ability to accept and love change successfully.

Cynthia has successfully built a strong customer base as a highly motivated, versatile professional who possesses exceptional organization, motivational, and leadership skills relating well with clients.

Cynthia has been mentioned in Good Housekeeping, This Old House, and interviewed on more than one occasion by the Spare Foot Blog, and was a Presenter at the NAPO Conference 2019, "A Radio Veteran. Shares Strategies and Tips on Selling an Intangible." Having navigated many challenges, both personally and professionally, she is passionate about helping clients "Live Their Best Life Yet"!

She loves to cycle, ride motorcycles, and has practiced YOGA for many years. The practice of YOGA and her faith in GOD has taught her the gift of stillness, acceptance, and growth in ways far beyond her imagination. She sees the good in people and enjoys looking for the strengths and talents people have and has studied the Gallup Strengths Finder for both her personal growth and with clients along the way.

Life is one big adventure, and she is honored to have worked with many amazing professionals, clients, and family who supported her along her journey.

KEEP MY EYE ON MY WHY - BETSY MATIAS

Why: I am here in my home office. It is in the quietest corner of my house. I've carved out a comfortable workspace that hums with productivity—on most days, that is. I have a big desk I refinished myself. It sits in front of a big window with a view of the street. I like that I can see the UPS truck when it arrives. It is the start of a new week. Mondays are always busy.

A few Zoom meetings down, files organized, marketing projects in process, appointments set the—week is off and running! My home office is thriving; humming along with productivity. Thursday is here. The week has taken a turn. A timeline gets off track, and a client goes another direction, an offer falls through, paperwork goes missing, the printer is jammed: the productive hum has morphed into an overwhelming drone.

There it is. I catch it in the corner of my eye. It's front and center in my home office, above a low bookshelf. I made it from a giant, beveled wooden frame found in the "free" pile one day at a South Seattle salvage yard. I gave it a coat of paint and added some cork. Over time I have curated a collection of personal photos, trinkets, images, keepsakes, affirmations, and quotes that keep me grounded in who I am, who I want to be, and how I want to feel. My giant vision board is a powerful personal Habit that centers me in those harried moments that sometimes tilt me off balance. My vision board feels like 'home base' when I need a moment to catch my breath. When uncertainty, overwhelm that is too many challenges at once, feel like they may take over, I make it a Habit to turn to my vision board for reassurance that everything will fall into place, somehow, some way. I can recontextualize the issue of the moment and use my creative problem solving and positive productivity to find a solution, amid that curated collection, with my greater goals before me. My vision board ensures that I keep 'my eye on my why.'

I make it Habit to visit this central place of focus in my home office that reminds me not to 'sweat the small stuff!' It guides my decisions, day in and day out, and provides a foundation for planning.

This Habit is key to staying true to my core values, character, purpose, and the people I love. It is all right there as a reminder that challenges will always crop up during a busy week, but it is the larger perspective that is vital to thriving. What I focus on expands; this, I know. Time and again, my vision board reminds me of just that!

The Un-Habit: Being a perfectionist

Why: Progress over perfection. Say it five times. Try and remember this powerful phrase the next time you allow yourself to get bogged down with perfectionism in your home office environment. I have it prominently displayed on my vision board. We all want to be the best we can be, right? Aiming for perfection in everything we do can hold us back from appropriate planning, keeping perspective, and moving forward. Perfectionism is a hard Habit to break, especially when working from home, where we may not have colleagues to mastermind with.

How many times have you labored over something, ripped it up, deleted it, thrown it away, and started over to get it perfect? It is a Habit truly worthy of change to create a thriving, productive home office. Only we know what perfect looks like in our minds. Only we know our intended outcome or result. Chances are, those around us admire our work, appreciate our passion, and see the value we bring. It is enough, I promise.

What truly needs to be perfect, and what needs to be 'good enough'? Can we consider something a first pass and improve upon it down the line? Which objectives will move us forward in achieving our goals? How about our client's goals? Letting go of perfectionism will change your life and take your home office energy from stuck to thriving. Striving for unrealistically high expectations can hinder progress, lower your confidence, and foster procrastination out of fear of failure. Letting go of unrealistically high expectations can be freeing, but how do we break this Habit in our home office environment? Practice saying "no" more often. Challenge your inner critic to be quiet and squelch negative thoughts in favor of positive ones. Trust that everything will fall into place and focus on one objective at a time. Most importantly, avoid holding those around you to the same unreasonably high standards—practice compassion. Embrace others' efforts and recognize that their way, though it may be different, can be equally brilliant.

About Betsy: Betsy Matias is a Realtor® in Bellevue, Washington, specializing in the sale of new and existing residential real estate in and around Seattle's east side. She approaches every home sale with a laser-sharp focus and strategic plan. She is paired with a calm, problem-solving demeanor that allows her clients to experience confident ease throughout the process.

WHAT SETS BETSY APART?

Her mission statement is essential to Betsy's business: to deliver an outstanding service experience to every client. You can see this interwoven into her communication and service-oriented systems to manage every aspect of a home sale or purchase effectively. From her initial client contact to searching for the right home to the listing, marketing, negotiations to contract, every client will feel like they are priority #1.

Betsy's experience as a successful business owner, educator, stints at Nordstrom, world-wide travel, and corporate relocation experience provide her with a solid foundation to understand the complexity of buying and selling real estate, no matter what stage of life you are in. Whether you are downsizing, a first-time homebuyer/seller, or relocating, she strives to prepare her clients for success in the marketplace, armed with the data-driven strategies, strategic marketing, and unparalleled service.

IN HER FREE TIME:

When she's not immersed in real estate, Betsy loves to entertain, travel abroad, and cook. She's an avid dog lover - first of her two doodle dogs and then contributing her time and energy as a liaison to Seattle Humane. She is a creative at heart, always channeling her background in design to painting, drawing, and decorating. She gives her all on the tennis court or a Par 3 course with her family and loves Seattle summers. She is extremely involved in the community, facilitating art workshops for children with special needs, children in homeless shelters, and other non-profits.

MINDFULLY DISCONNECT, EVERY DAY - NEELU GIBSON

Why: Whether you are an entrepreneur with a home-based business or a company employee working full time from a home office, taking time each day to disconnect is important for your well-being.

If you manage your time effectively, you may already incorporate this Habit. If, however, you are someone for whom taking a few minutes for bio breaks, lunch, or simply standing up and stretching, are activities relegated to the back burner in favor of meetings and calls, the Habit of mindfully disconnecting is worth considering.

Mindful disconnection means making a deliberate choice to walk away from your computer or your home office for a few minutes each day to do something entirely different - a quick walk, deep breathing, or a conversation with a friend or a loved one. You will be amazed at how energizing this is.

Let's take a quick step back - for some, working remotely for long periods and setting up an effective home office is a new concept. We don't get dressed for work, commute, socialize, do our job, then go home.

We are suddenly in a space without boundaries; there is no 'on/off' switch to transition from work to home. We can work anywhere we like, outside, on the couch, at the kitchen table... and dare I say it, even in bed before going to sleep.

Having worked remotely on occasion but suddenly finding myself 100% remote, managing a global team of professionals, and a packed calendar, was daunting at best. I quickly learned to embrace my new normal and made some changes that have proved to be effective:

A defined work space - I used to work in the living room or at the dining table but found that those spaces effectively became my 'office' and no longer felt like places to relax and unwind. My office now is our breakfast nook - my laptop, work phone, and iPad live here.

Set boundaries - and decide how flexible these boundaries should be. After my last meeting of the day, I spend time finishing tasks and plan the next day. I then close my laptop and walk away. I had to create this Habit too - it is far too easy to keep working or go back to the table when you know you should be spending time with your family.

Mindfully disconnecting each day.

My team and I have a scheduled 15-minute meeting each day to call in if we are able. Our cameras are on, and we talk about absolutely anything other than work. This short break, filled with stories and laughter is priceless.

The Un-Habit: Not Setting Boundaries

Why: Without boundaries we are on a trajectory to burnout. I have a confession to make. I have been guilty of accepting 6 am meetings knowing my day will end after 7:00 pm. On occasion, I took work calls at 9:00 pm and even 10:30 pm. I assumed my family understood these crazy hours and accepted them. What I came to realize was, the time I spent on emails and calls at all hours, was time I stole from myself and family. My availability without boundaries set an unsustainable norm, fractured my family life, and set me on my personal trajectory to burnout.

Thanks to feedback from friends and family (rather like an intervention, actually), I actively focused on cultivating the Habit of "Setting Boundaries." Now, in the remote space, working from home, there is a very real risk of falling back into the no boundaries/burnout trajectory.

There is no line between work and personal life when working from home unless you create that line. Above, I said, 'set boundaries...and decide how flexible these should be". This is something to consider and define. What are your hard boundaries? Not answering emails over the weekend? Only working during certain hours? You need to assess whether these are in line with business expectations. What about personal boundaries? Do your loved ones know what to expect of you?

By breaking the Habit of not setting boundaries, you are helping yourself, your colleagues and people in your personal life. Once you communicate, "I am not available on weekends unless there is an emergency" or "I answer my phone between 7 am and 7 pm", you are effectively helping your business partners who would otherwise be frustrated if, for example, they were expecting a response from you on Sunday morning and your phone had been off all weekend.

From a personal life standpoint, setting boundaries and communicating those to loved ones, helps them manage their expectations. When, for example, I am clear about needing to work late for a few days due to an emergency, my family understands, as they know, this is a temporary situation and not the norm.

Setting and adhering to your boundaries will help you be an effective business partner and to be present for your friends and family. I believe that the best gift you can give your loved ones is your focused time and attention.

About Neelu: Neelu is currently serving as the Worldwide Vice President of Regulatory Affairs for a major medical device company, based in San Diego, California.

Recognized as a strong, results-oriented executive, Neelu has enjoyed an impressive career, highlighted by obtaining multiple regulatory approvals & clearances from the U.S. Food and Drug Administration (FDA) and similar approvals from international regulatory agencies.

During her 20+ years with Johnson & Johnson, Neelu served on five management boards, holding leadership positions in Regulatory Affairs at 7 J&J companies. Neelu is passionate about personal and professional development and continues to share her leadership experiences with entrepreneurs, students, and others.

Neelu grew up in London, UK, moved to the U.S. almost 30 years ago, and refers to herself as "Brindian," to reflect her British-Indian heritage. She is a published author and continues to write about leadership, personal growth, and career development.

BE MORE PRODUCTIVE BY INTEGRATING PERSONAL TASKS IN YOUR WORKDAY - ANDREA DUFFIELD

Why: When I first started working at home, I set out to create a strict schedule. I was determined not to be distracted. Over time I came to realize that I was working longer days, often without getting up from my chair for hours at a time. I would end the day bleary-eyed and overwhelmed by the thought of all that needed to be accomplished before the next day.

I committed to creating opportunities that would make me move at regular intervals, allow me to complete tasks that I would otherwise have to do later in the evening, and provide space for focused reflection, problem-solving, and planning.

Example of what works for me:

Movement

1. Doing laundry: The buzzer indicating that the load of wash is finished is a great cue to get up and move. While it only takes a few minutes to transfer wash over to the dryer or throw in a new load, it still gets the blood flowing.

2. Exercising: If I have a project with extensive reading, I print a copy and hop on my stationary bike. Muscle memory kicks in, and I can focus just on the content of what I am reading.

3. Walking meetings: When the weather is nice, I will suggest a 1:1 walking meeting. Both parties put in earbuds and go for a walk. It works just as well virtually as it does when we do it in person.

Reflection, Problem Solving & Planning

1. Folding Laundry: I often find myself craving time in my day to have uninterrupted focus on a problem or plan. For me, folding laundry is a motor memory task; I can use that time to have a dedicated focus on something specific. Being away from the computer and my phone, I create an intention to focus my attention.

2. Making School Lunches: When our kids were too young to make their lunches, I would get everything set out first so that during the actual assembly of five lunches, I was performing rote tasks. Knowing that we were a blended family of seven, I am sure it makes more sense now knowing why laundry was such a daunting task at our house!

You can pick any number of household tasks that you complete to increase your movement and reflective sessions. The key is to plan, know what you want to focus on during that time, and stick to it!

The Un-Habit: Stop trying to compartmentalize yourself

Why: "Bring your whole self to work. I don't believe we have a professional self Monday through Friday and a real self the rest

Be More Productive by Integrating Personal Tasks in Your Wo...

of the time. It is all professional, and it is all personal." Sheryl Sandberg

I love to-do-lists; they make me feel like I have a sense of control. What I have learned over time is that just writing a list of all the tasks I have on my plate, without order, results in a chaotic day. When I started working at home, my list at my desk was only for work tasks, my home, and personal list was on the kitchen counter. I thought that by segregating the lists I would focus on just work during the day and magically, at 5:00, my focus would switch to home and personal. As you can guess, that didn't work. I spent days stressing about being done with work in time to call the orthodontist before they closed. I wasted hours calling furnace service companies until I found one who could send a technician in the evening or on weekends.

Over time, I learned that I need a different kind of list that divides both work and personal tasks into urgent, important, and can wait. Each day I need to acknowledge that if something is hitting my urgent column, I must take care of that first. On days when I don't, my mind is constantly distracted. Urgent doesn't have to be big. Urgent tasks often don't take a lot of time, but they consume a significant amount of thought and energy.

If you can, let yourself address what is urgent at the start of your day frees up time to be more productive, happy, and successful. You give yourself the freedom to focus on important! Stop creating separate lists based on work versus personal. Start creating whole self lists based on urgency and importance.

About Andrea: Andrea Duffield has worked in the Western Washington health care and non-profit world as an entrepreneur and executive for over 25 years.

Andrea has an elementary education bachelor's degree and is a licensed Speech and Language Pathologist with a master's degree from Western Washington University. After working as a speech-language pathologist in multiple settings, Andrea obtained her MBA and transitioned into entrepreneurship in 2003 with her businesses MOSAIC Physical Therapy and MOSAIC Children's Therapy Clinics. MOSAIC's array of services included speech-language pathology, physical and occupational therapy, behavioral health, psychology, and counseling services.

During her tenure at MOSAIC, Andrea received accolades for her entrepreneurial acumen from the Inc. Magazine, American Business Awards, and 425 Magazine. In 2014 and 2015, she was listed in the Puget Sound Business Journal's Top 50 Women-Owned Businesses. In 2016 she was honored to be named the Women Business Owners, Nellie Cashman, Woman Business Owner of the Year Award.

In 2020 Andrea accepted the CEO role at the non-profit, Bridgeways, located in Everett Washington. Bridgeways' mission is to provide services that promote quality of life for individuals living with mental illness in a manner that facilitates growth, independence, and a sense of community. This mission is carried out through a manufacturing social enterprise and an array of programs, connecting adults living with mental illness to life-changing opportunities through employment, housing supports, and engagement with mental health and other supportive services.

Andrea has passionately volunteered with local and international non-profit organizations. She is a past president of the Seattle Children's Hospital Autism Guild. She has also volunteered for the Seattle Children's Hospital Festival of Trees, The Seattle Children's Hospital Annual Vintage Races, and the Seattle Police Foundation. She also served on the Board of Directors for Manos Unidas, a non-profit school for special needs children in Cusco, Peru.

Andrea is a proud wife, mother, and stepmother. She thrives spending time outdoors with family and friends. While she loves to travel, she also feels lucky to live in the Pacific Northwest. She and her husband consider themselves foodies and thoroughly enjoy the amazing food and wine in the Seattle area.

DE-CLUTTER YOUR PHYSICAL AND VIRTUAL DESKTOPS - JANINE SARNA-JONES

Why: Most desktops accumulate clutter that is either an item that requires action or an item that has no home. The irony is that this is true for both three-dimensional desks and two-dimensional desktops on a computer. I encourage everyone to create a practice of clearing their desktops, both physical and virtual, at least once a week.

Taking the time to incorporate this Habit into your life helps limit wasted time searching for things, reduces frustration, and enables you to develop a sense of self-efficacy. It is widely believed that the average office employee wastes 1.5 hours looking for things. Have you found yourself searching through the clutter on your desk for a paper you left there to later take care of? And later is now. Have you found yourself trying to remember a file name while hunting through your computer desktop? Instilling this Habit will make you more mindful when you find yourself leaving items on your desktops, but it will also help you feel more effective in your workspaces, both physical and digital.

The first step for de-cluttering your desktops is to get a pad—paper or notes app—and a container—cardboard or a digital file. The pad is for creating a list of tasks related to the items that require action. The container is for the items that you want to keep, but don't have a home for. Once your desktops are clear, schedule a recurring appointments with yourself to prioritize your action items and make homes for homeless items you decided to keep. Also, consider using physical and virtual inboxes to contain action items and homeless items. Creating containers (or homes) for processing these items can help you feel less daunted by the process altogether.

Start tackling one of your desktops this week. Discover the clarity and calm an uncluttered desktop will bring to you.

THE UN-HABIT: TAKE CONTROL OF YOUR NOTIFICATIONS

Why: In our technological age, "pings," "dings," and "chirps" surround us on a daily, if not hourly, basis. Like Pavlov's dogs, we find ourselves exhibiting conditioned responses. We may not start salivating, but at the drop of ping or vibration, we pick up our phones or open our email to read incoming messages. In either case, the ability to focus on our work is easily dismantled by a simple sound.

We live in an age where we all expect instant gratification. Send a text. Expect an immediate response. How many times have you found yourself looking at the animated dot-dot-dot? Fortunately, the Habit of snapping your focus to a device that demands your attention has a simple fix: Silence your Notifications. Taking the time to change notification settings on your phone, tablet, and the computer gives you the gift of control. Control over your time, attention, and focus. So many productivity experts recommend that we start our day by focusing on the tasks and activities that are directly related to our goals and priorities. Yet so many of us start our day to a flood of notifications.

As a business owner, I tried to be available at a moment's notice; if someone reached out to connect with me, I believed that my instant response would increase my revenue. Ha! What I found instead is that my Pavlovian response to emails, calls, and texts interrupted my ability to focus my attention on the projects and activities that truly affected my bottom line. Then I turned off the email notification. Killing the email "ping" was a revelation! It also made me realize that the vast majority of my email does not have to be addressed in a moment's notice.

Then I selected different kinds of sounds for the notifications and alerts I wanted to hear. So my calendar gives me a 10-minute "ding" before an appointment. That gives me the gift of 10 minutes to prepare—text messages "chirp" as they arrive. If I am busy or involved, I know, I can check those messages when I am ready. My response times vary for the various notifications and alerts that I regularly use, but what is most important is that I made a conscious choice about the kind of pings and dings I want to hear.

About Janine: Janine Sarna-Jones is the founder and president of Organize Me Inc, based in New York City. She has been helping people get organized at work and home since 1992. Before becoming a professional organizer and move management consultant, Janine was a photographer and photo archivist at the Smithsonian's National Museum of the American Indian.

When Janine founded Organize Me in 2000, she offered residential, hands-on organizing. Today, Organize Me Inc. provides the services of a team of professional organizers. They offer services that extend beyond what a solo professional organizer can accomplish–move management, unpacking services, estate clearance, project management, and hands-on organizing for both homes and offices.

Janine is a master problem solver with a deep Rolodex who loves managing client projects—the more complicated, the better! Bringing calm to stress-laden situations is her superpower.

A member of the inaugural class of Certified Professional Organizers® (2007), Janine has helped a broad range of clients, including corporate executives, small business owners, real estate agents, growing families, seniors, artists, therapists, and non-profit organizations. She has been a member of the National Association of Productivity and Organizing Professionals (NAPO) since 2001, serving as president of the New York chapter (NAPO-NY) from 2005 to 2007 and a three year-term on NAPO's Board of Directors from 2007 to 2010. In 2019, Janine became a member of the National Association of Senior Move Managers (NASMM). She also earned a CD Specialist Certificate from the Institute for Challenging Disorganization.

As a member of Parenting Magazine's Mom Squad, Janine was regularly featured in the publication from 2004-2008 and has been heard on the radio, in print, and on podcasts. Janine stays up-to-date with developments in her field by regularly attending expert lectures, conferences, and professional association meetings.

Janine lives in New York City with her husband and daughter.

LEVERAGE YOUR PEAK PRODUCTIVITY - SHANNON MCGINNIS

Why: Do you know when you are most productive? If you could make your schedule, when do you get into the flow and do your best work? The goal of the "Leverage Your Peak Productivity Time" 1 Habit is to match your highest priority work with your most productive hours. When you leverage your peak productivity time periods, you are most likely to accomplished more in those hours than you might the rest of the day.

If you are unsure about when your peak productivity time is, think about what you do on the weekends or on days that you don't have much scheduled. Do you wake up excited to start on a project, or do you give yourself a long, slow morning to do nothing? Do you hit your stride in the middle of the afternoon or stay up late eager to keep going? Ideally, your Peak Productivity period would be a couple of 90-minute blocks of time throughout your waking hours. When we focus our energy intensely for too long of a period, we disengage. When we don't focus intensely enough, we get distracted or bored. Overuse or underuse creates disengagement.

Once you know your peak productivity time, mark it off in your calendar, and consider this time sacred. This is the time to focus on your most urgent and important work. Once you've completed your tasks, you can shift gears and focus on other priorities.

If you are a full-time remote worker, and most of us are right now your focus, productivity is your superpower — don't let it get ruined with constant interruptions like text or IM pings. Working from home also allows you to give yourself intermittent breaks. After an intense period of focus, shift your energy with brief home priorities such as watering the plants, brushing a pet, or putting in a load of laundry.

The most important aspect of leveraging your peak productivity time periods is to make sure you accomplish the most important priorities when you are at your best!

The Un-Habit: Stop Letting Others Monopolize Your Time

Why: If you keep your entire schedule open every day, colleagues and friends may unknowingly monopolize your most productive hours. Take control of your calendar and stop letting others monopolize your time by initiating time blocking. Time blocking means setting aside a specific time frame to focus.

Determine when to block your calendar, reflect on your typical workday schedule, and determine when you feel you are doing your best work. Once you know when your Peak Productivity Time is, block those hours on your calendar so that no one else can schedule meetings during your most productive time. I recommend giving yourself 15-30 minutes on either side of that window to transition time to the zone, so you are at your best.

During your Peak Productivity time block, it is up to you what you want to focus on. It could be your highest priorities, whatever is at the top of your To-Do list, or a time designated for your most creative or strategic thinking. Whatever you decide to accomplish during your Peak Productivity Time may vary each day. The goal is to block these hours on your calendar as often as possible so that you choose what to accomplish.

Without taking charge of your energy, you may experience overwhelm, fatigue, missed deadlines, or additional stress that could lower your immune system. It is also important to refresh yourself throughout the day, so when your energy dips, take a break by working out, going for a walk, getting something to eat, or sitting outside for a few minutes.

When you initiate time blocking and stop letting others schedule all of your time, you can set yourself up for greater success to get more done in less time.

About Shannon: Shannon McGinnis, PMP, CPO, and founder of Organized 4 Success is a meticulous detail-oriented self-starter with excellent organization skills and experience working with cross-functional teams. As a sought after speaker and author of two instructional organizing books: The 10-Minute Tidy: 108 Ways to Organize Your Home Quickly and The 10-Minute Tidy: 108 Ways to Organize Your Office Quickly, Shannon will be sure your projects are running as efficiently as possible from initiation to close.

She founded Organized 4 Success in 2003. A full-service organizing business leveraging her time-saving methodology, her company empowers individuals and businesses to release inefficient overwhelm and embrace easy-to-maintain organizational systems.

As one of the nation's first Certified Professional Organizers, Shannon offers expert advice on project management, process improvement, time management, office productivity, and general organizing principles. As a PMP certified strategic thinker, she has experience negotiating contracts, developing long-term relationships, and maintaining confidentiality within groups and across departments.

Her two books, The 10-Minute Tidy: 108 Ways to Organize Your Office Quickly and The 10-Minute Tidy: 108 Ways to Organize Your Office Quickly, offer quick tips to help you get more done in less time. Go to www.10minutetidy.com to learn more.

Shannon is an experienced as a Senior Project and Program Manager focused on business process improvement for global customer experience. Her ability to manage multiple, simultaneous, complex projects that support business requirements and strategic prioritization exemplifies her PMP skills.

With years of PMO leadership in Agile environments, and with a drive for continuous process improvement, she delivers value by establishing trust by building enduring relationships with cross-functional team members and clients. This enables global organizations to implement change based on data-driven decisions effectively.

Shannon is an enthusiastic and dedicated PM and Customer Success professional with 7+ years of experience working with global, Fortune 500 companies in a variety of industries, including technology, travel, education, and financial services.

Contact her online:

https://www.linkedin.com/in/shannonmcginnis/

MAKE TIME FOR CONNECTION - DENISE LLOYD

Why: Let's face it; human beings are wired for connection. We are not meant to be at home, squirreled away in our offices working from dawn to dusk. We are meant to be with people, sharing stories and experiences, sorrows and laughs. How much of this you need is very individualized (some need it daily; some once a week), but we all need that moment of being seen by others.

Years ago, long before we worked from home because of a pandemic, I worked from home and lived alone, and as an introvert, I loved it! I thrived from Monday to about Thursday, and then productivity took a dive. I lost motivation, interest, and energy by the time as the week went by. I realized that over the course of the week, I needed some inspiration, some interaction, and some connection! So, I started to set a lunch date or go to a networking event each week so that I could finish the week strong.

It is no different in today's work from home world. Many of us went from being a part of a bustling workplace with lots of people to our home offices, with very little in-person interaction.

It can be easy to close your door, put your head down and get to work, losing all sense of connection to others. No more lunch in the break room with people from other departments and no more conversations at the water cooler about everyone's weekend plans. Being in a home office doesn't mean you have to give up those connections though. It just means you have to be more intentional about making them happen, in person, or online.

In today's virtual world, connecting online can be easy. Set up a regular online meeting between 12 and 1 – a virtual kitchen of sorts – and invite others to join you. That invitation could go out to other team members, friends, or even your neighbors. Who knows who you might end up eating lunch with! Do you know others in your area who work from home? Set up a weekly walking group so that everyone (including you!) knows that at least once a week, they can connect and chat. Send a Happy Hour request to friends and co-workers to join you for an end of the workweek drink on a Friday. In days gone by, that was a meet up at a local pub, and in today's world, a BYOB over zoom can work just as well as the most important priorities when you are at your best!

The Un-Habit: You Can't be Available to Everyone All the Time

Why: There is such a thing as being too available, and when you do that, you leave no time for yourself to get anything done!

One of the biggest challenges about shifting to working from home and being online all the time is that people think you are always available. If you are using any kind of collaboration tool, you can get asks from people constantly, and this can mean that you never get any of your own work done. While connection is a good Habit that can help with productivity, it can be a double-edged sword as too much connection can be counterproductive.

You will notice that the connection Habit I encourage is strategic. You are deciding when and how you want to connect with others. When you do this, you organize your work around that schedule, ensuring you get your work done. The rest of the time, the choice is yours if you want to be available to support others, to answer questions, or to take time from your tasks and priorities to help someone with theirs.

Setting boundaries around when and how you are available to connect is important. It is easy to fall into the trap of making time for everyone, anytime they ask for it, especially if you seek connection. When what they need seems quick and simple, the answer is often "Sure, why not?" You might not want to do that because the interruption to your own flow and productivity may make it way more disruptive than anticipated.

Instead of being available at a drop of a hat, or the click of a mouse, have a clear schedule of when you are open to being interrupted, and when you are not, and communicate that. Block your calendar so that it appears you are in a meeting or put an out of the office on your email so that you can focus on your own priorities. This way, when you are doing tasks that aren't as high a priority, you can open your schedule and be available to others. Bring on the ask, my friends! This technique is a win/win – you can still be available to others, and those that need you, will know when to ask to get the help they need.

ABOUT DENISE: Denise Lloyd is the Founder and CEO of Engaged HR. She has been in the Human Resources field for over 25 years. She has a wide array of leadership experience, including building a very successful HR consulting firm in Victoria, British Columbia, that operates across Canada.

For as long as Denise can remember, she has always possessed a curiosity about what motivates people to do what they do. Fast forward many years, and she continues to ask these same questions and is driven to create workplaces where everyone can gain meaning from their work. Throughout her career, she has been keeping employees engaged – with the organization's vision and with their own personal goals – long before "employee engagement" became the buzzword.

After her many years of working within organizations as an HR leader, she recognized that many businesses and organizations are facing the same staffing, policy, and engagement issues that don't have any HR expertise to help them resolve their challenges, and they were suffering the consequences. Without this HR expertise and strategic thinking, it was clear that these organizations risked losing valuable employees, wasting time, money, and energy navigating the complex world of HR.

So, she decided to apply her passion for creating engaged workplaces in organizations that did not have access to full-time HR leadership and founded Engaged HR. As a wildly successful firm, her innovative and solution-focused approach has been proven to create great places to work!

Denise holds a Master of Arts in Leadership from Royal Roads University, A Senior Certified Professional from the Society for Human Resource Management (SHRM-SCP), and the prestigious designation of Fellow Chartered Professional in Human Resources (FCPHR) from the Canadian Chartered Professionals in Human Resources. Denise lives in Victoria, BC, Canada with her husband and business partner, Arie where they own two business, Engaged HR Inc and Libratum Workplace Investigations Inc. They love being on this wild entrepreneurial ride together!

PLAN FOR THE RIGHT BALANCE OF INDIVIDUAL WORK TIME VERSUS VIRTUAL MEETINGS - JENNIFER MCKIBBIN HARRIS

Why: Strike the right balance of human interaction and individual work time to suit your preferences.

Each of us has a unique internal pull, which guides us to an environment that naturally recharges our batteries. For some, this pull may be toward social gatherings of people, talking, debating, or cheering. For others, this natural pull may be toward a peaceful setting, quiet and meditative, without interference from others. Many recognize this natural pull as a preference toward extroversion or introversion.

Why is this important when creating a virtual workspace?

When working from your home office, there is an added element of flexibility. We get to call more of the shots about where we choose to work from (the couch, the den, kitchen table?), what our workday looks like (should I start work at 7 am or 10 am?), and how our time is spent (email, projects, meetings?). We must understand where we get our energy from (people or alone time) to make decisions that help create balance. Identify when we need to exert ourselves versus be in a more natural, calm place to conduct work.

Plan the right balance of individual work time versus virtual meetings.

Video conferencing has become a new way of communicating with partners, co-workers, clients, and customers. It presents a visual connection the old-fashioned phone call could not do. For some, video is the life line. Without it, they feel silo'ed and cut off from the rest of their peers. For others, they wish it was never invented.

Use video conferencing to your benefit. Understand if it helps recharge your batteries or drains them. Having this knowledge is critical for planning and scheduling your workweek. Ask yourself: what is the proper balance of individual work time, video conference calls, and phone calls that supports your completion of tasks and does not leave you feeling drained by the end of your workday?

Follow these steps to achieve the right balance for you:

1. Identify how you recharge your batteries. Is it fundamentally with or without people around?

2. Proactively block out time on your calendar for video calls, phone calls, and individual work time.

3. Observe how you feel at the end of each workday and write it down.

4. Adjust future workdays with a better balance of meetings versus individual work time.

Plan For the Right Balance of Individual Work Time Versus Vi... | 385

The Un-Habit: Stop apologizing for what matters most to you

Why: While many companies have dipped their toe in the flexible work arrangement pool, the rise of the 2020 Coronavirus Pandemic forced most businesses to reexamine their virtual work policies. With the blink of an eye, employees moved to working from home 100% of the time. Our stark office or drab cubicle is now the family dining room table, couch, or if we are fortunate, a home office with a door. There are members of our household surrounding us all the time and interrupting our day. We're on video conference, and toddlers walk up crying with an immediate need. Partners are on phone calls with loud voices that can be heard by participants in our meeting. There is just so much going on all at once in our households!

Remote workers have reached a turning point. With these home dynamics, we're forced to adapt quickly throughout the day, switching from personal to professional and back within minutes. Knowing this, identify what matters most; what do you value? I value flexibility and autonomy, which means I want to be able to diligently work hard on a project and then be able to stop in the middle of that project, to help my children with their schoolwork.

As an HR Consultant, I am virtual most of the time. However, when the kids were released from school for three months due to the Pandemic, the activity in my house amplified times three! Working remotely always aligned with my values. However, during that time, I felt exhausted and was constantly apologizing to clients due to my family's needs and interruptions. Then I realized I was worn out from apologizing for something that at the core was my most important value: family.

Now I'm changing that habit. I've stopped apologizing... most of the time. I've made an effort to be aware of when I am saying it and reign it in. The results, I feel less exhausted.

Join me by trying to stop saying, "I'm sorry." When you use the phrase, let it be because you're not in alignment with what's important to you, not despite what's important to you. Next time you're in a meeting, and an interruption happens, pause, and do not apologize for what just happened. We all have things going on in our lives, competing for our attention. No more apologies, this is just life, and it will be OK.

About: Jennifer McKibbin Harris is the Founder and Consultant of Look Within HR Consulting, where she guides, coaches, and consults clients to achieve their business goals through the lens of their employees. She is a trusted, strategic HR partner, and leader engaging with various types of professional small businesses on their organizational and employee-related needs.

For over 15 years of her professional career, Jennifer worked in HR management at large corporations, such as Washington Mutual, Liberty Mutual, and Microsoft. Her experience in these companies gave her access to a variety of HR tools, training, and services. She worked with leaders at all levels and supported clients across the globe.

In 2015, her career pivoted. She realized her calling was to share her HR experience, tools, and education with smaller sized businesses that generally do not have the opportunity to work with a strategic HR partner. Shortly after, Look Within HR Consulting was born.

Jennifer's specialty is looking at a company's organizational system to determine maximum efficiency and create opportunity to highlight the talent within. The name Look Within HR came from the idea that we should all look within ourselves, our team, and our organization to gain awareness and focus on what's important and then access the potential that exists.

Before a career in HR, Jennifer worked in the fields of government and politics, both in an official capacity working for a member of the US House of Representatives in Washington DC and on the campaign side, managing a race for a seat in the Washington State Senate.

In alignment with Jennifer's core values, she is often found with her family or close friends when she's not working. You'll find her cheering on her two boys playing baseball or taking her sweet Chocolate Labrador for a walk with her husband.

With a strong sense of commitment to her community, Jennifer has also volunteered on a variety of Boards serving in leadership roles. These organizations include Business Network International (BNI), Institute for a Democratic Future, Chi Omega Fraternity, and Highland Terrace Home-Owners Association.

TAKE YOUR DOGS TO THE PARK, EVERY DAY - DAVID SCHWARTZ

Why: For those of us that have them, we all love our pets. As important members of the family, they provide us with comfort and entertainment and ease feelings of anxiety and loneliness throughout the workday. As a full-time solo entrepreneur since I graduated college at 22, I have always found that the only thing I don't like about my work life is the lack of a team environment, and co-workers to keep me company. My pets have always been my co-workers, they're great at keeping me company, but they rarely contribute in any capacity to my productivity.

My pets can be a significant source of distraction. I mean, they're just so cute, and they continuously do silly things that put a smile on my face. I have two dogs and two cats. My two large high-energy mixed breed dogs like to wrestle loudly, poke their heads through the arms of my chair, bark at nothing, bring me squeaky toys, bouncy balls; you name it, they will do anything to get my attention.

While, of course, there is no way to prevent your dogs from distracting you every once in a while, you can do your best to minimize the distractions. The best way to do this is with proper exercise - because a tired dog is a well-behaved dog.

I make it a priority to exhaust my dogs in the morning before I ever sit down to write an email. It's the only way I can ensure that they will not disturb me for at least a few hours so I can get some quality work done. A walk around the neighborhood doesn't get the job done. I need to ensure these dogs expend as much energy as possible so that they sleep while I work. That means a trip to the dog park, a good fetch game, a long run, or whatever activity you enjoy most with your dog. The fresh air and activity do you good, but it will also make your dog's day, every day. Just make sure that they are getting a minimum of 30 minutes of rigorous cardio, run them to the point where their head hangs low, and they want to lay down in the grass. That's when you know they have had enough. If you find that your dog is constantly in your face and demanding attention while you work, you probably didn't run them hard enough. Remember, a tired dog is a good dog.

The Un-Habit: Play with your dogs, don't let them play you

Why: No one says that you shouldn't take breaks and play with your furry friends during the workday, but it's important to set boundaries for both you and your dogs around playtime. Play with your dog on your terms, not on theirs. Set aside doggie play breaks during the day where your focus is to play. Set a timer, throw balls, play tug-of-war, wrestle, have fun with your dog! Relieve some of that stress from your workday, playtime is as good for you as it is for your pooch. But when that timer goes off, you go back to work.

Take Your Dogs to the Park, Every Day - David Schwartz

A useful trick is teaching what I call an "all done" command to your dog. I can rile up my dogs to level 100, tails-a-wagging, an instant puppy party in seconds, but when I utter the command "all done," playtime is over, and they know it.

This comes in handy in many situations, but especially when I am working. If a dog brings me a ball and I decide to appease them with a few tosses, when I want playtime to be over, I say, "all done," The dog knows that playtime is over for right now. They may come back with the ball in a few minutes or immediately, but a consistent and firm "all done" coupled with a waving hand motion lets the dog know that you are not going to play right now. This isn't magic, and your dog has to learn this command like sit, stay, or any other. An easy way to train this is to play with your dog for a few minutes, then say "all done," coupled with a hand gesture of your choosing, and stop playing with it. Ignore them entirely and go about doing whatever other tasks you need to do. A few minutes later, go back to playing with them, get them excited, and then repeat the process by saying "all done" doing your hand gesture and changing your focus and energy away from the dog. This teaches the dog that you are the one to initiate play and that it starts and stops with you. It may take a few tries, but the dog will catch on after a while, don't get discouraged if it takes a while, practice makes perfect!

About David: David Schwartz is a nationally recognized, award-winning DJ/MC and founder of Orion Entertainment, a Seattle based DJ and Photo Booth company.

David started Orion Entertainment when he was a freshman at the University of Washington. He got his start playing house parties in the Greek System, and eventually transitioned into playing nightclubs, bars, and private events. Six years later, David has performed at hundreds of events all across the Pacific Northwest and beyond. Now a premier destination wedding and event DJ his love for music and travel has propelled him from Hawaii to Boston and beyond. David loves to blend unexpected genres and decades of music - his passion for music and DJing is always reflected in his sets, whether playing a wedding, nightclub, virtual or corporate event.

He recently received recognition from Honey Books and the Rising Tide Society, as one of their 20 on the Rise for 2019 in the Event Professionals Category. He was also selected by the Bridal Masterclass Experience to be a Hands-on Coordinator and share his experience with fellow wedding professionals. Orion Entertainment has also won 3 consecutive couples choice awards from Wedding Wire.

In 2020, David was nominated for DJ of The Year, a showcase competition of DJ talent nationwide. His most notable event performance was at T-Mobile's New Years at the Needle, widely considered Seattle's premier New Years Eve celebration.

David spends most of his time with his students, teaching and training the next generation of private event DJs. The Orion Academy's sought after training program provides students with a pathway to becoming a professional DJ. Orion Entertainment has also partnered with local school districts in Washington and will be speaking to students in 2020 about alternative career pathways for high school students.

In his spare time, David likes to go on adventures with his boyfriend, Austin, and his dogs Ranger and Rainier. He enjoys watching and playing soccer, running, hiking, camping, and cooking new and interesting foods.

START EACH AND EVERY DAY WITH GRATITUDE - MIKE NAKAMURA

Why: Is there a better start to a day then noticing the things for which we are grateful? As a long-time remote or solo entrepreneur, I know how isolating working from home can be. Even now, in my studio, with no appointments currently, I'm here alone.

We begin a day with various feelings, from tired to happy, excited, maybe sometimes dreading the day. Add in the new work from home routine we go right to the "office." It helps to take a few minutes to appreciate the many positives we have.

No matter your initial feeling when you wake, look out, and be grateful for something in your life. Find a few things, no matter how trivial they may seem at first. Think about and maybe even say out loud a few. It doesn't have to be, "I'm grateful for..."

It may seem silly; however, I look outside and say to myself, "What beautiful day." It's different than positive thinking or being determined to get myself "in a better mood." Somehow, my expressing gratitude changes my day, and I am off to a happier start. After all, we all work better if we are in a good mood!

Maybe, "What a beautiful cloud: or "I like the bathroom rug." Of course, there are many more important things than the bathroom rug, so consider how much family and friends help you create a full life. Just smile more. When you finish brushing your teeth, pause three seconds, and smile at yourself!

If you journal, occasionally make gratitude a topic of the day.

A 2018 paper "The Science of Gratitude" outlines increased happiness and positive mood, more satisfaction with life, less materialism, less likely to experience burnout, better physical health, better sleep, less fatigue, lower levels of cellular inflammation, greater resiliency, and encouragement of the development of patience, humility, and wisdom as benefits.

The Un-Habit: Be Grateful for Nothing and No One

Why: Breaking the Habit of showing little or no appreciation is important to living a full life. It's imperative not to feel negativity inside and express it by stopping ourselves from having the best relationships and accomplishments.

Philosopher Lucius Annaeus Seneca "ranked ingrates below thieves, rapists, and adulterers."

Staying gratitude-less is not a natural human condition; we want to thank others and welcome the beauty in our lives. We are aware of what we have and are less focused on what we do not have.

Other animals exhibit reciprocal altruistic behavior, and it seems offering kindness increases the chances of receiving kindness in return.

Start Each and Every Day with Gratitude - Mike Nakamura

Gratitude changes your mood and brings a positive feeling to the day. It reduces anxiety and can help overcome depression. Image the impact if you express gratitude for a partner or family member!

For all of us working at home and connecting online, the lack of face-to-face interaction and the reduction of body language makes overtly appreciating others especially important.

Consider how you feel when you receive a thank you card; someone made your day. You have this same power to pass this feeling along to others in your life and receive some of the positive results by showing gratitude.

Interestingly enough, the holiday Thanksgiving is all about gratitude. Even with political differences, we often end the day (or weekend) with positive energy and a relaxed sense of being. Prayer is much about thankfulness and has endured for millennia.

Physically, the neurotransmitter serotonin helps create a dopamine cycle of feeling good. This is triggered when you're in a state of gratitude. What's not to like about a self-fulfilling cycle of feeling good based on gratitude?

So, to break the Habit of ungratefulness, start small. Tell yourself, or your partner, something you appreciate about them. During one of those online meetings, let others know you support them. Look for the good in every outcome.

You are on your way!

About Mike: Mike Nakamura is a headshot, portrait, and corporate event photographer working out of a Kirkland Washington studio. His business is Mike Nakamura Photography LLC.

Commissioned to photograph Microsoft Store Grand Openings from 2011 to 2016, he traveled to the United States, Puerto Rico, and Canada, working with the team to generate immediate social media outreach and long-term marketing imagery. Mike was awarded the Emerald City Applause Award for best photography for his coverage of the flagship New York City Microsoft Store Grand Opening coverage.

He was trusted to work in high-security environments. He has photographed President Obama, First Lady Michelle Obama, Vice President Joe Biden, and Secretaries of State Madeline Albright and Colin Powell, and many other highly placed government officials. Additionally, he has photographed Jeff Bezos, Brad Smith, Steve Balmer, Senators, and Representatives.

Sports figures and bands have been part of Mikes's coverage, including Michael Strahan, Russell Wilson, Macklemore & Ryan Lewis, Kelly Clarkson, Tim McGraw, Blake Shelton, and Lenny Kravitz as many others.

In-studio and on location for corporations, Mike specializes in headshots, including board members, executives, and team members. Several clients fly Mike to their corporate offices for headshots. Executive groups, teams, and individuals are included in many sessions.

Branding portraits for entrepreneurs provide a portfolio of images for use in different applications and frequent updates for social media. Mike uses various backgrounds, lighting sets, corporate themes, and even unique locations to create your branding portfolio.

And corporate clients have families, so family portraits are often an additional session from the branding or headshot session. Knowing how important families are, including family sessions, are some of the most rewarding work done. The portraits are gifts to future generations.

Mike is a past-president and active member of the International Live Event Association (ILEA) and supports the event industry through involvement.

ARRIVE LIKE A BOSS - WHITNIE WILEY

Why: The benefits of working from home, whether you work for an employer or yourself, are widely documented. However, working in the same space you live in is not without its challenges. The good news is that with forethought and planning, those challenges are not insurmountable. Meeting the challenges will set you up for success in ways you may not have even imagined.

Martha Beck said, "How you do anything is how you do everything." In other words, how you approach the smaller, everyday, mundane tasks is how you'll also approach the bigger, more important challenges in your life and work.

When you work from home, if you are not intentional, there is the very real possibility of blending your work and life in such a way as to make it difficult to not only separate the two but to create undue tension and stress that prevents you from bringing your best self to your work or living your dream life.

So, ... how do you approach working from home? Is it with a cavalier attitude? Or do you treat your work and your office with the respect and reverence it deserves? One of the ways you can elevate your approach to working at home is to show up daily like a boss. Treat the experience as if you worked outside the home and get intentional about how you arrive at your office daily as part of your morning routine. Oh yeah! If you don't have a morning routine, now is the time to develop one.

Set your day up for success by starting it with a morning routine. According to US Navy Admiral William McRaven, one of the best Habits you can establish that sends you out into the world or your home office with a feeling of accomplishment is to make your bed. Making your bed, along with a host of other seemingly inconsequential tasks like brushing your teeth, making coffee, exercising, and more, when done with intentionality and on purpose, provides you a feeling of accomplishment and increases productivity and reduces your stress.

While making your bed daily is important, see it as a metaphor for how you approach life, your work, or your business. Stop to think about the daily routines that set you up for success: making your bed, brushing your teeth, praying, meditating, exercising, getting dressed, and putting your success goggles on, etc. Complete these activities and any others you've chosen, then show up to your office as the boss you are.

The Un-Habit: Don't Forget a Closing Time

Why: How difficult is it for you to stop working at the end of the day? Do you find yourself walking past your office nights and weekends, thinking, "I'll send one more email or return that one important call"?

Working from a home office makes it easy to blur the lines of work and home. Overworking at the moment may seem like the right thing to do, but doing so is detrimental to your long-term health, wellbeing, and relationships. Just as it's important to have an evening routine to wrap up your day and prepare for a good night's sleep, it's important to have a definite end to your workday.

Having routines and setting boundaries help you create the separation that will result in optimal performance in your work and harmony in your life. Integrating work and life is a blessing only if they are integrated in a way that honors and enhances your life. To get the best outcome, you must understand yourself, your work style, values, and priorities.

Once you're clear on what's important, you know what you are protecting and why. Setting an office closing time and sticking to it, you continuously send yourself the signal despite the fact you work where you live, work, and life are not interminably intertwined. Just as importantly, you send the message to others that your boundaries are to be honored and respected.

Notwithstanding the fact we live in an "I want it now society," your customers, clients, or boss, if you work for someone else, only respect your boundaries to the extent you do. Provided you are delivering quality service, there's no reason to think you'll lose market share or your job because your workday ends at a particular time. You'll be better able to deliver quality service and products, after establishing the Habit of first taking care of yourself through boundaries.

Regardless of who you work for, now is the time to break the Habit of working all day and into the night. Don't let endless working hours undo the many benefits of working from home;

instead, set office hours and, except on rare occasion, stick to them.

About Whitnie: Whitnie Wiley is the founder and chief evolution officer (CEO) of Shifting Into Action (SIA), a coach, consultant, author, speaker, and trainer.

As the premier next stagecoach, Whitnie has over 25 years of experience coaching in dream and goal achievement, career management and transition, and leadership development. She helps new and aspiring leaders build and manage careers that feed their souls, use their talents and gifts, and finance the lives of their dreams through training programs and retreats, 1-on-1, and group coaching. Additionally, she provides consulting and coaching services to organizations relating to succession management, leadership development and training, human resources, and talent development.

Before starting SIA, Whitnie was a lobbyist and the legal counsel for the Association of California Water Agencies. She was responsible for creating and managing the legal department, as well as the association's legislative intern/externship and mentoring programs.

Whitnie's other leadership roles have included chair of the Association of Corporate Counsel's New-to-In House committee, service on the leadership development institute, and the *Docket* advisory board. Also, Whitnie was a member and served as chair of the California State Bar's Committee of Bar Examiners, a member of the leadership development institute for the California State Bar and chair of the Volunteer Center of Sacramento. She currently shares her expertise with nonprofit organizations through Catchafire and Lepris, and she can be heard frequently as a podcast guest.

For almost seven years, Whitnie authored the *Lead the Way* column for the Association of Corporate Counsel's *Docket* magazine. She encouraged her readers to develop self-awareness and use their values and priorities to pave their path to enjoying their careers, better leadership, and improved teamwork.

Whitnie is a contributing author to the bestselling book 1 Habit for Success and TAG Talks. Using her experience as a leader, along with observations and the feedback received from her readers and clients, Whitnie is looking forward to the publication of her forthcoming book, "The SIMPLE Leader," and the official launch of The SIMPLE Leadership Method.

Whitnie holds a bachelor's degree in Organizational Behavior and Leadership from the University of San Francisco, a master's degree in Organizational Development and Leadership from St. Joseph's University and a Juris Doctor from Alliant International University's San Francisco Law School. She is a certified life coach with a specialty in career transitions and a Jack Canfield Certified Success Principles trainer.

She can be reached at Whitnie@ShiftingIntoAction.com

PRACTICE 10-10-10 - ANDREA HEUSTON

Why: To create a thriving home office atmosphere, I make sure to set a positive tone for each day. Before I begin my work, before jumping into the busy day ahead of meetings, video chats, and emails, I have a morning practice that sets me up for a successful day. I learned this practice from an amazing business leader, Warren Rustand. It's called the 10-10-10.

There is a Finnish proverb stating, "Happiness is a place between too little and too much." The 10-10-10 practice helps me focus my energy on that place of happiness. The practice consists of three separate 10-minute sections. I usually manage to do the full 30 minutes, but some days I do it in sections, and other days I may hit 20 minutes total, and that's okay. As long as I continue the practice, I realize the value.

The first 10 minutes is spent in gratitude. I'll focus on what I'm grateful for by writing it down or just thinking about it in a fully focused way. My gratitude can be for something as small as the sound of the waves crashing outside my window or the taste of that first spring strawberry or the quiet of the house before everyone awakens. A conversation with a dear friend, the feel of a child's hand in mind, the sunshine, the taste of an almond croissant – they're all things that I am grateful for. Just the small act of appreciating someone or something in my life creates a positive atmosphere for me to create value for my team and my clients daily.

The second 10 minutes is spent reading something inspirational. Many times, I read about positive things happening in the world. The Good News Network is a fantastic resource for this. I have a lovely book of inspiration I turn to periodically as well.

The final 10 minutes are spent in free-form journaling. It's all stream of consciousness. I don't choose a topic to write about, but sometimes a topic chooses me! Some of my best work ideas come from this journaling practice, be it a new podcast topic, an employee engagement tactic, or even a new service offering. I also love going back to read my older journal entries; sometimes, I find gold nuggets of thought I had forgotten about, or I get the privilege of seeing how far I've come.

THE UN-HABIT: STOP "SHOULDING" YOURSELF!

Why: We are so skilled at saying, "I should be doing this," "I should stop doing that," "I really should be further along in my career by now." While working at home, I often catch myself thinking that I should be working harder on a particular project, or I should be with my family instead of working or exercising. But constantly feeling like I should be doing something else is stressful and unproductive! Anytime I tell myself that I should or shouldn't be doing something, I'm headed down the highway of guilt at full speed. "Should" essentially means that we're using an external marker, an outside expectation, versus being present to our own needs and wants. I'm still a work in progress, but here's how I have learned to stop "shoulding" myself:

1. Create awareness around the Habit. If I can catch myself, I can rewrite the script. So when I hear myself saying something like, "I should exercise more," I stop and ask myself, "According to who? Me? Or someone else?" It takes the guilt out of the context of the thought.
2. Replace the word "should" or "shouldn't" with "I can," "I will," or "I want to." It's a mindset shift that changes my inner dialogue and helps relieve the pressure and fallback.
3. Give myself some grace. Having a home office is both a blessing and a curse. I love the ability to just move from work to family time so fluidly. However, work often calls when I'm with family, and family obligations are always present. By realizing that it's ok to shift my focus, I escape the need to tell myself what I should or shouldn't do.

Ultimately there will always be evidence to support any belief we have. Whatever we think or are looking for, we will find. Instead of thinking, "I should take a walk," I reframe it to "I want to walk outside this afternoon in the sunshine." The second thought is much stronger than the first and more likely to get me out the door.

About Andrea: Andrea Heuston, founder, and CEO of Artitudes Design, has been in the tech industry for 30 years. Her company, Artitudes Design, is a full-service creative service and experiential design firm specializing in providing high-level speaking and design support to top executives. Artitudes Design is an award-winning organization both in the categories of creative design and employee culture. Andrea is a respected business leader and entrepreneur who is sought after as a board member and a Keynote speaker.

Andrea is passionate about giving back to the community and sits on the Board of Directors for Encompass, a non-profit organization that partners with families to build healthy foundations for children of all abilities. She is also active on the Board of Directors of the local Seattle chapter of the Entrepreneur's Organization, a global network exclusively for entrepreneurs that helps leading entrepreneurs learn and grow through peer-to-peer learning, once-in-a-lifetime experiences, and connections to experts.

Recently she has developed into a sought-after keynote speaker with a voice on women's and leadership topics in the workforce —Which has given rise to her success as a LinkedIn Social network influencer. Last year, her article, "Leading Like a Woman," became the 3rd most viewed article on LinkedIn. And more recently, she started her podcast "Lead Like a Woman," focusing on empowering women leaders to empower others through topical discussions and interviews with female leaders. She is passionate about helping to close the gender gap for women in business.

All business aside, Andrea spends her free time with her husband and their two children, Aidan (18) and Owen (15) enjoying their second home on Washington's coast. Andrea enjoys nothing more than taking long walks along the beach with her Australian Shepards and reading novels. One of Andrea's real passions is traveling, learning languages, seeing different parts of the world, spending time in several countries, and fluently speaking a number of languages. As an artist, Andrea gets her inspiration from everyday things, but traveling also inspires her not only in her creative endeavors but also in her life.

68

USE A "MAYBE LIST" TO KEEP YOU FOCUSED - DENISE B. LEE

Why: To-do lists are standard tools of the home office. I often see people create a long list of things to do that includes the urgent and important items and the novel ideas that have captivated their imagination – the ideas that make them think, "Wouldn't it be great if…" These novel ideas land on the to-do list because the person doesn't want to forget them, and it seems much better to put these ideas on a to-do list than a random piece of paper that is likely to get lost. Capturing novel ideas is important because they can lead to a new way of doing something, personal growth, adventure, a new business project, or any number of beneficial things. But there's a cost to putting these ideas on the to-do list.

A to-do list represents tasks and projects that you are committed to doing, and ideally, the tasks have a sense of concreteness in the steps associated with them. While novel ideas can be exciting and fun, there may only be a vague notion that they should be pursued rather than a firm commitment to doing so. Placing novel ideas on the to-do list muddies priorities and distracts from the important and urgent items. The to-do list gets longer, and the sense of stress and overwhelm grows – hardly the basis for an effective and efficient home office.

Rather than capturing novel ideas on the to-do list, put them on a "maybe list." Reserve the maybe list for anything that might be worth exploring. Block off time at regular intervals to review the maybe list - maybe once a month or once a quarter – and set up some reminder system to do so. During the review, jot down a few quick notes about what it would take to implement an idea so the benefits and costs can be considered. Use the review time to cull ideas that no longer seem viable, organize ideas by context, and decide if it is right to implement an idea.

By capturing novel ideas that hold potential apart from our to-do list, we can focus on completing what we've committed to doing and still have room for creative growth. But it is the review time that will turn the maybe list into a place where ideas can incubate rather than a place for them to languish. Creating a maybe list is a fruitful Habit to adopt for a productive home office.

The Un-Habit: Ignoring Your Inner Dialogue

Why: You can set up your home office to maximize productivity, but you won't get the desired results unless you have a productive mindset. The first step towards creating a productive mindset is to bring awareness to your inner dialog. The internal dialog shapes perceptions and resulting behaviors. In his book, The 7 Habits of Highly Effective People: Powerful Lessons in Personal Change, Stephen R. Covey said, "To change ourselves effectively, we first had to change our perceptions." One particularly powerful word to notice in your inner dialog is "should."

Use A "Maybe List" to Keep You Focused - Denise B. Lee | 415

"Should" can be useful in encouraging health and safety - "You should look both ways before crossing the street" or "You should wash your hands before eating." It can also be used critically to promote someone else's priority system, impose what someone else considers normal and acceptable, and declare someone else's expectations of compliance. When "should" is used critically, it can skew your perceptions by eclipsing the possibility of asking if this is important for you, if you want to do it, or if there is a better way of doing things.

Your productivity is tied to how effective and efficient you are. "Effective" means working on the things you need to be working on to accomplish the goal. "Efficient" means working with the fewest resources to accomplish the goal. Working on what others say you should work on can diminish your effectiveness if those goals do not resonate with your values. If the prescribed way to work doesn't mesh with the way you think, your efficiency can be reduced because it takes more effort to act in a way that does not come naturally to you. "Should" can create roadblocks to productivity because it makes you less effective and efficient, and it limits your perceptions of other possibilities.

When you first start paying attention to your use of "should," you may be surprised by how frequently it pops up. Once you've caught yourself saying "should," pause for a moment and consider if what you "should" do reflects your priorities and your higher good. If the answer to that query is "no," consider alternatives that fit your values and how you do things. It is far easier to be active and efficient when working on goals that reflect your values, and you are working in a way that fits the way you think. When you Ignore Your Inner Dialogue, you open the door to a more productive mindset and a thriving home office.

ABOUT DENISE: Since founding Clear Spaces, LLC in 2005, Denise Lee has helped hundreds of homeowners, small business owners, and students reduce the frustration, overwhelm, and embarrassment of chronic clutter and disorganization. Denise is a sought-after organizing expert who has appeared on St. Louis local television and A&E's Hoarders, and she has been interviewed for radio shows, newspapers, and magazines. Certified Professional Organizer® and coach Denise works with her clients to find individualized holistic organizing solutions and life strategies so they can confidently live the life they want to live: free from clutter and overwhelm. Her clients appreciate her gentle and supportive approach. It is not unusual for Denise to work with several generations within the same family.

Denise holds ADD, Hoarding, and Chronic Disorganization Specialist certificates through the Institute for Challenging disorganization. In 2019 she earned the Certified Senior Advisor® designation. She is a graduate of the Coach Approach for Organizers and is pursuing certification as a coach. She has degrees in Psychology and Information Technology from the University of Missouri-St. Louis and St. Louis Community College, respectively. Her experience in social work and Information Technology has provided a framework to understand the logical side of organizing while being sensitive to her clients' emotional needs. In 2012 she was honored by her colleagues by electing her as the President of the St. Louis Chapter of the National Association of Productivity and Organizing Professionals– a position she held for three years.

She currently serves on the Board of Certification for Professional Organizers.

Denise and her husband Sherman live in St. Louis, Missouri, where they enjoy the company of their two adult children and geriatric cats. In her spare time, Denise is an active volunteer for Boy Scouts of America. She enjoys hiking, camping, and trying to get her garden to grow beautifully and weed-free.

BE SUPER ORGANIZED FOR SUPER SUCCESS - BRANDON B. KELLY

Why: People that are leaving a corporate nine-to-five job have had structure and organization done for them, and sometimes overlook the extreme value of being organized in all they do once they are no longer in that corporate space.

As you look around your room or office, it is likely cluttered and even in dismay, leaving you stressed, unable to perform at your best, or losing critical items needed for clients and closing business. Thus, affecting your productivity and other areas of your life and needs to be fixed. Several years ago, I was broadsided from a dump truck in an accident that left me with a half a brain-quite literally- and I found out that I was getting overwhelmed and out of patience, creating a high level of unneeded stress in my life and my business. I found that I had tons of piles, projects, follow-ups, and bills that were too hard to deal with. But the tip that I needed-and pass on to you- is to have everything organized and focused.

I created a color-coded filing system for importance, priority, clients, and their industry, as well as color-coded for areas and territories, to group together. Another color for potential clients in a territory, follow up materials, etc. Every bin and file had a printed label identifying contents, projects, and dates so that they could be quickly sorted and found. I trained my brain to look for the color, and the date started/due date so that nothing would fall through the cracks anymore.

I would also caution you from using plain manila folders or handwriting on the tabs and suggest instead color-coded file folders and a labeler to give it a crisp look. Everything should be labeled systematically, including daily action files, daily wins, books, products, almost everything is organized and in its place. This will leave you in a calmer state able to focus on the needs of the day. For example, in my world, red files are permanent for auto titles or high priorities that are costing me money. Green files are ideas, money makers, or revenue-based. Blue files are topics and client-based. Yellow files are reoccurring or monthly based (billing to my business or company accounts etc.). Purple are family-oriented projects, activities, or trips. However, you organize and sort, make it a system that works best for you while helping give you an edge over your competition.

The Un-Habit: Being Messy

Why: Being messy and overwhelmed affects all areas of your life and can cap your potential. It also leads to not being prepared and not finding important items when you need them fast. It can also lead to laziness and procrastination and show up in your scheduling, follow-up, and even affect your health. By forming a Habit of active organization in your life, it will lead to your success and keep most stresses out of your life.

The longer you remain unorganized, the less productive you and your business will be. It is critical for success to get organized and have great systems in place.

About Brandon: Brandon Kelly is the author of 6 books, started or sold nine businesses, 1 Private Equity Hedge Fund, set 3 high jump records, competed for a spot on the US Olympic High Jump team, part of two Guinness Book of World Records, and was presented an award from the King of Sweden for serving youth around the world. He has survived two critical wrecks from dump trucks then won two rounds of cancer. He is the founder of the International CEO Super Summit and The National Society of CEO's as well as Magnitude Investments & Capital. Brandon has written or contributed more than 150 national courses and training on leadership and goal setting. He serves on 4 National Committees and Boards of Directors for Non-Profit Organizations. He married his teenage sweetheart, and together they have four children and recently celebrated their 23rd anniversary.

MOVE YOUR PAPER! - SHARON DAVIS

Why: Paper moves through our hands or someone else's hands, lands on our desk, shoots out our printer, or gets placed in our "to do" pile. More frequently, papers are shuffled back and forth in our home office, piled or set aside to deal with later; and important and vital work does not get done.

Having a process in your home office for moving paper will keep work flowing and projects moving forward toward completion. Moving papers in a systematic way creates a rhythm that lessens the required mental energy to process each task. You will be able to think more clearly about the work right in front of you rather than being distracted by the various piles on your desk and around the home office and wondering what to do first. Your desk will remain clear so you can be more productive and creative.

In my work as a professional organizer, there are many facets to my business; but the most important aspect is taking care of my clients. In my home office, I created a system so that no one slips through the cracks, as has happened in the past. My system for moving paper in my home office looks something like this: 1) have initial conversation gathering contact info and notes; 2) add this paper to new client folder (already made up) 3) place client folder in wall file 4) place paid invoices and business expense receipts into the appropriate wall files.

By moving your paper to a standing file placed on your home office desk or the wall, you will see where you are in the process from "lead" to "closed sale" so that when you are interrupted or distracted you will be able to easily jump back into the rhythm of moving papers through your system and pick up where you left off. This process helps me stay focused on the most important and vital aspect of my business from day to day.

At the end of each day, before I leave my home office, I lay out what I want to work on the next day, whether it is a project box, folder or a list of leads. If what I am working on is already in front of me when I step into my home office and sit down at my desk in the morning, I am less likely to be distracted by e-mail, social media or whatever else may pull me away from my primary goal.

Developing the Habit of moving paper through a process in your home office on a consistent basis will not only keep the daily routines of your business moving in a positive, productive pattern, it may also create new opportunities to grow and expand into other areas.

The Un-Habit: Stop Piling Papers

Why: Piles of papers and clutter in your home office are a constant visual reminder of unfinished business, procrastination and postponed decisions. Your mind wanders from the task in front of you to wondering what is in that stack. You get overwhelmed with the distraction, which takes you off the vital and important work that needs to be done. You get side-tracked then overwhelmed with the distraction and become less productive, maybe even reverting to mindless activities, such as checking social media or playing video games.

Stacks of papers on the floor in your home office can attract dust and bugs and become a tripping hazard. Stuffing papers into files without taking time periodically to purge old, outdated policies, procedures, resources and contracts will inhibit you from finding the current document that you urgently need to resolve an issue and will further delay a favorable outcome. Having to peruse through a stack of papers to find some document that you currently need is time consuming and mentally draining. Looking at the various papers will no doubt raise questions: Do I need to keep this? If I keep it where will I file it? Should I act on it? If I throw it away, will I need it later? Mind boggling and confusing, isn't it?

I urge you to block out time to deal with your piles and stacks in your home office one chunk at a time. Work in 15-minute blocks and ask yourself the previously stated questions. I think you will find this task empowering and freeing. You will realize that about 80%-90% of the papers you were keeping are no longer relevant. When your files are purged, you will be able to locate documents that are relevant within a few seconds or minutes at the most, thus saving precious time that can otherwise be spent on those important and vital functions of your business.

About Sharon: Sharon Davis is a Certified Professional Organizer with over 15 years of experience, education, and training in the field. She holds a business degree from Camden County College in New Jersey, where she grew up. In her first job out of college as a legal secretary, she used her organizing skills to excel at her job and keep her attorney on track. After meeting her husband, Patrick, a Navy man, she found herself moving frequently and began assisting neighbors and friends in getting ready for a move or setting up their new home. Even after her family expanded to include three children, maintaining an organized home and making sure family members stayed on schedule became second nature.

Upon settling in Pensacola in 1998, Sharon began a series of part-time jobs, from which she acquired more experiences that would inspire her to help people get organized in their homes and businesses.

In 2007 Sharon began substitute teaching in the Escambia County School District and further saw a need for organization. She helped teachers organize their homes and their classrooms. By working with students who were academically challenged, Sharon taught organizing techniques specifically tailored to help students with ADD and other learning challenges.

In 2009 she joined the Institute for Challenging Disorganization, where she earned her Certified Professional Organizer in Chronic Disorganization credentials. Since receiving her professional credentials, she has earned Specialist Certificates in hoarding, chronic disorganization, ADD, and aging.

Sharon continues to help home-owners, small businesses, entrepreneurs, and home-based businesses to eliminate clutter and create systems that lead to increased productivity.

Sharon has been featured in a 2006 series of articles in the Pensacola News Journal, "Holiday Harmony." 2017 brought about several opportunities, including another article in the Pensacola News Journal, "Clutter Have you Stressed?" an article in Bella Magazine, "Positive Purging," and was a guest break-out speaker at The Hoarding Awareness Conference in Philadelphia where she spoke about the Hazards of Hoarding.

Sharon's philosophy is simple--live a comfortable, balanced life following the words of Luke 12:15, "A man's life does not consist in the abundance of his possessions."

CREATE A SPACE THAT SPEAKS TO THE WHOLE PERSON - MIND & BODY - PAUL ANDRÉS TRUDEL-PAYNE

Why: Wholistic Design, not to be confused with Holistic, is when we design a space that speaks to the whole person; both Mind & Body. Using proven techniques from various alternative and scientific modalities, we infuse a space with different elements that serve to address the needs of a specific person or the desired purpose of a specific room. You can use it to transform a bedroom into a master retreat where you can escape the busy of every day, or turn a small room into a development sanctuary for your little one, in which they can discover skills, self and independence. In the home office, wholistic design can impact productivity and success.

The power of wholistic design in the home office can be boundless. The techniques are all pulled from proven scientific and alternative health and wellness practices. At its core, wholistic design is simply the art of optimizing your home office, by transforming it into a space that supports and serves you both emotionally and physically. To make that happen, the trick is to focus on our key 4 senses that draw energy and influence from outside our bodies: Sight, Sound, Scent and Touch. When designing a home office, to ensure wholistic properties are incorporated into your design, one just must check to confirm each one of these four senses has something in the space speaking directly to it. Following these simple guidelines, you can transform your home office into a true sanctuary of productivity and wellness that will speak to you energetically, and help evoke balance, grounding, and growth in your everyday life.

Utilize Wholistic Design concepts to have a thriving home office in which you can do your best work and be your best self.

THE UN-HABIT: IGNORING THE IMPACT YOUR ENVIRONMENT PLAYS ON PRODUCTIVITY AND YOUR POTENTIAL FOR SUCCESS.

Why: In the busy of every day, it is easy to become overworked, exhausted, and stuck in the hamster wheel of life. And when it comes to working remotely, from your own home office, your ability to thrive and your potential for productivity and success have never been more influenced by the space you create and fill every day. We have all been taught to leave work at the office, or to not bring your personal issues to work. So what then happens when both spaces become one? When our place of work, a space we are meant to thrive and find success, and actual home, a space where we are supposed to unwind and recharge, become one in the same?

More times than not, many of us turn to the newest sales and productivity secrets, or the hottest newly published multi-step success program we can find online, to act as the remedy. When in fact like a band aid, at most these things will act as a quick solution to help with a symptom, versus an actual solution for the real problem. When we think of creating a home office where we are thriving, forgetting to first address our space and environment, can be the exact reason we are unable to thrive and find success.

This is why a home office is a prime space to see the true benefits of wholistic design. By focusing on creating a space that speaks directly to our mind and body, we then can create a dedicated space where we can ensure all the things our work and home should do for us, can truly co-exist within one space. Serving us, by becoming a space where we can focus to find productivity, and ground us to find balance, so we can make sure our environment is optimized for us to find success and truly thrive.

About Paul: Paul Andrés Trudel-Payne is a trusted home & lifestyle expert and entrepreneur. He is a highly sought-after industry pro that is focused on helping others design the life they deserve, both at home and at work. Paul pulls from his many roles and varied experiences to make this happen. He draws from his experience and time as a licensed Realtor, an Interior Stylist & Designer, a Business Strategist, a Lifestyle Coach, a Published Writer and an Equality & Mental Health Advocate.

Paul Andrés recently relocated from Seattle, WA where he started his career as a Realtor. He sold 10 homes in his first 10 weeks, built a 100% referral based business after just 1.5 years with a 3-day work week, secured Corporate Partnerships with globally recognized industry giants based out of the PNW, grew his businesses into a Lifestyle brand with a team of award-winning Brokers that each net over 100k annually with roughly 96% of all leads closed being company sourced. In the summer of 2019 after hitting 70mil in sales annually, he brokered a deal and sold his lifestyle brand and companies to pursue more alignment with his purpose, and create high impact by helping other creatives achieve the level of success and work/life balance that he was able to create.

Now in sunny San Diego, Paul is the owner and Creative Director of Casa Consult+Design, offering interior styling and e-design services to homeowners, developers and RE investors, as well as creative business consulting and strategy coaching to home industry professionals. Even before his new business was 1 year old, Paul had already been voted Best Kitchen & Bath Designer by 425Magazine and Interior Design Innovator of the Year by Build International. In addition, Paul is regularly featured as a guest contributor or industry expert on numerous blogs and industry magazines such as Huffpost, realtor.com, GaysWithKids, ApartmentTherapy, Shondaland and more where he covers topics such as real estate, home styling and design, entrepreneurship, parenting, diversity & equality and the impact of mental health.

In between time with his businesses and his role of loving husband and doting father, Paul still finds time to do more. Most recently starting In Your Mind, his new podcast. After years helping others find, sell, style, design and even create homes from nothing, it's no shock that Paul innately understands the desperate desire we all have to find our home. But with In Your Mind, Paul approaches the idea of home in a very new and raw way. He explores the idea of being at home with who you are or who you've become.

Create a Space That Speaks to the WHOLE Person - Mind & ...

Every Week, Paul will be deep-diving into the minds of Thought Leaders & Industry Game Changers. He'll help share the unfiltered journey each took to find success and become who they are today—allowing us to find inspiration and aspects of ourselves in the stories of others and giving us a glimpse into what it takes to truly feel at home from within.

TIME BATCHING - KAMELIA BRITTON

Why: Wholistic Design, not to be confused with Holistic, is when we design a space that speaks to the whole person; both Mind & Body. Using proven techniques from various alternative and scientific modalities, we infuse a space with different elements that serve to address the needs of a specific person or the desired purpose of a specific room. You can use it to transforming a bedroom into a master retreat where you can escape the busy of every day, or turn a small room into a development sanctuary for your little one, in which they can discover skills, self and independence. In the home office, wholistic design can impact productivity and success.

The power of wholistic design in the home office can be boundless. The techniques are all pulled from proven scientific and alternative health practices. At its core, wholistic design is simply the art of optimizing your home office, by transforming it into a space that supports and serves you both emotionally and physically. To make that happen, the trick is to focus on our key 4 senses that draw energy and influence from outside our bodies: Sight, Sound, Scent and Touch. When designing a home office, to ensure wholistic properties are incorporated into your design, one just must check to confirm each one of these four senses has something in the space speaking directly to it. Following these simple guidelines, you can transform your home office into a true sanctuary of productivity and wellness that will speak to you energetically, and help evoke balance, grounding, and growth in your everyday life.

Utilize Wholistic Design concepts to have a thriving home office in which you can do your best work and be your best self.

The Un-Habit: Multitasking

Why: Multitasking is the opposite of Time Batching, and it's hurting the value of the work you're putting in. How many times have you caught yourself trying to complete multiple tasks at a time? We've all been there.

When working from home, you're more likely to multitask and engage in time-wasting activities. There's no one there to keep you on track.

When you attempt to multitask it's very easy to get distracted. Your brain can't actually focus on multiple things at once. If it could, then we'd all be reading full emails while driving down the freeway without even so much as a swerve.

So even if you think you're a master multitasker and are able to pull it off, you're still not actually doing your best work. If you're not doing your best work, then are you really serious about your business or career?

Trying to do two things at once will usually result in getting less done, poor performance, and frequent mistakes. We all make mistakes, but when you're fully focused, you'll make them much less often.

When your thoughts are going everywhere you'll still get things done, but not nearly as well as you could. I believe if you're going to do something, then you might as well give it your best. This has served me well and has led to many years of success.

Where attention goes, energy flows. Giving your full undivided attention to one task at a time ensures that you're giving it the best of you. Everything is energy. Being fully present and working through with more mindfulness will help you excel and move you closer to your goal. Plus, it just feels better to do good work that you can be proud of.

So do one thing and do it extremely well. Take pride in your work and focus. Then take a break. You've earned it. You'll feel more productive and this will boost your confidence. Your business or career will be better for it too.

About Kamelia: Kamelia Britton is a Business Coach & Instagram Strategist who helps entrepreneurs grow a profitable personal brand with purpose.

In 2016, she started a travel blog while still working as a nurse. Travel was her passion and she always loved photography, taking endless photos of everything she experienced. Brands took notice of her work on Instagram and she was offered paid partnerships through her content within her first year.

By 2018, she was able to quit her nursing job and was pretty much exploring a new country once a month as a full time travel blogger. All of her hard work paid off and others started asking how she did it.

That's when she began coaching others on how to create a successful personal brand of their own.

In 2019, she received an unexpected cancer diagnosis that helped her find her true passion and purpose.

Now Kamelia empowers others to create a life of freedom by working online. She helps you create a business from who you already are, your true essence.

Everyone is endowed with their own unique gifts and experiences, and Kamelia helps you discover these attributes that are part of your story.

She also teaches you how to share your story in a meaningful way to attract a loyal audience for your business. Her clients are from all walks of life and she works with many niches.

As a travel influencer and content creator, she has a deep understanding of how Instagram works, and has helped many of her clients create successful businesses from it.

Kamelia has also worked on numerous campaigns with major brands such as GoDaddy, Expedia, The Four Seasons, and many more.

You can find Kamelia on Instagram at @Kamelia.Britton.

You can get a free strategy session with Kamelia by going to her website at Kamelia.Britton.com.

73

FOCUS ON THE VALUE AND NOT THE MONEY AND THE MONEY WILL COME - ROBERT J MOORE

Why: If you focus on the money, you will stay in scarcity and always worry about paying your bills. Working from home allows me to save a lot of money as you do not have to pay for an office, commute fees, and it will enable you to manage my time better.

If all you do is focus on money, this would be life. You become focused on achieving your own goals without help from others. Although, as an entrepreneur, it's easy to get caught up focusing on money and profits. After all, – money is tangible. We can see it in our accounts. We can spend it. We can buy things we like.

It's easy to ignore value because we can't see it, touch it or count it. To trade it for money, we need to nurture it, invest in it, and make it legible. When you start showing other people the value you have, that's when you become needed. Otherwise, they will come to you for your services as it's been demonstrated that it's helpful to them already.

When I first started my home business, I was scared as all I could do is focus on how to pay the next bill. Still, finally, I took my coaches advise and started to really focus on what value I am to others, what was my gift to enhance others business, this is when I really started to enjoy what I was doing, and the money began to come in without thinking about it.

Today I don't feel that what I do is work as I enjoy it way too much.

I then realized that when you show value:

To clients – they give us reviews.

To an audience – they like to share our content.

To employees – They work harder.

The Un-Habit: Staying in Your Comfort Zone

Why: One bad habit you need to kick is staying in your comfort zone. Sure, it can feel great to play it safe. But, being an entrepreneur is all about taking risks and breaking out of your comfort zone. Not to mention, stepping out of your comfort zone has tons of perks.

Learn new business and life lessons, have more organic relationships, grow yourself and your business, spark creativity and innovation, boost productivity, learn how to handle curveballs.

I had to step outside of my comfort zone when I started each of my ventures. I'll admit it wasn't my favorite thing to do at first. But, leaping outside of my comfort zone forced me to do things I never thought I would or could do. It made me a better business owner and led my company down the path to success.

While most of us would agree that we don't enjoy being uncomfortable or that we "don't like change," probably none of

Focus on the Value and Not the Money and the Money Will C... | 441

us would say that we don't appreciate growth. We know on an innate level that growth is what it's all about, and it's when we get out of our comfort zone that we stretch and grow. Our comfort zones are generally reliable places where we can catch our breath in a crazy world, but it's easy to get stuck there without realizing that's what's happening.

Forcing yourself into discomfort, then seeing the result will keep you pushing yourself. When there's an element of uncertainty, and you come out on the other side either the same or better than you were before, you'll have the confidence to take the opportunity to kick it up a notch toward something that has the potential to be amazing.

When you feel in control, you can deal with anything that comes out of it. Even when things turn sour, you know it's temporary, you know you can bounce back, and you're more likely to push past your comfort zone again.

About Robert: Robert J. Moore is a Therapist, 5x's internationally Awarded Bestseller, Speaker, Business Coach, and a publisher, A Guinness World Record holder, that has impacted the lives of many through the work associated with Magnetic Entrepreneur Inc. Robert has impacted the lives of over 140,000 people through an emotional tale that has provided insights on how to determine one's worth and create a life worthy of joy and success.

Robert has impacted the lives of many through the work associated with his International Award-Winning Best-Selling books," The Better Way Formula – Principles for Success" & Magnetic Entrepreneur. Robert has co-authored with Jim

Rohn's 18-year business partner Kyle Wilson and world series pitcher Todd Stottlemyre, Les Brown's Daughter Serena Brown Travis, etc...

Robert has hosted many events with his brand Magnetic Entrepreneur Author Awards, Magnetic Entrepreneur Guinness World Records Attempt, high-end Mastermind, allowing his students to reach the levels they could only dream off.

Robert has been interviewed by magazines from around the world, national TV programs, radio shows. He has also been invited to speak on world-class stages with Jack Canfield, Eric Thomas, Les Brown, Bob Proctor, Eric Thomas, Kyle Wilson, Douglas Vermeeren and Raymond Aaron, etc. But not so long ago, Robert was destitute. Homeless and alone, he had alienated his friends and family with his delinquent behavior and had nowhere to turn.

Robert J. Moore has studied 51 of the top achievers in the world in the past decade to build his amazing brand. Robert has partnered up with Lori A. McNeil, and they have made one of the first coaching and media certificate programs in the world. Robert states that "this is by far one of the greatest works I have ever created. I am honored to share it with you".

ACKNOWLEDGMENTS

We greatly appreciate the following contributors for offering their own 1 Habit™s to this book.

- Debbie Rosemont - Co-Author of 1 Habit For a Thriving Home Office, Certified Professional Organizer, Productivity Consultant, Business Owner, and Speaker
- Steven Samblis – Creator of 1 Habit, Celebrity Interviewer, Entrepreneur
- Alan Berg - Certified Speaking Professional, Global Speaking Fellow Summit, Founder of National Society of CEO's, Motivational Speaker, Business Coach, Author
- Randy Dean, MBA - The E-mail Sanity Expert(R)
- Michael A. Gregory - Founder of The Collaboration Effect® a professional speaking business & Michael Gregory Consulting, LLC a firm focused on collaboration over conflict
- Darlene Law - The "Brains" of AJL Communications Ltd (aka: Chief Financial and Logistics Officer)
- Christopher Jossart - 16-Time Award-Winning Writer &

Editor, Top 10 National Nonfiction Author, Educator, and Communicator of the Year
- Louise Tyrrell - Transformational Health Coach, Stress Consultant, Speaker
- Kathy Gruver - International Speaker, Award-Winning Author, Coach
- Mary Nestor - International Speaker, Author, Trainer and Executive Coach, Owner, MJN Consulting
- Katie Goodman - Creator of internationally touring comedy show, "Broad Co
- Reade Milner — Marketing Consultant, Entrepreneur
- Kamia N. Kindle - Founder and CEO of SPG Web + Marketing, LLC (Soda Pop Graphics), Mother of Two & Mogul for Life
- Irene Zamaro - Founder of Tradeshows Today
- Kirsten Jarvi - MS RDH Founder of CERDH.com
- Gaurav Bhalla - Creator of Better Businesses Better Lives Blueprint, Author, Educator, Speaker, Coach
- Cynthia A. Peel - Owner Peel's Maker Studio, Speaker, Best Selling Author, Business Coach
- Jennifer Mastor- Owner, MASTOR Recruiting & Consulting
- Heather Denniston DC CCWP NASM - Wellness Strategist, author and keynote speaker
- Regina F. Lark, Ph.D. - Owner, A Clear Path, LLC., Co-Author, 1-Habit for Chronic Disorganization
- Tabitha Colie - Remote Work Evangelist, Multipotentialite
- Scott Schweiger - Computer Support and Consulting, Owner of Cascade Computing
- Melinda Slater - Principal Designer + Owner of Slater Interiors
- Jim Hessler - Founder, Path Forward Leadership

- Liz Jenkins - CPO - Owner, A Fresh Space
- Kelly Smith - Owner, Willow & Oak Business Solutions
- Lauren Burgon - Business Attorney
- Silvia Peterson - Owner, SLP Consulting LLC
- Dan Faulkner - Founder of the Dan Faulkner Group at Compass Real Estate
- Jessica Riverson - The Feminine CEO, Business Mentor
- Aubrey Armes - PHR Chief Change Officer, Coach, Mentor, Speaker
- Laurie Nichols - Creator of the Triple-Win Formula for Succession Success
- Brooks Duncan - COO of Asian Efficiency, Host of The Productivity Show
- Kirsten Sandoval - Founder/CEO Mesa de Vida, LLC
- Jen Taylor - Owner of Jen Taylor Consulting
- Lori Vande Krol - Award Winning Productivity Expert, CEO, National Speaker, Mom
- Jill Nichols-Hicks - Founder/Owner Illuminating Women, LLC
- Gazala Uradnik - Founder of GFS Events
- Ron Rael - CEO, Leadership Speaker, Consultant Author
- Stacey Sorgen, Certified Personal Trainer, Holistic Coach, RYT200
- Kristin Bertilson - Certified Professional Organizer. Owner of Queen B Organizing, Corvallis OR
- Yvonne D. Hall - CFP®, CIMA®, Managing Director – Investments, Hall Wealth Management Group of Wells Fargo Advisors
- Jackie Ramirez - Broker Windermere Real Estate/East Inc.
- Nicole Mangina - Real Estate Expert

- Reisha Holton - founder One on One College Essay and creative writer and reporter
- Daphne Michaels - Human Potential Trainer and Consultant
- Ashok S. Ramji - CERTIFIED FINANCIAL PLANNER™
- Andrew Hinkelman - Executive Leadership Coach
- Leona Thomas - President and Founder of Enabling Investments, LLC
- Sarah Frink - Digital Marketing Expert & CEO & Founder of Real Marketing Solutions
- Lisa Fischer, Personal Wardrobe Stylist, Image Consultant, Speaker
- Rose Harrow - ChangeMaker Catalyst, Author, Executive Coach, International Speaker
- Jeff VandenHoek - Owner | Consultant, Intentionality, LLC
- Mindy Garrett - Founder or Mind & Body Elite, Health & Fitness Coach
- Andrea Duffield MBA MA CCC-SLP – CEO, Communications Coach & Consultant
- Cynthia Lindsey - Professional Organizing Consultant, Move Manager, Life Manager Partner, Its Arranged
- Betsy Matias - Real Estate Broker
- Neelu Gibson - Worldwide Vice President, Regulatory Affairs
- Janine Sarna-Jones - Founder of Organize Me Inc., Certified Professional Organizer
- Shannon McGinnis - Author of the 10 Minute Tidy, PMO Leader
- Denise Lloyd - Founder and CEO of Engaged HR Inc.
- Jennifer McKibbin Harris - Founder & Consultant at Look Within HR Consulting

- David Schwartz - Professional DJ/MC and Owner of Orion Entertainment
- Mike Nakamura - Photographer
- Whitnie Wiley - Founder at Shifting Into Action; Creator of The SIMPLE Leadership Method; Author, Speaker, Trainer, Coach & Consultant
- Andrea Heuston - CEO of Artitudes Design Inc. and Host of the Lead Like a Woman Podcast
- Denise B. Lee - CPO®, CSA
- Brandon Kelly - Motivational Speaker, Business Coach, Author, Founder & CEO of CEO Super Summit, Founder & CEO of CEO Super Summit
- Sharon Davis - CPO-CD, Certified Professional Organizer, Owner of Efficient Home Organizing
- Erik Swanson – Author, Speaker, Habits & Attitude Success Coach
- Paul Andrés Trudel-Payne — Home & Lifestyle Entrepreneur, Creative Director of Casa Consult+Design, a Business Solutions & Innovation Consultant, a Strategy & Discovery Coach, Podcast Host & Speaker
- Kamelia Britton, Business Coach & Instagram Strategist
- Robert J Moore - Founder of Magnetic Entrepreneur Inc, Guinness World Record Holder, 5x International Award Bestselling Author / Speaker

ABOUT THE CREATOR OF THE 1 HABIT™ MOVEMENT

Steven Samblis is the creator of the 1 Habit book series.

He is the founder of 1 Habit Press. Before creating Samblis Press, Steven had a meteoric career in business that saw him go from being ranked among the top 50 rookie stockbrokers at Dean Witter, to speaking before 250,000 people for The Investors Institute. He has spoken before congress on shareholder's rights representing T Boone Pickens' "United Shares Holders Association."

In 1989 he founded "The Reason For My Success". which grew into one of the largest sellers of self-improvement programs in North America. The Company expanded into production where Steve collaborated with Chicken Soup for the Soul co-creator

Mark Victor Hansen on the audio program The program, called "The Worlds Greatest Marketing Tools".

As a consultant, Steve created a new name brand for a struggling gym in Dover New Hampshire called Coastal Fitness. He then created a $9.95 a month business model which helped to turn the single gym into one of the most successful fitness franchises in the world, Planet Fitness. In November of 2015 Planet Fitness went public with a 1.6 billion dollar market valuation.

For six years, before launching 1 Habit Press, Steve was the on-air host and Editor in chief for Cinema Buzz, a website and syndicated television show in North America and the UK. On the show, Steve has interviewed over 1000 of the biggest actors and directors in entertainment one on one on camera.

facebook.com/samblis
instagram.com/samblis
amazon.com/author/samblis

ABOUT CO-AUTHOR - DEBBIE ROSEMONT, CPO

Debbie Rosemont, Certified Professional Organizer and Productivity Consultant, started Simply Placed in 2003 to help clients increase productivity, maximize efficiency and bring balance and control into their work and lives. Simply Placed associates work with individuals and businesses to create effective organizational systems, clear clutter, successfully manage time, focus on priorities and achieve goals. They help people work smarter, not harder, to increase their bottom line and peace of mind through consulting, hands-on organizing, and group training.

Debbie teaches individuals and groups productive Habits and organized systems that allow them to maximize their email, time, tasks, teams and workspace, resulting in improved client service, employee retention, revenue and reduced stress. Simply Placed can help you and your business focus on what's important, ultimately helping you achieve a level of efficiency that allows you to get not just more, but more of what you want, out of business and life.

Rosemont is an engaging speaker, an effective consultant and trainer, and has been interviewed numerous times for TV, print, radio and online media. She is also the author of the book <u>Six-Word Lessons to Be More Productive</u> and the creator of several information products.

Rosemont is one of a small number of Certified Professional Organizers in Washington and was a founding member of the Seattle chapter of NAPO. She is an active member of NAPO (National Association of Productivity and Organizing Professionals) and Women Business Owners (WBO). She was a proud finalist for the 2015 WBO Nellie Cashman Business Owner of the Year award.

Rosemont, who wears many hats in her own life as a wife, mother, volunteer and business owner, understands that "life happens" and that it can be a challenge to get and stay organized. However, she's seen the benefits of an organized life and wants that for her clients. Her goal is to ultimately save her clients time, money and stress, and allow them to focus on the things that matter most.

Simply Placed, and Debbie Rosemont, can be reached by phone at 206-579-5743 or by email at debbie@itssimplyplaced.com. More information about the company, services and seminars can be found at www.itssimplyplaced.com.

- linkedin.com/in/debbierosemontsimplyplaced
- amazon.com/author/debbierosemont
- facebook.com/simplyplaced
- instagram.com/simplyplaced
- twitter.com/simplyplaced
- youtube.com/simplyplaced

AVAILABLE FROM 1 HABIT PRESS

The Book That Started a Movement.

1 Habit™

You know the joy you feel when you are so passionate about your "why" that you can't wait to wake up and jump right into life? That motivation will get you started, but to be able to follow through, you need the Habits that will help you place one foot in front of the other when things get tough.

Get your copy at 1Habit.com/product/1-Habit/

1 Habit™ for Women Action Takers

In this book, you will find stories from Women Action Takers who are on a mission to make a significant impact on this planet by sharing their Habits and unHabits to help you place one foot in front of the other when you need it most.

Get your copy at www.1Habit.com/product/wat

1 Habit to Beat Cancer

Helping Cancer Suck Less: Daily Habits that Helped Incredible Cancer Thrivers Survive and Enjoy Life

1 Habit To Beat Cancer is a simple, easily digestible book that shares the new Habits that inspired these people to overcome their cancer as well as the bad Habits they did away with on their journey.

This book will teach you ways to overcome stress, feelings of despair, and overwhelm to feel instead determined and empowered to live your greatest life, and often, it takes JUST 1 Habit to change your life.

Get your copy at https://www.1Habit.com/product/1-Habit-to-beat-cancer

Made in the USA
Monee, IL
27 July 2020